Servant of the Word

Servant of the Word

The Life and Ministry
of C. F. W. Walther

August R. Suelflow

SAINT LOUIS

To
Gladys Gierach Suelflow
for her consistent support and
lifelong encouragement,
unequalled excellence,
and devotion as wife and mother.

Copyright © 2000 Concordia Publishing House
3558 S. Jefferson Avenue, St. Louis, MO 63118-3968
Manufactured in the United States of America

9 780570 042716

Library of Congress Cataloging-in-Publication Data

Suelflow, August Robert, 1922–1999
    Servant of the Word: the life and ministry of C.F.W. Walther / August R. Suelflow.
        p.   cm.
    Includes bibliographical references.
    ISBN 0–570–04271–2
    1. Walther, C. F. W. (Carl Ferdinand Wilhelm), 1811–1887. 2. Lutheran Church—Missouri Synod—Clergy—Biography. I. Title.
BX8080.W3 S85   2001
284.1'092—dc21   00-009354

1   2   3   4   5   6   7   8   9   10   09   08   07   06   05   04   03   02   01   00

CONTENTS

PREFACE

[*Editor's note:* Our gracious Lord called August R. Suelflow to eternal sainthood on August 28, 1999 after he had finished writing the following preface.]

Servant of the Word is an account of the fascinating life and ministry of Carl Ferdinand Wilhelm Walther, founder and first President of The Lutheran Church—Missouri Synod. This great leader, whose influence was widespread both in America and in Europe, was a prime theological preceptor, seminary professor and administrator, essayist, lecturer, and organizer of American Lutheranism.

Walther was a devoted scholar of Martin Luther's writings and had mastered the Lutheran Confessions as well as or perhaps better than anyone in America during the 19th century. He initiated publication opportunities for the wider distribution of Luther's works, and for that reason frequently was referred to as "the Luther of America." In typical humility, however, Walther rejected that designation as inappropriate and insisted that he was merely "Luther's Archivist."[1]

Walther worked tirelessly in the biblical languages (Greek and Hebrew), never ceasing to encourage others in the study of the Scriptures, especially Pauline theology. He also had the gift of a marvelous memory and throughout his life delivered learned essays on doctrinal subjects, with ample quotations from the Scriptures and other documentation—all without the help of modern technology.

Initially Walther's theological writings were prepared in German. Over the past twenty years much of this material has been translated into English, a project significantly supported by Concordia Publishing House, St. Louis. These sources especially demonstrate what a multi-faceted man Walther actually was: an outstanding theological professor, a sincere and effective parish pastor, a master teacher of doctrine and practical theology—in short, a devoted servant of God's Word and the church.

Writing about Walther, John Alden Singmaster (1852–1926), onetime professor at the Lutheran seminary in Gettysburg, Pennsylvania and President of the General Synod, stated:

Dr. Walther was a man of extraordinary energy and apostolic devotion. His zeal for the truth and his self-denial in its advocacy mark him as a heroic example worthy of study and emulation. His courage and constancy in trial in the Fatherland and in America must evoke the sincere admiration of all who read the story of his life. His achievements are quite as wonderful as his endowments and his character. ... The future historians of the church of America will give him a very high place on the roll whose memories should be honored for what they were and what they did.[2]

The task of future generations is to study, critique, and learn God's message of forgiveness as revealed in His Son Jesus Christ, our Savior and Brother. In a day when there is much discussion about the doctrine of justification as the doctrine by which the church stands and falls, a study of Walther's life and writings should be of great help.

This biography is not intended to give detail to Walther's extensive theological writings. Rather, it is more concerned with depicting Walther as a human being who lived in mid-America at a time when St. Louis was becoming the center of westward travel and expansion, and when Lutherans in America were becoming more aware of their distinctive theology and their life in mission. This book also focuses on the institutions founded by Walther and on Walther's role as husband, father, and grandfather.

Two resources were especially helpful to me in writing this book. The author is most grateful for having had the privilege during a sabbatical leave to do research in Saxony and to walk in Walther's footsteps. This made it possible to personally see his birthplace, the schools he attended, and his first parish, all of which were extremely informative for learning about the young Walther.

A second major source of information came directly from Walther's own personal correspondence, which provides an intimate look into his theological stance, his thinking, and his emotions—indeed a unique means of "getting into Walther's head." His correspondence was extensive. In a letter dated May 18, 1882, Walther wrote to Heinrich Stallmann:

Daily I must answer so many letters, sometimes big bundles, which have asked me for doctrinal and sometimes questions of conscience. Answering these, I rarely have enough time to write other letters that do not contain such questions. This is true because these people are waiting anxiously for an answer from me.

It is estimated that Walther wrote about 800 letters per year. Over a twenty-five year span, this may have added up to some 20,000 letters. However, only about 1200 letters have been preserved because once he had responded to a letter, he usually destroyed it. Apparently it never occurred to Walther that someday his letters might be published.

The author expresses deep gratitude and appreciation to several organizations and individuals: Aid Association for Lutherans of Appleton, Wisconsin provided a financial grant to Concordia Historical Institute in order to engage Rev. Werner K. Wadewitz to transcribe Walther's handwritten letters into type-written form; the Marvin M. Schwan Charitable Foundation and Rev. Larry Burgdorf provided funding for this publication; and Concordia Seminary and Mr. James Waltke provided funding for a sabbatical leave. Special thanks are due to all those who at various times rendered most valuable assistance, including especially Rev. Kent J. Burreson, Mrs. Brigitte Conkling, Dr. Curtis P. Giese, Seminarian Thomas A. Egger, Roy Ledbetter, Dr. Thomas Manteufel, and James Ware.

August R. Suelflow
June 23, 1999

With great determination, Dr. Suelflow studied and researched the life and teachings of C. F. W. Walther. In his quest for historical accuracy, Dr. Suelflow was captivated by the legacy left to God's people by this great American Lutheran father and sought to capture the countless indelible marks Walther left on life's highway in order to share them with others.

Both Dr. C. F. W. Walther and Dr. August R. Suelflow left their marks on God's people. Though divided by time, their kindred spirit drove Dr. Suelflow's desire to share the life story of this remarkable servant of the Word. The most prominent similarity between these two keepers of the faith was their shared gift of humility. Neither man sought glory for self nor viewed himself as standing in a light which others tried to shine upon them.

Dr. Walther refused to be known as the American Luther and instead considered himself as merely "Luther's Archivist." Though Dr. Suelflow disagreed with Walther's own humble self-view, he recognized himself as merely the keeper of historical Lutheran records. Both men seemed blind to the multi-faceted way that God, in His grace, utilized them as confessional Lutherans to keep the rich heritage of Luther alive in America.

Dr. Suelflow, in presenting this fresh account of Walther's life, sought to provide the reader with much more than the typical window into Walther's theology. Wading through reams of Walther's personal correspondence, Dr. Suelflow has provided the reader with insight into the life journey of this Servant of the Word. He provides a glimpse into Walther's life as more than a theologian or writer. Here we are able to see into Walther's home, his university studies, his marriage, children and grandchildren. Dr. Suelflow was able to bring us this wealth of insight into Walther's legacy because of his own remarkable memory and astute retention of historical facts.

With heartfelt gratitude, we express deep appreciation to the late Dr. August R. Suelflow for sharing this biography of the most influential person in our synod's history. The Lutheran Church—Missouri Synod is deeply grateful for Dr. C. F. W. Walther and Dr. August R. Suelflow and their relentless homage to the truth of Christ. It is with heavy hearts of grief that we close this chapter in August R Suelflow's life. However, we rejoice with unending joy that he lives in the arms of Jesus forever.

Soli Deo Gloria!
Craig A. Du Bois, son-in-law
Epiphany 2000 A.D.

NOTES

[1] Walther's Norwegian Lutheran friend, J. A. Ottesen of Utica, Wisconsin, referred to him as the Luther of America. Walther responded to this in a letter dated Feb. 8, 1870. See Ludwig Fuerbringer, *Walthers Briefe*, vol. II (St. Louis: Concordia Publishing House, 1919), 183. For additional insight, see Paul Burgdorf, "Keeper of Luther's Archives," *Concordia Historical Institute Quarterly*, vol. XIII, no. 4 (Jan. 1941), 115.

[2] *Lutheran Quarterly*, 47 (July 1917), 454–55.

1

IT BEGAN IN EUROPE

One of the greatest historians of American religion, Sydney Ahlstrom, wrote about Carl Ferdinand Wilhelm Walther:

> His private life became literally a part of the [Lutheran Church—Missouri] Synod's life and his thoughts very nearly came to be its thoughts. What these thoughts were, however, cannot be quickly stated, for he ranged over the entire field of Christian dogmatics and brought to his pronouncements a depth of historical erudition and type of theological acumen which no survey can convey.[1]

During Walther's lifetime, most American denominations had engaged in serious discussion and debates concerning their theological integrity. Many of them were involved in attempting to bring their theological heritage to bear upon the new social, cultural, and geographical changes that had been introduced into American life in the middle of the nineteenth century. Walther was well-aware of the situation.

What is particularly of interest to us is Ahlstrom's evaluation of Walther's role in the midst of all of this:

> Walther's influence was especially significant in that he stood almost alone in the nineteenth-century American theological scene as one fully aware of the crucial importance of the problems of Law and Gospel to the Christian faith.[2]

Who was this man C. F. W. Walther? What kind of man was this leader of the church who, like Martin Luther, shaped the thinking of future generations, especially in The Lutheran Church—Missouri Synod?

WALTHER'S FAMILY BACKGROUND

Conditions in the kingdom of Saxony (today a part of the Federal Republic of Germany but at that time a separate, independent kingdom) were chaotic and showed the ravages of war in the early 1800s. Napoleon had subdued Prussia in October 1806 and had fought victorious battles close to Walther's hometown of Langenchursdorf even before he was born. At that time, his parents had only three young daughters, all under the age of four.

Walther had not yet attained his second year of life when the Napoleonic battles came near to Langenchursdorf once again. By 1812 and 1813, Napoleon was making his way back to France from the charred ruins of Moscow. As Napoleon left Russian territory, the Austrian and Prussian troops joined the Russians and pursued him into Saxony. At the battles of Lützen on May 2, 1813, and Bautzen on May 20, 1813, Napoleon's spirits seemed to have been lifted temporarily when he rallied his troops until he suffered one of the greatest defeats since the occupation of Moscow. Even though Napoleon was victorious in the battle of Dresden on August 26–27, 60,000 men lost their lives, and the tide had turned. In another battle fought on October 16–18, 1813, with a loss of 15,000, Napoleon's victories turned into defeat. By March 1814, the victorious allies who had invaded Paris crushed Napoleon Bonaparte.

In the midst of such blood, warfare, and uncertainty, Carl Ferdinand Wilhelm Walther was born on October 25, 1811. His father, Gottlob Heinrich Walther, and his mother, Johanna Wilhelmina Zschenderlein, were the parents of twelve children, only a few of whom reached adulthood. Young Ferdinand was the eighth child and the fourth son.

The twelve children of Gottlob Heinrich and Johanna were:

1. Moritz Wilhelm, born January 11, 1801; died March 5, 1803.

2. Theresa Wilhelmina, born February 23, 1802, and died February 15, 1832, eight days before her thirtieth birthday. She was married to Arch Deacon Magister H. W. F. Schubert who was the Associate Director of the *Gymnasium* at Schneeberg. They had two children, Maria born in 1823 and Theodor born in 1828. (See also Mariane Louisa.) These two children would play an important role in the 1838 immigration.

3. Augusta Constantine, born on May 9, 1803, and died on May 28, 1881. She married Johann Gottlieb Engel. It was Engel who objected to bringing the Schubert children to America in 1838. They were the parents of Robert Engel, who served at one time as Walther's secretary and later as language teacher at Concordia College, Ft. Wayne, Indiana. He returned to Germany after that.

4. Henrietta Juliana, born August 21, 1804, and died on February 10, 1868. She married Pastor Franz Adolph Wilhelmi (born 1791) on July 4, 1824. Walther's widowed mother spent her last years in the Wilhelmi home at Hartmannsdorf, Saxony.

5. Julius Theodor, born October 18, 1807, and died on September 10, 1813.

6. Otto Hermann, born September 23, 1809, and died on January 27, 1841. He participated in the immigration to America in 1838. In America, he married Agnes Buenger and had one son, Johannes, before his premature death at age 31.

7. Mariane Louisa, born October 3, 1810, and died October 20, 1834. After her older sister Theresa died, she married Theresa's widower, Heinrich Wilhelm Friedrich Schubert (born in 1796). He taught at Schneeberg. Young C. F. W. Walther attended the *Lateinschule* at Schneeberg and stayed with Theresa and H. W. F. Schubert from 1821 to 1829. Schubert buried his first wife in 1832 and his second in 1834. That same year he also died, leaving two orphans.

8. Carl Ferdinand Wilhelm, born October 25, 1811, baptized on October 30, 1811. His sponsors were the Rev. August Theophilus Niedner, a pastor at Braeunsdorf, Miss Friedericke Wilhelmine Friedrich of Zwickau, and Wilhelm Benjamin Walther of Waldenburg. Interestingly, Pastor Niedner was Walther's predecessor at Braeunsdorf, having served there from 1804 to the time of his death in 1836. It is very likely that Miss Friedrich was related to Walther's mother. W. B. Walther may have been an uncle of Carl Ferdinand Wilhelm, who died on May 7, 1887, having lived to a much riper age than any of his siblings.

9. Anna Natalia born November 2, 1812, and died on July 15, 1813.

10. Amalia Ernestina, born July 7, 1815, and died in 1842 in Frohna, Missouri. She married E. G. W. Keyl (May 22, 1804– August 4, 1872). Together with their infant son Stephanus, they immigrated to America in 1838.

11. Marie Rosalie born June 27, 1816; died seven days later on July 3, 1816.

12. Klara Philistiana born June 11 1817; died three months later on September 12, 1817.

Walther only got to know six of these eleven siblings. The infant mortality rate was very high in those days. The cause of the deaths is simply mentioned in the church records at Langenchursdorf as *Stickfluss* (suffocating catarrh) and diarrhea.[3]

Life in Langenchursdorf

Walther was born in Langenchursdorf, a small village northwest of Hohenstein near Langenberg in Saxony. The homes were built very close to the brook that quietly flows through the lengthy village. Most of the inhabitants were farmers and weavers. Historians surmise that the town had its beginning around the twelfth century and originally may have been called Konradsdorf.

Moritz Heinrich, Walther's great-grandfather had been pastor at Oberlungwitz. Walther's grandfather and father both served as pastors at Langenchursdorf. The grandfather, Adolf Heinrich Walther (1728–1802) served from 1763 to 1802. C. F. W. Walther's father, Gottlob Heinrich, was born in Langenchursdorf and became his father's assistant on April 8, 1799. Walther's brother Otto Hermann, born there in 1809, became his father's vicar or assistant on November 9, 1834, but in 1838, he immigrated to America along with sixteen members of the church.

Thus, Langenchursdorf had been the center for the Walther family. C. F. W.'s father was born there on November 15, 1770, and died there on January 13, 1841. He lies buried next to the church in the old cemetery. Strangely enough, his son, Otto Hermann, died just a few days later on January 27, 1841, but across the Atlantic in St. Louis, Missouri.

The first church in Langenchursdorf was built in 1201 and was enlarged several times. The last additions were made in 1764 under the pastorate of Adolf Heinrich Walther, the grandfather of C. F. W. Walther. The church, barn, parsonage, and school form a little village by themselves. The barn for the pastor's horse and other animals was built in 1763. The present parsonage was built in 1844–45 and is constructed very similarly to the previous parsonage, in which Walther lived as a child.[4] Thus, all of the present church buildings, except the parsonage, were standing at the time Walther grew up.

The church itself still stands on a prominent spot in the village and has its steeple in the center of the roof, a style that is quite rare. The parsonage had a wide front entrance with a long hall running the width of the house. The house also contained a stairway to the second floor. Usually these homes had four rooms downstairs and four upstairs. Such parsonages were adequate and comfortable.

Walther's parents lived comfortably here, but by 1834 had mourned the early death of six of their twelve children. Just four years later, their only two living sons and one daughter sailed for America.

The home of young Walther was a typical Lutheran parsonage of that time. It was marked both by an upper-middle class culture and by parsonage discipline. Two interesting stories about Walther's youth have come down to us. When he was only three years old, he experienced his first pre-Christmas visit by St. Nicholas, who came to the Walther home on December 6. Also known as *"Pelznickel,"* the saint inquired about the progress the children had made in studying the Bible and the Catechism. Children were asked to give an account of themselves and recite a poem or a prayer of some kind. The little three-year-old, standing in awe before St. Nicholas, shyly said:

> Jesus, Thy blood and righteousness
> My beauty are, my glorious dress
> Wherein before my God I'll stand
> When I shall reach the heavenly land.

Quite a memory feat for a three year old! So thought Walther's father who was so overjoyed and proud of his little boy that he gave him a three-penny piece. Ferdinand (as C. F. W. went by) concluded this must be a very special verse to be worth such a generous response from his father. The youthful mind had been indelibly impressed with this theology, which was to become the center of his entire life.

Martin Guenther, Walther's first biographer,[5] wrote that Walther's father was stern in bringing up the boys and wanted his sons to grow up strong and masculine. Discipline and character building were part of the home training. The father used a little ditty to impress them:

> A youth must many trials endure
> before he can become a sir.

("*Ein junger Mann viel leiden muss Eh' aus ihm wird ein dominus.*")

The parlor in the Walther parsonage was rarely entered by the family, used only for the family Christmas celebration and when company came. It had a special sofa that was a seat of honor reserved only for guests. But on one occasion little Walther sat down on that soft seat and was promptly punished. Both parents loved all of their children dearly, and such strictness was an expression of their concern that the children learn discipline and respect.

Walther's brother, Otto Hermann, has left an interesting glimpse into the Walther home. Preparing for his own ordination, he wrote in a biographical sketch about his parents:

> Exhausting themselves with solicitous care, they left nothing undone
> till the end that I might begin from infancy to be instructed most dili-

gently in our most holy religion. Already then (if I may speak thus) I had been destined by my parents for the holy office, but since my father was hindered by his pastoral duties, so that for that reason he was unable to instruct his little boy in the first elements of a proper education, he entrusted my education to his close friend Vollmar, whose ministry as pastor at Waldenburg was ended by his recent death.[6]

Clergymen had become part of the upper middle class in Saxony. Clergy families intermarried and very often the sons of clergymen studied for the holy ministry, while the daughters married pastors. They almost constituted a class by themselves and a class that could rather easily move either horizontally or vertically in society through marriage, their status, and friendships.

Economically the clergy may not always have been a match to others of equal standing, yet their real strength lay in their superior education. Walther's father, who had studied at Leipzig University, insisted that his sons be well-educated. Walther received his earliest education at home in the two-story building which had been erected as an educational unit by the Langenchursdorf congregation. The school was located right next to the parsonage, and the deacon of the congregation gave instruction there.

HOHENSTEIN

Even though the congregation still had a deacon (Johann Christian August Grosse), when young Walther was seven years old he was sent to Hohenstein near Chemnitz.[7] This may well have been the closest Christian community school.

The question has been asked whether Walther walked the six miles daily or how he commuted, if he was staying at home. This riddle can be resolved. Walther's uncle (his father's brother), Franz Friedrich Wilhelm Walther, was a teacher at the *Knabenschule* (boy's school) there from approximately 1806 to 1830. What a convenient opportunity to board at his uncle's home during this time!

The huge St. Christophorus Church in Hohenstein dominates the village. In 1817, a year before Walther's arrival, it celebrated the 300th anniversary of the Lutheran Reformation and placed a bust of Luther and Melanchthon in the church. Behind the church is a large four-story building in which Uncle Walther and his nephew lived on the second floor. The school is a bit down the hill; part of it is still standing, although a number of additions have been made over time.

There is another facet to this story. The village consisted almost entirely of weavers. Many of the children of the weavers began working at home at this trade when they were five or six years old. The pastor, Karl Friedrich Wagner, who had begun his service in 1806, became embroiled in a controversy with Kantor or Rector Walther over the so-called "factory children." These children were to receive special education during the lunch hour in school. Uncle Walther demurred, saying he was unable to conduct these classes because he was too exhausted from all his teaching responsibilities. Not surprisingly, some ill will resulted.[8]

Walther always appreciated and enjoyed music. It is quite possible that the noted composer Christian Gotthilf Tag, choirmaster at the church in Hohenstein from 1755 to 1808, influenced Walther's interest in music. The impact of Tag undoubtedly was still alive at Hohenstein when Walther arrived there at the age of eight; the choirmaster during Walther's time at the school was Johann Gottlieb Werner, Tag's successor who served from 1808 to 1818. Tag has been characterized as a second-generation musician in the tradition of the great Johann Sebastian Bach (1685–1750).[9] His life also indicates that sacred music in Saxony had never really deteriorated. Yet it seems to be reasonably certain that, in spite of Tag, Walther did not become acquainted with Bach music itself.

The educational system Walther experienced in his youth was one of the best. There were village schools which Martin Luther and Philip Melanchthon had established early in the Reformation period. Because of the assumption that the study of Latin grammar was the best means by which to arrive at an understanding of Holy Scriptures and hence religion, the Latin school was emphasized in Saxony. Here promising children from any part of the state, generally supported by public funds, could attend.

Any school which taught at least two ancient languages was called a *Gymnasium*.[10] In contrast to the *Gymnasium*, the Latin school put an even heavier emphasis on languages and grammar. The school system was somewhat modified under the influence of pietism. The pietists placed a much greater stress on the meaning and understanding of Luther's Small Catechism, rather than on memorization. Under this influence, the *Spruchbuch* or collection of Bible verses for use in school became very popular. Schools came to be seen not only as a place of preparation for civilized life, but also as the workshop of the Holy Spirit.

Walther attended the schools just as the influence of Johann Heinrich Pestalozzi (1746–1827) was being felt. Pestalozzi was no friend of the Catechism and contended that the study of Bible history had but little educational value. "The general effect of his philosophy was to maintain classes in religion in the schools, but to use them for ethical and moral, not doctrinal purposes."[11] Later, under the influence of Friedrich Adolf Wilhelm Diesterweg (1790–1866), schools became secular institutions as they were separated from the supervision of the clergy.[12]

STUDENT DAYS IN SCHNEEBERG

In 1821, at the age of ten, Walther began his studies at the *Lateinschule* (not a *Gymnasium*) in Schneeberg. The city of Schneeberg, together with its church, St. Wolfgang, sits at the highest point in the Erzgebirge. The eleventh century church is enormous. As a result of World War II, the entire church interior has been gutted because of extensive fire and damages. Prior to that time, the village had already faced various fires. In fact, in a 1719 conflagration, only three houses were saved in addition to the church and some other buildings.[13]

The community was famous for its silver mining. It is said that in 1416 the largest piece of silver known in Europe up until that time had been discovered right across from the church. Even though the coal, silver, and other minerals except uranium have all been depleted, since the 1670s the city has continued to celebrate an annual *Bergmannfest* (miners' festival) to commemorate the extensive coal mines found everywhere in the area. A festival service is conducted in the church each year. Walther was a witness to these festivities.

Founded in 1485, the school Walther attended in Schneeberg had gone through various phases. Some of these changes were caused by fire, others by changes in the philosophy of education by the time young Walther enrolled. The building in which Walther studied still stands except that it has been enlarged on several occasions. This school is approximately one block away from the church, St. Wolfgang Church, which stands on the hill.

The names of most teachers and instructors throughout the years have been lost. Whoever they were, the teachers had a reputation of being extremely strict and applying corporal punishment. A deeply revered Rektor by the name of Gottlob August Voigtlaender served the school from 1820 to 1828, Walther's years as a student. Although he was only twenty years old when he came to head the institution, educated people and the instructors held him in great respect. The school chronicle indicates that he had great organizational talents and was always deeply concerned about his teachers and students. Unfortunately, Voigtlaender died when only twenty-nine years old.[14]

It was during this time that Walther's brother-in-law, Magister Heinrich Wilhelm Friedrich Schubert, served as "Con-Rektor, *auf Probe.*" This means he was an associate principal while still a trial teacher. At the time Walther was at Schneeberg, Schubert was married to Walther's older sister, Theresa Wilhelmina, and during this time the two Schubert children whom Walther tried to bring to America in 1838 were born. However, Theresa died in 1832, after which Schubert married another of Walther's sisters, Mariane Louisa. Both the second wife and Schubert died of an unknown cause in 1834. (Schubert lived to be only thirty-eight years old, his first wife only thirty, and his second wife only twenty-four.)

It is regrettable that none of the records including the curricula, the names of the instructors or the students have survived. At the time Walther attended the school, there were over 200 students. Shortly after Walther graduated, it was converted into a *Bürgerschule* (a citizen's school). Histories of the institution indicate that the majority of the teachers were theologians.[15] Nevertheless, rationalism had taken over. Walther later recalled in an 1872 address to the Synod: "I was eighteen years old when I left the *Gymnasium*, and I had never heard a sentence taken from the Word of God out of a believing mouth. I had never had a Bible, neither a Catechism, but a miserable '*Leitfaden*' [a manual or guide] which only contained morality."[16]

Historian Kurt Krauss reports that the curriculum included French, English, Italian, arithmetic, and Latin. At one time, the old records state, even Syriac and Arabic had been taught. The Schneeberg pastor gave six hours of instruction on the introduction to the biblical books.

While attending the school, Walther entered an interesting item in his diary on February 8, 1829:

> Today my parents came and surprised me, which was most welcome.
> I can honestly admit that I am more pleasantly satisfied in the midst
> of my own family, even though I have been trying to tell myself that
> I like it best in the midst of my fellow students.[17]

Introspectively he wondered why he was no longer pleased to be in Schneeberg when only a few weeks before he had thought of leaving only with the deepest pains because of the separation. He continued:

> I am counting the minutes that are still left before I will be depart-
> ing from here. I reached a real understanding today—I am going to

bother my father until he will finally give me permission to leave here at Easter.

The young Walther also recorded that he was frequently saddened because he recognized how superficial his thoughts often were, even when his father as well as his fellow students and teachers assured him that he was a very optimistic person. But he had discovered that he was miserable, without end! Later in that same diary entry he recorded:

> I feel that I am born for nothing but music, within which I don't see myself making enough headway. Perhaps I could contribute something if I would study the doctrine of pure composition. But where is there an opportunity? Where are the means for that? Besides, the only instrument that I can play is the piano and that is certainly most pitiful. May God lead me out of this labyrinth. A dark veil seems to be covering my future and I am looking at it as though mesmerized. … But who knows, who knows, what the dice that will be cast from the urn will hold for my future.

In his diary entry of January 30, 1829, Walther showed both his understanding of music and his highly developed tastes. He had attended a concert in the Liebhaber Theater in Schneeberg, which he admitted was well worth a *Groschen* (a sum of money). But how critical he was of the composer, the chorus, the overture, and the adagio!

At about the same time he recorded his attendance at a "ball" and admitted secretly in his diary: "I must admit it, I found it extremely difficult at first not to participate [in the dance] but I got a hold of myself and gradually I became accustomed to withdrawing from the number of dancers."

He noted further in his diary on February 2 that he had not intended to engage in dancing, but simply wanted to have some entertainment with his evening meal. The next day, February 3, he recorded that he had attended another dramatic presentation. It was entitled "*Die Sucht zu Glänzen*," which literally means "the craze for glitter." This time Walther said that he was deeply affected by the presentation and totally identified with the writer.

Instead of leaving at Easter time, as he had hoped, Walther left the academic institution at Schneeberg on September 23, 1829. He received an excellent report card and his instructors acknowledged him as being "deeply honorable, with excellent knowledge." He was described on his dismissal report as "*Imprimis dignus*," especially worthy.[18] This meant that he was exceedingly well-qualified for academic studies and that he had never become guilty of any offenses while he was a student. The "Pastor Primarius," the head pastor who was also the superintendent at Waldenburg, wrote on November 21, 1829, to the University of Leipzig that he was commending the promising youth, Carl Ferdinand Walther, to be totally worthy, deserving, and honorable ("*Würdig*" and "*Bedürftig*"). He further stated that the letter was being written with the permission of his honorable academic teachers as well as other high patrons and sponsors of knowledge and academia of the school.[19]

While Walther was in Schneeberg the village suffered another fire, which broke out very suddenly. Walther ran to the house as it was being destroyed in the dead of winter. He wrote that he was not physically able to work hard in extinguishing the fire, but finally joined the bucket brigade. The buckets were frozen with ice outside and inside! This made any effort far less effective, since the amount of water transferred from one person to the next was limited.

In typical fashion, even until late in life, Walther denigrated himself because of his inadequate academic training. He wrote in his journal:

> This is exactly what makes my soul depressed, that I know, even though my knowledge is still very superficial in every respect; nevertheless, my father reminds me, yes, my teachers and especially also my fellow students, that I do have the knowledge, yes, even more that I am a promising student. I am very much afraid of the moment when that error will be discovered. I am miserable and without any limits or parameters to hang onto.[20]

On October 15, 1829, he recorded in his diary a moving departure from Schneeberg on his way back to his hometown of Langenchursdorf. It was difficult, he wrote, to separate himself from his fellow students and teachers. It was particularly hard for him to leave behind his "good Theresa," perhaps a high school friend. He stated:

> Such a parting I have not expected—such large and emphatic signs of loving well wishes. All of this, I became aware, humbled me very much because I realized that I was not worthy of any of them. But it engendered in me the conviction and goal that I should become worthy of them. So we departed and sixteen students accompanied me to Hasel [about two and one-half hours from Schneeberg] and thereafter four students followed me and stayed overnight with me [Zoffel, Stuebe, and two Guenthers]. The next day I left for Zwickau where I was received in a very friendly manner and showered with gifts. Soon I was on my way back to Chursdorf [as he recorded the name of the

village]. At Lichtenstein my brother [Otto Hermann] came with the red horse to pick me up. [It is humorous that some have looked at this part of the diary and saw that Walther referred to a *Fuchs*. Literally translated this would be a fox. Some have translated this section that his brother came to pick him up with a fox!]

Soon my brother and I were engaged in extremely interesting conversation, especially about the blessings that together we had experienced. He had given me a copy of Schubert's biography of Oberlin.[21] This filled my entire spirit and demonstrated to me that the possibilities a theologian has are the best ... The noisy doubts whether one could earn enough money [in the ministry] were completely overcome, since it was confidence in God, a firm faith in God's care and preservation that "provides the foundation to live."

He continued in his diary that he had been significantly encouraged by his "dear good brother" and prays that God will give him the grace to keep him in that faith, which has made him so blessed at this moment of his life.

During his Schneeberg days he was interested in nothing but music, but Walther was transformed by the biography of Oberlin. In addition, his brother Otto Hermann must certainly have been a strong factor in inclining Walther toward the study of theology.

Having left Schneeberg with a visit to Zwickau[22] and deep discussions with his brother, Walther arrived in Leipzig to enroll in the University on October 21, 1829. On December 5, he entered in his diary his arrival and praised and thanked God for unending love and protection.

CHARACTER BUILDING AT LEIPZIG

Walther was only eighteen years old when he matriculated at Leipzig University,[23] and he was a student there from 1829 to 1833. After arriving, Walther moved in with his older brother on Seidel Street. He received a cord of wood from a foundation because of his academic accomplishments. His father generously gave him a Thaler (perhaps a dollar) each week. We have a good glimpse of his university life from the biography which Walther wrote of his brother-in-law, Johann Friedrich Buenger.[24]

As our Buenger at Easter 1829 entered the University of Leipzig, conditions as concerned the true Christian faith, were as dismal at the highest school of the land as they were in all of Saxony. Precisely from this university for many years already there had flowed, as a living spring, the poisonous stream of rationalism, of unbelief, of sham enlightenment and the most frightful distortion of Scripture upon all the congregations of Saxony. The preachers whose misfortune it was to be prepared at that time to serve the church in Leipzig, proclaimed from their pulpits in the congregation that, naturally, which their professors had given them as the great new wisdom. At the very top of the whole church there stood at that time the Chief Court Chaplain and Vice President of the Chief Consistory, Christoph Friederich von Ammon, who had written a book with the title *Continuation of the Building of Christianity Toward a World Religion* [*Fortbildung des Christentums zur Weltreligion*].

The brother of this biographer rightly declared concerning this book that the title ought really to have been "The Perversion of Christianity Toward a Worldly Religion." Indeed, rationalism had perverted and watered down Christianity into "a different Gospel—which is really no Gospel at all," against which the Apostle Paul had warned (Galatians 1:6–9).

The called professors of theology at Leipzig at that time were August Hahn, Friedrich Wilhelm Lindner, Johann August Heinrich Tittmann, Karl Gottfried Wilhelm Theile, Christian Friedrich J. Illgen, Julius Friedrich Winzer, and Johann David Goldhorn, who were later followed by Christian Wilhelm Niedner, Georg Benedict Winer, and others.

According to Walther, the best of these professors were the first two mentioned. Hahn had fought against rationalism and carried forward no less than the pure Christian doctrine, but Lindner, although he appeared resolute, published a massive book against the Lutheran doctrine of Holy Communion in the year 1831. The other professors, Tittmann excepted, were outspoken rationalists. Walther continued, "There was then great danger for our Buenger, that he might yet lose even the little that he had brought away with him from his father's house and that had been saved during his school years."[25]

Yet Buenger came to Leipzig exactly at that time when a small group of students found themselves together. They had come to faith in the divine authorship of the Holy Scriptures and in the grace of God in Christ, the Savior of sinners, not so much through the lectures of the better professors as through the witness of believing laity, so called, and particularly through one old candidate [H. Johann Gottlieb] Kuehn, who lived in his own house in Leipzig. From the very beginning he had been a dedicated Christian. Although he had graduated from the university, Kuehn served a deaconite in Rochsburg and Lünzenau when he died prematurely on August 24, 1832 after a brief illness with fever. The pious Graf [von Einsiedel], who was the patron of the church of that place, then called Ernst Moritz Buerger who married Kuehn's widow and later immigrated to America with the Stephanites.

This handful of awakened students gathered on specific dates of every week for common prayer and for the common reading of Holy Scriptures to their edification and for a mutual exchange with respect to the one thing needful. For a while (at the invitation of August Hermann Francke), Professor Lindner also privately conducted a so-called Collegium Philobiblicum, in which he applied the Scriptures in an edifying manner and gave instruction in the derivation of servant themes from biblical texts. The students, who had come to faith and had withdrawn completely from the world, naturally had to submit to much ridicule and derision.

Mystics, as one tended to call these believers in Saxony, pietists, hypocrites, obscurantists, bigots, were not the worst names that men gave them. In part hated as contemptible deceivers, and in part sympathized as unfortunately misguided religious enthusiasts, they were ostracized by the living world and to some extent by their own closest blood relatives. But despite this, they remained inwardly joyful in their God and Savior. All who remained loyal among them looked back in future years to this time of their first love as the most blessed time of their entire life.[26]

Also in that small group, sometimes referred to as the "Holy Club," was Walther's older brother Otto Hermann, who had taken him along to the first meetings and introduced him to this New World. Thus Walther experienced a strong emphasis on the pietistic life. It was a legalistic mindset that kept goading the young men to lead a more acceptable life in the eyes of God. One is reminded of Luther, whose concern was to seek a loving and forgiving Father in heaven. Walther could not find him either because of all the pietistic legalism he had absorbed.

For Walther the dilemma was intense. On the one hand, the majority of his professors were rationalists, accepting only what was reasonable in the Bible. What was not, they totally rejected. On the other hand, he was deeply involved with the "Holy Club" pietism, which emphasized that the person must be engaged in self-denial, mortification of the flesh and a conscious avoidance of everything that was evil in the world. Regardless of what exercises Walther tried, he was unable to find a forgiving, loving God.

In Walther's biography of Buenger, he described the reading habits of the group of theological students as they tried to make themselves more holy:

The less a book invited to faith, and the more legalistically it urged contrition of the heart and total mortification of the old man preceding conversion, the better a book we held it to be. And even these books[27] we read only so far as they described the sorrows and exercises of repentance; as this was followed by a description of faith and comfort for the penitent, we usually closed such a book, for we thought this did not as yet concern us.[28]

Walther still had not found the spiritual consolation he was looking for. Encouraged by his friends, he wrote to Martin Stephan, a notable confessional Lutheran pastor in Dresden. Stephan had preached the Gospel in an age of faithlessness and rationalism. His sermons and devotional exercises brought countless people to his church. Sometimes entire families walked many miles to attend his worship services.

Walther was desperate. He wanted to have assurance that God loved him. He explained his situation in a letter to Stephan and then waited for a reply. When the letter finally came, Walther first prayed fervently that God would not permit him to receive further misleading comfort. Then he finally opened it, and years later he recalled: "When I read his reply I felt as though I had been translated from hell to heaven. Tears of distress and sorrow were transformed into tears of heavenly joy."

He was unable to resist. He had to return to Jesus. Stephan showed him that the repentance which he was seeking was on the basis of the law, and he had already experienced it; that he was lacking nothing but faith. He was exactly like the person who had fallen among the murderers and was then saved by the heavenly, merciful, and caring Good Samaritan.[29]

Walther also found effective comfort and help in the home of Friedrich W. Barthel in Leipzig. At the time that Walther studied at Leipzig, he frequently entered the Barthel home, where he was always comforted and directed to the Gospel. At the age of thirty-four, Mrs. Barthel, along with her husband and five children, would participate in the Saxon immigration. They were passengers on the *Olbers* and the steamboat *Selma*. Her husband, who became the first treasurer of The Lutheran Church—Missouri Synod, died in 1857. Her son Martin became the first manager of Concordia Publishing House, serving from 1869 to 1891. At Mrs. Barthel's funeral service in 1881, Walther spoke these words beside her coffin:

At that time it was particularly the dear deceased who carried me in her motherly heart. As often as I stepped over her threshold, there flowed from her mouth not only evangelical words of comfort for me, but also day and night she prayed in fervent prayer for me, a young stranger and behold! God heard her supplication. Finally I found peace in Christ. And now a bond of blessed fellowship with Christ embraced us that nothing was able to break until her death.[30]

A third experience at Leipzig further helped to mold Walther's character. During the winter of 1831–32, he temporarily discontinued his university studies because of his poor health. It was the old lung problem, which some have identified as tuberculosis or consumption coupled with a very frugal lifestyle and constant self-accusations and spiritual uncertainty. During his semester out, he returned to his paternal home and spent whatever energy he had reading Luther's works in the library of his father.

Instead of celebrating the three hundredth anniversary of the transmission of the Augsburg Confession on June 25, 1530, the townspeople of Leipzig celebrated on June 24, 1830 the two hundredth anniversary of the arrival of Gustav Adolph of Sweden to support the Protestants in the Thirty Years War. Walther recorded in his diary that there was a great celebration in the city, the ringing of bells and jubilation: "Today I heard Goldhorn, who really sent me into a mood that I am hoping to retain tomorrow, to consider earnestly the year 1630, thirty years of Ferdinand's persecution of Protestantism, and joy over the present and hope for the future."

There were especially two pastors in Leipzig who still preached the old Gospel under whom believing students could attend worship services. The first was Pastor F. A. Wolf who served at St. Peter's Church. Later these students attended worship services at the Orphan's and Penitentiary Church where Pastor F. M. Haensel delivered the sermons. Haensel's sermons were always filled with the biblical message. Walther was greatly comforted by these gospel preachers at a time when he felt that he had been thoroughly rejected by God because of his inability to atone for his sins.

Out of all of this emerged two mottoes to which Walther adhered throughout his lifetime. The first was "Back to Luther," and the second was "The nearer to Luther, the better the Theologian."

Although Walther had been at a very low level of spiritual life, at Leipzig things took a turn for the better. A strong transformation took place in him, from unbelief to rationalism, to pietism, and then to Lutheran confessionalism.

Walther returned to the University of Leipzig shortly after Easter 1832. He spent the next year there until Easter and completed his prescribed courses.

There is an interesting side aspect of Walther at Leipzig that we should not omit. Walther served as a tutor to Eduard Sander (perhaps Cander) whom he described in his diary. Eduard had written a note, probably for himself, about how grateful he was that Walther had been his tutor "to whom I owe my entire salvation [*sic*]. I did not know before he came to me whether or not I was a sinner, I knew something about Christ and His grace, but nothing from the Bible. For everything I thank my present tutor [Walther]. I as a very weak sinful man cannot repay him sufficiently, but God will do so, because he has led my soul to heaven."

Walther expressed in his diary how great, blessed, and caring our God is: "He has given this child the Spirit. Please do not let him be disappointed; to you belong the praise, the thanks, and the honor in all eternity. Oh Lord Jesus, complete the work that you have here started so very impressively; do not let him be torn out of your hands. Help him now and continue to lead him to your heavenly kingdom."

DISPUTES AT KAHLA

From 1834 to 1836 Walther served as a tutor at the Friedemann Loeber estate in Kahla. Friedemann was the oldest brother of Pastor G. H. Loeber who participated in the Saxon Immigration and later was called to Altenburg, Perry County, Missouri. As tutor, Walther served not only the Friedemann Loeber children but also the August Loeber children. This must have been an exciting place for Walther because he frequently had an opportunity to discuss and even to dispute significant religious matters with his principal.

An 1886 issue of *Der Lutheraner* gives us an interesting and quite contemporary description of what they were disputing.[31] The principal, Friedemann Loeber, argued with Walther that not everything in the Bible was totally dependable and divine truth. Walther observed that his principal was not an enemy of Christianity, but in his youth there had been many rationalistic ideas which he had absorbed and which were still clinging to him. For example, the principal held that the Holy Spirit did really not inspire the Bible account of the stars, and therefore the stars were lights on which creatures similar to those on earth were living. Walther wrote:

> I tried to talk this out of him as well as I knew how at that time but without results. On one occasion he was beaming all over and came to my room and showed me a newspaper. He said, "My dear Mr. Candidate, you have been beaten. I have just read in this paper that at

the beginning of this year 1834, the great astronomer Herschel had taken all of his giant telescopes to Africa in order to see whether there were people on the moon. Now just read it." he said.

Walther responded that he read it and that in truth there really was a news item that confirmed what the principal had said:

> But I responded to him: "My dear Mr. Principal, I petition you that you not believe that. Yes, because I am telling you that if I myself would look into this telescope and would see that there were some kind of people on the moon such as we are and were running around up there I would not believe it. The moon does not have inhabitants. I believe that the people that were seen in the telescope were not on the moon but actually inside it." To that my Mr. Principal responded, "I cannot convince you of anything," and in a kind of huff he left me.

Both Walther and Loeber were men of their time. One wonders how the conversation would have turned at the announcement "The Eagle Has Landed," when on July 20, 1969, Neil Armstrong and Edwin Aldrin Jr. landed on the moon. Perhaps Friedemann Loeber and Walther would have shared a laugh.

BEGINNINGS IN THE MINISTRY: BRAEUNSDORF

The time had now come for Walther to move on to his first parish assignment in Saxony. The place was Braeunsdorf, an old community which may have gotten its name from "Brauen," the brewing industry that thrived there.

We do not know exactly when the parish was established. Obviously it was Roman Catholic until the Reformation transformed the congregation in 1543 at the time when the von Schoenburg family traded the territory with Duke Moritz in the famous Weckselburg.

The Thirty Years War created havoc in the community. In 1640 the first church and parsonage were burned to the ground. Between 1641 and 1643, the congregation did not have its own pastor because the members were unable to support one. The story is still told today that during the Thirty Years War the Swedish soldiers encamped at Braeunsdorf and used the church for their cooking, with a rather large fire going inside. The local teacher had been asked to put the fire out, but he failed to do so, whether in stubbornness or forgetfulness we don't know, and the ancient church burned to the ground.

Following the war, that church was replaced by a new building in about 1652. This is the edifice in which Walther preached his inaugural sermon on January 15, 1837. By 1899 the congregation finally built its third church, the one visitors see today at Braeunsdorf. It was built on the exact spot where the earliest ones had been. It stands on a prominent hill, and one can see to the northwest both Hohenstein and Wolkenburg. Walther occupied a parsonage built in 1773, since the former parsonage of 1652 had also been destroyed by fire.

There is an interesting note that the first Lutheran pastor was Johann Sosenloh (sometimes spelled Hosenloch). He had been a schoolteacher and was ordained by Luther himself in Wittenberg on February 10, 1538. The first full-time resident pastor was Caspar Altwein who served from 1643 to 1694. The twentieth pastor of the congregation was August Theophilus Niedner, born 1760, who served from 1804 until the time of his death on April 26, 1836, at 76 years of age. He was survived by seven children, some of whom emigrated to America and became prominent in the St. Louis printing operation as well as in the ministry.

Carl Ferdinand Wilhelm Walther became the twenty-first pastor of this historic congregation. Walther had successfully completed his second examination for the office of ministry known as the "*Examen pro Candidatura*" in the fall of 1836.

There were two examinations that the Saxon Church required of its divinity school graduates prior to their entrance into the ministry. The first was the "*Examen pro Licentia Concionadi.*" After passing this successfully, the candidate was permitted to preach. The Commission of Professors from Leipzig conducted this exam. In his diary, Walther recorded an interesting result of this examination. One of his former professors, Dr. G. B. Winer, asked Walther to explain Romans 3:28 and whether it had been legitimate for Luther to insert the word "*allein*" (alone)—that we are saved by faith alone not by the demands of the law. Walther replied emphatically "yes." The professors and students who were present poked fun at this pietist and mystic for his ignorance.

Winer continued the examination, but Walther stood his ground and gave strong evidence for his stance. Then Professor Winer addressed the audience and said, "Gentlemen, this young mystic understands St. Paul better than any one of you."[32]

He had invited Otto Hermann to the second examination. In his biography of his brother-in-law Buenger, Walther states:

The second examination, to which one could not be admitted until two years later, was ... the examination before the State Consistory in order to qualify for appointment. ... At that time it was almost an impossibility for an orthodox candidate, who confessed and practiced his faith, to get a place in Saxony under royal patronage through the unbelieving State Consistory.[33]

Ernst Moritz Buerger, a Leipzig University graduate of 1829 and a member of the 1838 immigration, has left some more information about the second examination. He himself went to Dresden together with thirty other students to be examined. From four to six students were examined each day. The chief chaplain to the prince and the general superintendent of the church were the primary examiners. The examination lasted three hours and included delivering a sermon and some catechetical exercises.[34]

After his examination, Walther was soon to see emphasized that the ecclesiastical world was dominated by very strong rationalists, those who believe that only reason could be employed in the church, and that Bible believers who centered their faith in the Gospel were called mystics, pietists, and separatists. The differences were still extremely pronounced, even though Claus Harms had initiated a return to confessionalism or "Old Lutheranism" as early as 1817.

That Walther received an appointment to Braeunsdorf was due to the influence of Count Detlef von Einsiedel, prime minister in the cabinet of the Saxon king, Friedrich August I. The king was Roman Catholic, while Count von Einsiedel was a strong Lutheran. However, the king had abandoned almost all of his participation in ecclesiastical matters in Saxony.

The superintendent of the Braeunsdorf area and pastor of the imposing church at Penig, Heinrich Otto Siebenhaar, was in charge of Walther's induction. After Walther had passed his examination, he wrote to the superintendent from Langenchursdorf on November 10, 1836, indicating that he was now ready for the examination by the congregation and for ordination and installation.

Siebenhaar announced this to the congregation and asked that it be read on the first two Sundays in Advent, informing them that Walther had been named pastor of the congregation as successor of the deceased, August Theophilus Niedner. All people, he urged, ought to be present at the service.

Siebenhaar wrote to Walther on November 25, 1836 that the third Sunday in Advent had been chosen for Walther to deliver a trial sermon and catechetical demonstration in Braeunsdorf. The text suggested to

Walther was John 1:19–27. The catechesis was to be based on Ephesians 1:3–6, the Epistle reading for that Sunday. Siebenhaar asked that a summary of each be sent to him in advance. At the same time Siebenhaar invited Walther to bring his honored father and his brother to be present for this festive day, and then wished blessings upon the young candidate.

The schoolmaster at the church, J. G. Neidert, made the announcements to the congregation. In addition, Siebenhaar asked him to check with the congregation whether they could have the carriage in Penig at 7 A.M. to pick him up, or whether he was to arrange for his own coach. We don't know how the superintendent eventually got to Braeunsdorf.

At the preliminary event, Walther submitted the probationary sermon outline on John 1:19–27. Walther's theme was on witnessing to Christ and having the proper qualifications to do this. Such witnessing must be in harmony with Holy Scriptures. The substance of such witnessing must be based on one's own faith, experience, and humility, with love, not self-seeking. He stated finally that their witness must be grounded in and based on a divine call, which takes place in true confidence in God, without fear of men, and to God's honor without being a man-pleaser.

An announcement was made to the congregation that Candidate Walther would assume his ministry on the second Sunday after Epiphany, January 15, 1837. At that time the ordination and investiture would take place. Siebenhaar informed the congregation and Walther that the new pastor should receive the Holy Sacrament in order to give testimony that he really held membership in the Evangelical Lutheran Church. A Pastor Poetzchke of Kaufungen was to administer private confession to the candidate.

The superintendent designed the following order of service for the January installation:

1. Opening hymn
2. Ordination with celebration of Holy Communion
3. Investiture after which the autobiography is to be read together with the call document.
4. The main hymn
5. The Gospel
6. The confession of faith
7. The sermon
8. A hymn
9. Intonation, collect, blessing, and an expression of the Walther name
10. The final hymn[35]

The ordination was somewhat of a test case for Walther with respect to the deep tensions, which existed between the Confessional Lutherans and the Rationalists. Siebenhaar was soon identified as a Rationalist and supported by the Braeunsdorf schoolmaster, J. G. Neidert. Walther's big fear was that in preparation for his installation, the superintendent would alter the pledge to the Confessions. By this time Walther had already made the Augsburg Confession his own. Fortunately for Walther, the superintendent did not include any rationalistic ceremonies, although the sermon he delivered seemed to be unchristian at times. Walther's ordination followed the practice of the Apostolic and the contemporary church. Perhaps somewhat surprisingly, the Lord's Supper had not been modified and Walther received it after the Confession and Absolution.[36] Throughout his life, Walther's ordination vow was always a source of great comfort to him.

It is interesting—something we might well emulate today—that the ordinand also prepared an autobiography, which was read to the assembled congregation. At this time, Walther again expressed his humility in accepting the responsibility of the office and felt he was lacking something for the position.

Both Walther's father and his brother were able to participate in the installation service in Braeunsdorf on January 15, 1837. Attending the installation were five men and one woman, namely Frau Bretschneider, an occupant of a home in Braeunsdorf. The men were either farmers or gardeners. Participants were:

Heinrich Otto Sibenhaar, Superintendent
Gottlob Heinrich Wilhelm Walther, Pastor
Johann August Gottlob Goebel—Undesignated
Christ Gottl Wilhelm Eckhardt—Undesignated
Otto Hermann Walther, P. Vicar
Carl Ferdinand Wilhelm Walther
Ernst Gerhard Wilhelm Keyl, Pastor
Gottlieb Frischmann
Johann Gottlieb Tchoke
Gottfried Landgraf

The records indicate that both Tchoke and Landgraf were gardeners and were representatives of the congregation. The rest of those participating were clergymen.

Walther preached in his inaugural sermon on Jeremiah 1:6–8:

Then said I, Ah, Lord God! Behold, I cannot speak; for I am a child. But the Lord said unto me, Say not, I am a child: for thou shalt go to all that I shall send thee, and whatsoever I command thee, thou shalt speak. Be not afraid of their faces: I am with thee to deliver thee, says the Lord.

This text could be considered the theme of Walther's entire life. In his sermon he made three assertions:

1. A pastor does not come because of his own will, but because God is calling him.
2. He does not come with his own wisdom, but with the Word of God.
3. He does not come with his own ability, but with the assistance of God.

In an undated letter written to Detlef von Einsiedel, Walther described his own installation and evaluated the spirituality of the congregation. It was not a very pretty picture.[37] According to Walther, the congregation had been sadly neglected for almost forty years; the living Word of God had not been preached! He wrote that respect for the Word of God and for the minister was only superficial, and only insofar as it was compatible with carnal security. The sins of lewdness, lack of church attendance, drunkenness, shamelessness, and rudeness could be detected everywhere. The educational level of the people was very low; only a few adults were able to write their own name correctly.

The school, on the other hand, he considered to be superior. Order, diligence, and obedience were apparent in it. Walther spoke highly of the teacher and the impact he made on the children. He said that generally they were better taught and less rude than most children. Still, almost prophetically he talked about the schoolmaster J. G. Neidert by saying that the religious instruction was no more than moralizing and a unique mixture of truth and lies.

In the same letter Walther also expressed his goals for the congregation—goals that could still be valid today. He aimed to teach the fundamental doctrines of Scripture, and thereby bring his hearers to acknowledge their blindness, helplessness, and sinfulness, while at the same time sharing with them proper insight into the true essence of saving faith in Jesus Christ, and thus lead them into a truly Christian life. He hoped to arouse a love and desire to search the Word of God and, as much as possible, to overcome prejudices the congregation had against sacred Scripture and pure doctrine. All these concerns demonstrate to what depths rationalism had penetrated the Lutheran congregations.

Walther further wrote that he was preaching two sermons on every communion and festival day and that he had introduced church examinations (*Kirchenexamina*) on the Catechism. He described his superintendent, living on the hill in Penig, as a rationalist.

Parish Work at Braeunsdorf

Walther served this congregation for almost two years. Parish records indicate that during this time he conducted sixteen marriages. Of special interest is the fact that he had his first Baptism on February 3, 1837; he performed a total of twenty-five infant Baptisms in that year, and twenty-seven in 1838. The last Baptism he performed was on September 19, 1838, just a few weeks before his departure for America. It should be noted that of all the Baptisms he performed, six or seven were those of illegitimate infants. It demonstrates Walther's total commitment to Baptism as a means of grace, essential for infants. The church records reveal that Walther attached a likely father to such illegitimate children. The mere numbers of such out-of-wedlock births reveals the social and spiritual condition of the congregation.[38]

Walther's handwriting in these parish records is unusually legible (for Walther!). The records are neat. He signed off on the last entry he had made, testifying that the records above his signature were all entered by him.

On one occasion Walther was accused of being over-zealous in his pastoral ministry.[39] A wife, who worshiped regularly as a member of the church, sought spiritual counseling from Walther because her husband had physically abused her. The husband considered Walther a mystic and pietist, was incensed, and demanded that she return home with him. In efforts to get away from her husband, the woman walked to the school nearby, weak and confused. There she fainted and had to be cared for in the schoolhouse for three days.

Later, in March 1838, as she was leaving the parsonage, her husband struck her so that she became unconscious. Walther drafted a petition that the couple be separated for the sake of the wife's physical protection. The case was brought to Superintendent Siebenhaar who mildly reprimanded Walther, suggesting he exercise greater caution in the future. Walther defended himself in a letter dated July 31, 1838.

One of the questions asked was whether the wife had become interested in the emigration that was already being planned, to which Walther answered with a resounding "no." Yet she and her son appeared on the immigrant list. The case actually went to court in Leipzig and a fine was imposed on Walther; later it was dismissed. This was the prelude to all the intricacies involved with the Saxon Immigration. It also provided material for Walther's *Pastoral Theology*, which he was to later write.

The profound theological differences that existed between Superintendent Siebenhaar and Walther can best be illustrated by their disagreement about the meaning of subscription to the *Book of Concord*. Walther had testified that death had come into the world through the fall of our first parents into sin. The rationalist superintendent held that this doctrine had been abandoned ages ago.

When Walther reminded the superintendent that he himself had pledged Walther to the symbolical books, the superintendent smiled: "You were not pledged to the letter but to the spirit of the Confessions." Walther countered that this kind of interpretation had not been included in his ordination vow and that Scripture very clearly states: "The day that thou eatest thereof thou shalt surely die." The superintendent replied: "Nonsense! Spiritual death is meant there." But Walther did not remain silent and asked: "Does not God immediately after the fall say to Adam, Dust thou art and to dust shalt thou return? Is spiritual death meant there too?" The superintendent closed his eyes, remained silent, and dismissed Walther.[40]

In a letter to his good friend Brohm, written at Braeunsdorf August 17, 1837, Walther related the difficulties he had in selecting confessional Lutheran books for the school that the teacher Neidert did not want. Neidert had strongly objected to Walther's choice and suggested that they ask the superintendent to make a decision. The case was resolved, when shortly thereafter Count von Einsiedel stopped for a visit and confirmed Walther's choice. Von Einsiedel also reminded both the pastor and the teacher that according to Article VIII of the school's constitution, the pastor was authorized to select the books, and if there was a dispute, the district school inspector would decide the issue. That settled it.[41]

The parish school was of great importance to Walther as he witnessed the children maturing. When confirming children, Walther asked each confirmand to add another Bible passage after his confirmation verse; in this way, they gave first hand testimony of their faith in Scripture itself. Walther was trying to reintroduce the Gospel and confessional Lutheranism to this congregation. He regularly visited the school and kept records of these inspections. His last entry in the school record was dated

June 21, 1838. This laid the groundwork for his lifelong concern with Christian education.

Walther submitted his resignation to the Braeunsdorf congregation on September 30, 1838, with a bleeding heart and severe inward and outward struggles. He preached his farewell sermon on the same Sunday. The congregation responded with loud sobs and sighing.[42] In his chronicle of the Braeunsdorf parish, G. H. Seifert said that Walther's sermon "made a deep impression on the assembled hearers, so that some were sobbing loudly." Later, when he was faced with difficulties in Perry County, Missouri, Walther regretted that he had left his parish so precipitously. Nineteen members of his parish had joined him in the immigration that year.

In leaving, one of the more difficult issues facing Walther was the case of the Schubert orphans, his niece and nephew. The two children, Marie, age fifteen, and Theodor, age ten, had lost both their parents in 1834. During the intervening years until the time of the immigration they had been cared for by relatives.[43] And now came the immigration. What to do with the Schubert orphans? The Walther brothers wanted to whisk them out of the country, so they transported the minors illegally, took them to Bremen, and entrusted them to the mother of John F. Buenger. Thereupon, Johann Gottlieb Engel, who was married to Walther's sister, asked for the arrest of the children's custodian, who turned out to be J. F. Buenger's mother. This landed Mrs. Buenger in jail. Just a day earlier Walther had sailed to America on the *Johann Georg*, a few hours after the *Copernicus* had left Bremerhaven on November 3, 1838.

It is regrettable that a rumor has persisted that Walther was scheduled to sail on the *Amalia* in order to flee the country. The *Amalia*, which was lost at sea, did not leave port until November 18, 1838, fifteen days after Walther had sailed.

Great misfortune surrounded Mrs. Buenger as she was planning to embark. She was under arrest and in a Bremen jail. Her son, Johann F. and a daughter, Agnes, who was to marry O. H. Walther in America, stayed behind to be with her. Six of her children had already left for the United States. It was stark agony for her to watch the other ships sail out of the harbor. She was finally released and with her two children sailed on the *Constitution* to New York, arriving there on February 18, 1839. They traveled from New York to Perry County, where they arrived on May 18, 1839, just before Martin Stephan, the pastoral leader and bishop of the immigration, was deported to Illinois.

The Schubert children sailed on the *Olbers*, November 18, 1838, together with O. H. Walther and Martin Stephan.

Walther's ship, the *Johann Georg*, arrived at the port of New Orleans on January 5, 1839, four days later than the *Copernicus*. The group waited anxiously for the *Amalia* to arrive, but with great sadness finally gave up. No one knows where it sank. The waiting group then took steamboats up the Mississippi River to St. Louis. Walther traveled on the *Clyde*, and set foot on the wharf on January 24, 1839. While in St. Louis, Walther temporarily stayed with Gottlieb Kluegel in a large house on Broadway between St. Louis and Bremen Streets near the landmark called Indian Hill.

God had great things in store for C. F. W. Walther in St. Louis.

NOTES

[1] Sydney E. Ahlstrom, "Theology in America: A Historical Survey," in *The Shaping of American Religion* (*Religion in American Life*, Vol. I, J. W. Smith and A. Leland Jamison, eds. [Princeton, NJ: Princeton University Press, 1961]).

[2] Ahlstrom, "Theology in America: A Historical Survey," in *The Shaping of American Religion*, 275.

[3] I recorded this information on the basis of the baptismal records of the parish in Langenchursdorf, Germany. No records of the siblings are to be found anywhere in the U.S. The Langenchursdorf church records go back to 1612. The earlier ones, including baptismal records, were destroyed during the Thirty Years War (1618–48). The earliest entries were made in Latin, although some also appear in German. The Lutheran Reformation was introduced into the congregation on November 18, 1542, and one of the early pastors, Paulus Reissmann, signed the Formula of Concord in 1580.

[4] A picture of it appears in W. G. Polack, *The Story of C. F. W. Walther* (St. Louis: Concordia Publishing House, 1947), 2.

[5] Martin Guenther, *Dr. C. F. W. Walther: Lebensbild* (St. Louis: Concordia Publishing House, 1890).

[6] O. H. Walther's documents submitted in preparation for his ordination after graduation from Leipzig.

[7] Since 1898 the village has been known as Hohenstein-Ernsthal.

[8] Private transactions Akta, filed in St. Christophorus Church, Hohenstein-Ernsthal.

[9] Friedrich Blume, *Protestant Church Music* (New York: Norton, 1974), 237, 351, 365–369. Over a hundred of Tag's cantatas are known, probably written during the 1760s and 70s. Tag's choral writing marks a transition into the age of the Liedertafel style, in which "extreme sentimentality is coupled with the pathos of unison writing and solo entrances by bass or tenor, whose . . . tone may elicit a *forte* entrance by the other voices."

[10] Ernst Christian Helmreich, *Religious Education in German Schools* (Cambridge: Harvard University Press, 1959), 19.

[11] Helmreich, *Religious Education in German Schools*, 41.

[12] Helmreich, *Religious Education in German Schools*, 42.

[13] August R. Suelflow, Personal notes from oral interviews in Schneeberg, 1987.

[14] Wolfgang Meyer, *1485–1985: 500 Jahre Höhere Schulen in Schneeberg/Erzgebirge* (Munich, Germany: Oschatz Marktheidenfeld), 19.

[15] See Kurt Krauss, *Schneeberger Heimatbüchlein*, No. 19, 1986, 14, 17. Page 21 states that the records of this school were lost.

[16] 16. *Synodolbericht 1872*, 69; cited by Guenther, *Dr. C. F. W. Walther: Lebensbild*, 5.

[17] *Tagebuch gehalten von F. Walther, Primaner zu Schneeberg* (Den Ersten Januar, 1829 [Walther's Diary, 1829–1831]), *C. F. W. Walther Papers*, M-0004, f. 373, Concordia Historical Institute.

[18] Guenther, *Dr. C. F. W. Walther: Lebensbild*, 4.

[19] Guenther, *Dr. C. F. W. Walther: Lebensbild*, 4.

[20] *Tagebuch*, Feb. 8, 1829.

[21] G. H. Schubert, *Züge aus dem Leben von Johann Friedr. Oberlin, gewesenen Pfarrer in Steinthal* (Reading, PA: Verlag der Pilger-Buchhandlung, no date). It is unknown what edition Walther had read of this extremely fascinating biography.

[22] Because of Walther's mother, the family remained close to the Zschenderleins in Zwickau. This family became noticeable once more when in 1871, Walther's aunt, Marianne Zschenderlein, left him a legacy. Instead of keeping it, he immediately gave all the money to the poor in Braeunsdorf.

[23] Leipzig University was opened on December 2, 1409, during the stormy days of the great papal schism, 1378–1429. This was the period when two popes headed the church. The Germans, Italians, English, Danes and Swedes supported Urban VI, elected in 1378. During that schism students and teachers left the University of Prague, and those from Saxony, Bavaria, and Poland went to Leipzig. At the Council of Pisa, Saxony had obtained from Alexander V, a successor, a bull granting permission for the establishment of the university.

[24] C. F. W. Walther, *Kurzer Lebenslauf des weiland ehrwürdigen Pastor Joh. Friedr. Bünger* (St. Louis: Verlag von F. Dette, 1882).

[25] Walther, *Kurzer Lebenslauf des weiland ehrwürdigen Pastor Joh. Friedr. Bünger*, 7.

[26] Walther, *Kurzer Lebenslauf des weiland ehrwürdigen Pastor Joh. Friedr. Bünger*, 7–9.

[27] For the sake of completeness it may be well to include a few titles or authors of the literature that the Holy Club used at Leipzig. Included in their regular reading were Johann Arndt, August Hermann Francke, C. H. von Bogatzke, Philip Jacob Spener, J. C. Schade, Johann Jacob Rambach, and Johann Phillip Fresenius.

[28] Walther, *Kurzer Lebenslauf des weiland ehrwürdigen Pastor Joh. Friedr. Bünger*, 17–18.

[29] Walther, *Kurzer Lebenslauf des weiland ehrwürdigen Pastor Joh. Friedr. Bünger*, 29.

[30] Henry J. Eggold, trans., *Selected Writings of C. F. W. Walther: Selected Sermons* (St. Louis: Concordia Publishing House, 1981), 188.

[31] "Gibt es auf dem Monde auch eine Art Menschen?" *Der Lutheraner*, Vol. 42 (March 1886), 46.

[32] C. L. Janzow, *Life of Rev. Prof. C. F. W. Walther, D. D.* (Pittsburgh: American Lutheran Publication Board, 1899), 16.

[33] Walther, *Kurzer Lebenslauf des weiland ehrwürdigen Pastor Joh. Friedr. Bünger*, 16, 20.

[34] Edgar Jochim Buerger, *Memoirs of Ernst Moritz Buerger* (Lincoln, MA: Martin Jullian Buerger, 1953), 19–20.

[35] Auszug aus den Acten der Evangel. Superintendent Chemnitz, 1836–1838 in the collection of Concordia Historical Institute, St. Louis. W. H. T. Dau may have copied this material in the 1920s.

[36] Guenther, *Dr. C. F. W. Walther: Lebensbild*, 20–21.

[37] Guenther, *Dr. C. F. W. Walther: Lebensbild*, 19–24.

[38] Most of this material was excerpted from a chronicle of the congregation written by one of its pastors, T. H. Seiffarth in 1901.

[39] Auszug aus den Acten der Evangel. Superintendent Chemnitz, 1836–1838.

[40] Walther, *Kurzer Lebenslauf des weiland ehrwürdigen Pastor Joh. Friedr. Bünger*, 32.

[41] Guenther, *Dr. C. F. W. Walther: Lebensbild*, 26.

[42] Guenther, *Dr. C. F. W. Walther: Lebensbild*, 33.

[43] Walter O. Forster, *Zion on the Mississippi* (St. Louis: Concordia Publishing House, 1953), 194.

2

NEW HORIZONS IN AMERICA

STEPHAN AND THE RELIGIOUS CLIMATES IN GERMANY

Martin Stephan excelled in his Gospel ministry as a laudable leader in his congregation, St. John's, Dresden. Shortly after the immigration to America in 1838 he became a depressing disappointment to many who knew him.

His greatest *forte* in his ministry in Haber, Bohemia and in Dresden, Saxony was, as Walther had noted, that he preached the Gospel having experienced its power in his own soul.[1] In the midst of rationalism in the church and the decline and denial of the apostolic doctrines, Stephan stood his ground for confessional or "old Lutheranism."

Stephan was born on August 13, 1777 in Stramberg, Moravia and orphaned early in his life. In his youth he lived in poverty and received only a limited education. Since his father had been a weaver, Martin took up the same trade and became a journeyman linen weaver in Breslau, Silesia from 1797 to 1799.

The decades following Stephan's birth were extremely difficult for most German religious people. Confessional Lutheranism—that is, a Lutheranism that advocated a return to the Reformation doctrines of Martin Luther and a binding subscription to the Lutheran Symbols—was arising. This was a strong reaction to the Rationalism that was prevalent in the universities, the congregations, and the state government. Rationalism was considered the "new wisdom" which had been discovered mostly in academia. Scholasticism and reason were applied to theological matters. At first in their apologetics or defense of the faith, pastors tried to make the Christian faith be as "reasonable" as possible in argumentation. In the process, reason became more important than revelation. In some areas, such as colonial America and England, Deism, which rejected revelation completely, became very popular.

Following an age of Lutheran systematic formulations, Rationalists emptied the church doctrines, since they no longer accepted Scripture as

God's revelation, and developed a kind of humanistic philosophy. One of the first promoters of the movement was Christian Wolff (1679–1754), for whom reason became the final authority.

Pietism, which had preceded Rationalism, was strong, especially at Halle under the leadership of Philip Jacob Spener (1635–1705). He has often been referred to as the "Father of Pietism." His *Pia Desideria*, published in 1675, strongly influenced parish life because of the renewed emphasis on Bible studies and private devotional gatherings. He opposed the evils of Orthodoxism. His later followers, such as A. H. Francke, became most influential at the University of Halle, which was founded in 1694.

In his *Six Books on True Christianity*, Johann Arndt (1555–1621) combined Lutheran Orthodoxy with Pietism. With the commissioning of two missionaries to India in 1703, Pietism was responsible for the first foreign mission work in which Lutherans engaged.

By the 1750s however, Pietism was already being overshadowed. J. S. Semler (1725–1791) became the "Father of German Rationalism." He too became a professor of theology at the University of Halle but largely replaced the Pietism of Spener and Francke with Rationalism.

The battle between Orthodoxy and Rationalism reached a climax in the early nineteenth century. In 1817, Claus Harms (1778–1855) threw down the gauntlet when he issued a new set of Ninety-Five Theses in commemoration of the three hundredth anniversary of the Lutheran Reformation. He reissued Luther's Ninety-five Theses and added ninety-five of his own. The church was in the process of turning. The best brief description of changes and criticisms of the church is encapsulated in Thesis number 50:

> The Confessions of the Lutheran Church give us a correct interpretation of the Bible, but at the moment, the church is in a sad state … reason is running wildly through the church, driving Christ away from the altar, throwing God's Word out of the pulpit, mixing slime with holy water in the baptismal font, erasing the superscription over the confessional and driving the priest out of the sanctuary.[2]

In Thesis 77 he asks a penetrating question, one that is especially relevant today.

> To say that time has removed the wall of separation between Lutherans and Reformed is not to speak directly. The question is: Who has fallen away from the faith of their church, the Lutherans or the Reformed? Or both?[3]

During the prevalence of Rationalism, the vicarious atonement, justification by faith, the fall into sin, and related doctrines were rejected. Sermons became mere discourses on current events, science, careless bathing, and the necessity of planting trees.

It was during that same time that King Friedrich Wilhelm III of Prussia developed a plan for the protection of his homeland, which had been severely beaten by Napoleon's troops and conquered in 1806. He felt it would help stabilize his country if the Reformed and Lutherans would be merged in a single national church. Again, the occasion was the three hundredth anniversary of the Reformation in 1817. The opposition to the royal decree to merge was particularly vocal from the "old Lutherans" in Prussia. Ultimately this produced the "Old Lutheran Immigration" under J. A. A. Grabau (1804–1879), who led about a thousand immigrants to Buffalo, New York and to Wisconsin in 1839. It is estimated that ultimately between 5,000 and 6,000 emigrated for the same reasons. Although it was not always easy to receive permission to emigrate, the argument was based on the "*Beneficium Emigrandi,*" which since 1555 had established as a law that if you disagreed with your government in religious matters you had the right to emigrate.

Although Walther was not a Prussian but rather a Saxon, as noted in the first chapter, he opposed Rationalism wherever it was apparent, and specifically against his superintendent, Siebenhaar, in Penig as well as his school teacher, J. G. Neidert, in his parish in Braeunsdorf. In the meantime, Rationalism continued to empty the Scriptures. New agendas and hymnbooks were produced denying the fundamental doctrines of Lutheranism. It seemed that all of European Lutheranism as well as Lutheranism in America was in convulsion.

In America, for example, H. F. Quitman (1760–1832) prepared a new English Catechism in 1814 for the congregations of the New York Ministerium. To a specific question in the catechism, "What is faith in Christ?" Quitman answered: "A firm belief in the divine authority of Jesus, and of His doctrine and promises, expressed by a sincere zeal to cherish Christian sentiments and dispositions, and to cultivate Christian graces."[4] Many other such examples could be added. Conspicuous by its absence is the very center of Luther's theology, "justification by faith." Lutherans on both sides of the Atlantic had come to deny this chief tenet of the Reformation.

Walther and his fellow students at the University of Leipzig began their protests against such doctrinal deterioration through their membership in the "Holy Club." The members of this group, particularly when they were placed into pastorates in the Muldenthal (the valley of the Mulde), became convinced "Old Lutherans" or "Reformation Lutherans." At this point, Martin Stephan became an important leader of the group. He had been called to the Bohemian Church, which was joined to St. John's, Dresden in 1810. With the support of his friends, at twenty-five years of age Stephan had studied at the University of Halle and at Leipzig. He graduated from the latter in 1809. As noted in chapter 1, Stephan had helped Walther back to faith in Christ as his Savior.[5]

IMMIGRATION

Under the leadership of Stephan, Pastors E. G. W. Keyl, G. H. Loeber, E. M. Buerger, and the two Walther brothers, in addition to several candidates for the ministry, began arrangements for their immigration. The group consisted of about 700 people along with these candidates and pastors. It was really a fairly youthful group as one considers the ages of the clergymen and candidates: Martin Stephan, 61; Loeber, 42; Keyl, 35; Buerger, 33; O. H. Walther, 29; C. F. W. Walther, 27; Ottomar Fuerbringer, 28; and Georg Albert Schieferdecker, 24.

Because of Stephan's continued teaching and preaching of the Gospel at a time when people were surfeited with "rationalistic rot," he attracted huge numbers of people in his St. John's Church just outside the city walls of Dresden. They came from all areas, usually on foot, arising at sun-up on Sunday mornings so that they could get to his church in time.

One of those to attend Stephan's services was a Lutheran churchman from Gettysburg, Pennsylvania, named Benjamin Kurtz, who has left an interesting description of his visit to the church:

> The crowd was so dense that we could scarcely press into the church, and but for the distinguished rank of our noble companion [Count Detlef von Einsiedel?] we should probably have been compelled to remain outside. Mr. Stephan was then about fifty years of age, remarkably plain in his appearance, and his countenance and the contour of his head reminded us very forcibly of Dr. Dwight, the late President of Yale College. His sermon was plain, vigorous and evangelical, and well calculated to enlighten the mind and affect the heart. There was nothing like an attempt to show-off to advantage; no playing of the orator; no effort for applause (nothing of that kind). Fancy a very plain matter-of-fact man, rather tall, somewhat inclined to austerity, with a slight tinge of melancholy in his features, addressing a

crowd and deeply interested congregation in a most solemn manner, on the awful interests of the eternal destiny of man, holding up Jesus Christ as the only hope of a perishing world, and demanding faith in him and obedience to his precepts, as one who in the name of his Master has authority to insist on a compliance with these requisitions, and you'll have a tolerably correct conception of one of the most devoted and consistent and successful ministers then residing in the kingdom of Saxony. ...[6]

By 1838, five ships were ready to sail for America from Bremerhaven. The chronology of the ships was as follows:

Name of Ship	Date of Departure	Arrival in New Orleans
Copernicus	Nov. 3, 1838	Dec 31, 1838
Johann Georg	Nov. 3, 1838	January 5, 1839
Republic	Nov. 12, 1838	January 12, 1839
Olbers	Nov. 18, 1838	January 20,1839
Amalia	Nov. 18, 1838	Sunk in the Atlantic

The ships traveled in a southerly direction. Soon after embarking, they experienced hardships. Already on November 20, Franz Adolf Marbach's little two-year-old boy died on board the *Olbers*. Nor was the sailing smooth. The ships weathered extensive storms from November 21 to 28. A second little boy, Ernst Wilhelm, the one-year-old son of Carl Gottlieb Zeibig, died on December 19, also on the *Olbers*.

On December 9 Martin Stephan preached on board the *Olbers* for the first time since beginning the journey. Moreover, O. H. Walther, the poet of the immigration, produced a series of interesting poetry printed for the immigrants entitled *Exulanten Lieder*. Dedicated to Martin Stephan, published on October 31, 1838, it is a beautiful collection. One of the poems, sung to the tune of Paul Gerhardt's famous evening hymn "Now Rest Beneath Night's Shadow,"[7] expresses strong confidence in Christ:

> Now rest my child, and slumber
> No cares thy bed encumber
> But angels undefiled
> Our ship is still a-sailing
> Our pilot-true unfailing
> Is Christ the dear and Holy Child.[8]

The passengers recorded favorable winds, followed by storms as they came closer to the Gulf of Mexico, and the very warm temperatures they experienced as early as December 23, something they had not been accustomed to in their homes in Saxony. With great interest they watched the porpoises swimming alongside the ships, jumping ahead and then falling back and following them like pet dogs. They sighted Puerto Rico, the Santa Domingo Islands, and Cuba. They entered the Gulf of Mexico in mid-January, at which time they also elected Martin Stephan the Bishop of the immigrant family. The other passengers confirmed the election as soon as they arrived in the port of New Orleans.

The *Amalia* never arrived. Friends and relatives remained in the port to await the possible late arrival. Later Otto Hermann Walther, wrote an emotional poem as in dialogue with our Lord Jesus Christ.

> Lord Jesus, Lord Jesus, the ship has not come,
> The ship named *Amalia* is missing!
> When wilt Thou, O pilot, convey her back home
> From the storms that are howling and hissing?
> Have we, Lord been favored Thy mercies to share?
> Was their ship too small for Thy kindness and care?
> Lord Jesus, come, still all our yearning
> And hasten *Amalia's* returning!
>
> I granted her prayer
> For kindness and care.
> She was not too small
> For tempest and squall.
> My love went with her a-sailing,
> My power and presence prevailing.
> My sheep, neither hopeless nor craven,
> Were led to a beautiful haven.
>
> Lord Jesus, Lord Jesus, where dost Thou abide,
> And where are the people we cherish?
> Oh, help us, dear Savior, in Thee to confide,
> Renewing our hope lest it perish!
> We thirst for our brethren, to see them we long,
> And walk to the temple together in song.
> Lord Jesus, come, still all our yearning
> And hasten *Amalia's* returning!
>
> Away with all fear!
> Thy Lord is still near!
> The lilies at morn
> With dew I adorn;
> I feed all the birds of creation;
> My children shall see My salvation.

My sheep, neither hopeless nor craven,
Are led to a beautiful haven.

Lord Jesus, Lord Jesus, oh, point out, we pray,
The course where her banners are flying!
If she has succumbed to the storms on her way,
Then help us remember her dying!
Has she been devoured by the waves of the sea
Like Pharaoh's hosts of antiquity?
Lord Jesus, come, still all our yearning
And hasten *Amalia's* returning!

She was not forsaken;
Her people were taken
By Love's own behest
From toil unto rest.
No anger has dashed her to pieces;
But homeward her voyage now ceases.
My sheep, neither hopeless nor craven,
Have entered a beautiful haven.

Lord Jesus, Lord Jesus, oh, do not be grieved,
That we are still crying and weeping.
Thy Word has assured us, and we have believed,
Thy loved ones are safe in Thy keeping
For they who are steadfast in trials and shame
Shall meet there in heaven, proclaiming Thy name;
To Jesus, our Savior, returning,
His welcome shall still all our yearning.

My grace e'er shall be
Sufficient for thee.
Though darkness be here,
There all shall be clear;
And faithful My promise believing,
The crown of salvation receiving,
My sheep, neither hopeless or craven,
Shall enter the heavenly haven.[9]

Even prior to their departure, the immigrants had adopted several official documents. On May 17, 1838 in Dresden, the "Emigration Code" had been developed. The "Travel Regulations" indicate how Stephan became incredibly enamored by his success, starting with the manner in which he attracted worshipers to his parish in Dresden. Because he knew the Gospel and applied it successfully to the needs of the people, Stephan forgot that he had been successful by proclaiming the Lord Jesus Christ and not by proclaiming Martin Stephan. Pride and arrogance built up in him because his followers virtually worshiped and idolized him. His response was complete acceptance of this adulation, foolishly placing enormous value on his own person. This change of character caused him, with the consent of his loyal supporters, to put into the "Travel Regulations" several revealing paragraphs. Paragraph three of this code declares:

> The chief management of all affairs of the entire *Gesellschaft* [immigration society] shall be exercised by its primate, who accordingly will combine in his person the supreme authority in spiritual and civil matters. All arrangements for worship will emanate exclusively from him until the "Ecclesiastical Code" comes into existence after permanent settlement has been effected.[10]

The same document also established special rules on how the head of the immigration was to be treated. Paragraph six says:

> The primate shall at all times be treated by members of the *Gesellschaft* with a reverence due his high office and great wisdom; he shall receive the title 'Very Reverend Sir'; offenses against his person and disobedience against his orders shall be punished with severe civil and ecclesiastical penalties.
>
> Only his *Herr Colleagues* [fellow pastors] in office and the members of the board shall be granted immediate and free access to the primate— on ship the cabin passengers, and otherwise those to whom he expressly grants it. All other members of the *Gesellschaft* shall appear before him only after previous announcement.[11]

Later, on board the *Olbers* on January 14, 1839, they also signed "Stephan's Investiture." Upon arrival in America, additional signatures were gathered, including the names of Carl Ferdinand Wilhelm Walther, his brother Otto Hermann, Gotthold Heinrich Loeber, and Ernst Gerhard Wilhelm Keyl. The document includes this significant paragraph pledged to Martin Stephan:

> In consequence of all this, therefore, we approach you with the reverend, urgent plea: accept, Reverend Father, also for the future the office of Bishop among us bestowed upon you by God, and grant that we may now already express with this name our unqualified confidence in your fatherly love and pastoral faithfulness toward us, and the assurance of our sincere complete and childlike obedience toward you.[12]

Bishop Stephan had determined and convinced the signatories as they were approaching America that it was urgently important that he be identified as Bishop.[13]

Further this adulation of Martin Stephan is found in the "Pledge of Subjection" to Stephan which reveals abject submission:

> Further, we solemnly pledge ourselves, as we have already promised by signing the Emigration Code, par. 3, to submit with Christian willingness and sincerity to the ordinances, decrees, and measures of His Reverence in respect both to ecclesiastical and community affairs, and not to regard them as an irksome yoke, but as the means of promoting our temporal and eternal welfare.[14]

The climax of complete submission was expressed in the "Confirmation of Stephan's Investiture" dated February 24, 1839. It, too, contains Walther's signature followed by "formerly pastor at Braeunsdorf in Saxony." Incredible as it seems, the following is a sample from this document:

> And the more we have come to know of your doctrine, your message, your intention, your faith, your long-suffering, your love, your patience, your persecution, and your tribulations, the more we cannot but give thanks that the gracious and merciful God has kept you for His Church until now, and that your paternal, faithful care for the blossoming forth of this dear Church did not permit you to refuse at this perilous time the Episcopal office offered to you.

A few paragraphs later, we read:

> Therefore, also we and the three candidates subscribing with us herewith promise solemnly and before God that we will at all times and with unqualified confidence follow your further paternal leadership for which we plead, as well as comply with childlike, willing obedience with your Episcopal ordinances in all things.[15]

The document was duly signed on the *Olbers, Johann Georg, Copernicus,* and the *Republik* by the four clergymen, three candidates, and twelve congregational deputies. One could say that in this document Stephan had reached the absolute height of his professional life.

But the total collapse came less than two months later when the colonies were plunged into extreme chaos, doctrinal errors, and ethical questions that they had never faced before.

THE DOWNFALL OF STEPHAN

Before they arrived in Perry County, the immigrant group purchased 4,475 acres of both government and privately-owned land for $9,234.25.[16] This averaged out the price to $2.06 per acre. Careful divisions were made and each plot of ground was divided among the settlers. Together with the first detachment of immigrants, Stephan moved to the colony on April 26, 1839.[17]

In late April and early May 1839 the turmoil began and opposition to Stephan mounted steadily. In St. Louis at this time were Pastors G. H. Loeber, E. G. W. Keyl, E. M. Buerger, and C. F. W. Walther, as well as laymen Eduard Vehse, Gustav Jaeckel, F. W. Barthel (Walther's warm friend in Leipzig), and H. F. Fischer, all of whom were prominently involved in the leadership of the immigration.

An unusual event occurred following the service in St. Louis conducted by Pastor Loeber on May 5, 1839. The sermon Loeber delivered no longer exists, but apparently it was a most soul-searching sermon. In response, two women, each independently without the knowledge of the other, made detailed confessions to Loeber of improper relations with Stephan. These were outright admissions of adultery; in the days which followed, other women came forward, claiming that Stephan had attempted to seduce them.[18]

In response to these events, the St. Louis clergy determined that C. F. W. Walther, being the youngest of them and probably the most expendable, and one who had expressed greater opposition to Stephan, be asked to convey the allegations. He assumed this stressful task and traveled down the Mississippi without Stephan's approval to be admitted to the colony. (This regulation was part of the policy in existence at that time.)

With a companion, Walther arrived in Perry County where the Brazeau and Mississippi Rivers meet. Landing on the opposite side, Walther had to cross the Brazeau River in a boat. Upon landing, they were met by a big campfire at the place where the village of Wittenberg soon would be established. Stephan was present with some of the company. He totally disapproved of Walther's arrival.

The following day he engaged in discussion with Stephan, but apparently Walther did not share the charges which he was about to make against the leader. It was clear that Walther had disobeyed Stephan and consequently felt the antagonism of the new bishop. Walter Forster relates these events as follows:

The younger Walther, however, now proceeded to do everything he could to undermine Stephan's authority in many small ways without actually coming out into the open at once. In the services Walther disregarded the order of worship which Stephan had heretofore insisted on. In going through the colony, the agent of the St. Louis group encouraged the people in Perry County to disobey Stephan's orders for the construction of roads and bridges, and rather to devote their time to building dwellings and planting crops—which, of course, was advice both popular and sound. In general, C. F. W. Walther seemed to have deliberately conducted himself in such a way as to give the impression, without studied insubordination, that something was very wrong. Meanwhile he informed the key figures of events and plans in St. Louis.[19]

While Walther was still in Perry County, a group of immigrants from New York arrived. Included in the group were Christiane Buenger, age fifty, the pastor's widow from Etzdorf and her two adult children who had remained with her in Bremerhaven, Johann Friedrich Buenger, a candidate of theology, and Agnes Ernestine Buenger. (The six siblings of Christiane's family had traveled on the *Olbers* earlier, except Emilie, Walther's future bride, who sailed on the *Copernicus*.)

The new arrivals were shocked when they were informed of the recent developments. Some of them, however, did not understand or were unable to believe the Stephan disaster. By this time the entire colony, as well as Stephan himself, were already aware of what would develop. On Pentecost Sunday, Stephan had ordered all members living in the colonies to come to the landing place (Wittenberg) where he was to preach. Walther, on the other hand, encouraged the people to come to the settlement at Altenburg, where he was serving as the guest speaker. It is reported that only two or three people attended Stephan's service and the rest came to Altenburg to hear Walther.

By the end of May a large portion of the group who had remained in St. Louis decided to leave and to resettle in Perry County. About 400 left in two river boats. The first riverboat reached the mouth of the Brazeau at 4 A.M. on May 29 and the second arrived at 5 P.M. the same day. Some 120 immigrants stayed behind in St. Louis.

This brought together for the first time all members of the immigrant group except the relatively few who remained in St. Louis. A "Council" was formed the following day to take care of their urgent problems. Stephan considered this nothing but a "rebellious faction," even though his house was put under heavy guard.

On the morning of May 30, the "Council" invited Stephan to meet with them. Stephan, however, was most emphatic in declining, saying that no one had the authority to place him under investigation. Because of this refusal, the "Council" removed him from his office and excommunicated him. (This was the procedure the clergy had suggested.) The decisions of the Council were shared with the entire group. The accusations against him included being guilty of teaching false doctrine, of major mismanagement in administration, and of sexual immorality.[20] Both Walther brothers, together with the other pastors, signed the statement of deposition.

In spite of hearing the indictment, Stephan refused to vacate his home. The crowd gathered and people milled about the house. Mob psychology prevailed. What had been abject adulation now became venomous hatred. The angry new leaders were determined to expel Stephan from the colony. In heart-rending submission to the edict of total exile from the community, Stephan resigned all his responsibilities and gave up any obligation to the community. In addition, he promised never to return to the settlement in the state of Missouri.

This document is on file at the Concordia Historical Institute, and even today one can see the second signature of the deposed bishop and especially observe the extremely shaky hand, which signed his name to the list of the effects he was permitted to take. He had dipped the feather pen into the inkwell and as he finished signing "Martin" a stream of ink fell off almost one inch in length. The same thing happened when he was signing "Stephan."

After a thorough search of his house and his personal effects, the fallen leader was removed and was obliged to spend the night from May 30 to May 31 in a tent. Forster observes:

> Few hearts, it seems, were softened among those who found him bowed over his Bible the following morning. On May 31 at 10:30 A.M. Stephan, stooping over a cane and professing his innocence with visible emotion, was conducted to the waiting ferry. Not many people were present. Stephan's request had been granted that the crowd be kept away. The ex-Bishop was rowed across the Mississippi River by two men. He was also given a spade and an ax and other personal effects. He was now in Illinois.[21]

WALTHER'S ROLE

What was Walther's role in all of this? Most of what we know about Walther from the period of his resignation in Braeunsdorf to the expulsion of Stephan has been largely a matter of speculation and debate. There are those who claim that Walther saw through Stephan almost from the beginning. This is not likely. Walther had received a comforting letter from Stephan. Although Dr. Rudelbach had personally urged Walther to break company with Stephan, Walther responded: "Should I forsake a man who by God's grace rescued my soul?"[22]

Did Walther sign the documents of "Stephan's Investiture" and "Confirmation of Stephan's Investiture"? Even though it has been said that these may have been forgeries of Walther's name, there can be no doubt as one views the two original documents with Walther's signature that he did indeed sign them.

While Stephan's leadership was evaporating, Walther's was gradually increasing. He would go on to become the organizing president of the Missouri Synod in 1847 and the chief theological professor and president of Concordia Seminary, St. Louis, Missouri. His work was just beginning.

After expulsion from the community, Stephan served a very small group of people in Kaskaskia, Illinois, preaching in the courthouse every two weeks. Finally he had the opportunity to organize a congregation in Horse Prairie near Red Bud, Illinois. A woman, about thirty-eight years old, took care of Stephan in his Horse Prairie log cabin-church until the time of his death.

There is an interesting letter dated July 6, 1846, written from St. Louis by Johann Samuel Guenther to Maria Stephan and her siblings, the children of Martin Stephan.[23] The letter contains information on the death and burial of Bishop Stephan. Guenther relates that Stephan had died at midnight on February 21, 1846. The cause of death is listed as *Geschwulst*, a kind of swelling, possibly a tumor. Guenther's daughter Louisa had been Stephan's housekeeper in a dilapidated log cabin that served the congregation as church, school, and parsonage in Horse Prairie, Illinois. It was located in the center of the cemetery. Farmers lived quite far from the church. A German preacher, Adolf Hermann Frantz Baltzer of the "United Church," conducted Stephan's funeral on Tuesday, February 24.[24] The members of the congregation, all farmers, carried the body around the church to the grave. A painted white fence was erected around the grave, and after the funeral, a twelve-foot high cross-made out of oak, painted brown was erected. The cross was shipped from St. Louis to Horse Prairie on a wagon. The inscription reads:

Here rests Herr [Mr.] Martin Stephan Ev. Luth. Pastor of the local congregation, born at Stramberg, August 13, 1777 and died February 21, 1846.

Also inscribed are these words based on Hebrews 13:7:

Remember your former leaders, who spoke God's message to you. Think back on how they lived and died, and imitate their faith.

The letter goes on to say that Stephan had been called to this congregation five months prior to his death and that he had also taught school. His salary was extremely low because the congregation was so small and scattered. The congregation's log house was described as being financially worthless and as weak as paper.

So ended the life of Martin Stephan, a man who was born in poverty, lost his parents at an early age and was orphaned; a man who reached climactic heights in Dresden, emigrated to America as a prominent leader, and died in abject poverty. Stephan's wife, Juliane Adelheit Knoebel, had died earlier.

Some of our information on Martin Stephan has come from the pen of Walther himself. A little known fact is that Walther wrote the first chapter of Koestering's *Auswanderung*.[25] It had originally been written in 1864 and was circulated within the congregations to celebrate the twenty-fifth anniversary of immigration. Walther's section is entitled "Cause for the Immigration."

Somewhat confidentially, Walther mentions that the Stephans had marital difficulties in Dresden, but that those loyal to Stephan in the immigration put most of the blame on Mrs. Stephan. Walther also relates that Stephan's doctrine was not totally Lutheran, but had a strong element of Pietism. According to Walther, Stephan's position on the office of the ministry was hierarchical, based on priestly authority and blind obedience. He held that ordination was instituted by God in an unbroken succession since the apostles. The role of the lay people and the councils was to serve merely as witnesses.

The initial impetus for the immigration came in 1837 at about the time Stephan was suspended from the ministry because of breaking curfew laws. In early 1838 he declared to his congregation in Dresden that the time for the departure was near. As early as September 4, 1838, 707 people had declared their willingness to emigrate. This information is significant as an expression of Walther's analysis of Stephan.

In closing the discussion of Stephan, there in an interesting story about his hollow cane. Rumors had persisted that when Stephan was transported across the Mississippi in 1839, he had taken a hollow cane, which he filled with gold pieces. Vehse was the first to write about his presumptions that when Stephan was expelled he was stooped over and supported himself with his right hand on a cane. But on his left arm he carried what was speculated to be a hollow cane. One of the people on the scene, Carl Eduard Vehse, of whom we will hear more in a moment, believed that Stephan slyly had placed about 700 "piasters" in that cane and showed them to his host in Illinois. Vehse likely embellished a bit, claiming, "it has become known that he once had such a hollowed-out walking-stick made in the mountains, of which he boasted that therein 'spies might carry their dispatches.'"[26]

The story continues that Theodor Brohm, who had been a confidant of Martin Stephan, received that cane as a personal memento. Brohm's son, also named Theodor (1846–1926) was called to Concordia College in Addison, Illinois, and served there from 1879–1913. Oral history states that when Theodor Julius Brohm, his father, came to visit, some of the faculty homes in Addison were under construction. The old gentleman, in his curiosity, climbed up the ladder to the roof to see whether he could better observe the construction. The buildings were frame houses, with an open space between the inside and outside walls. As Theodor Julius got up there with his cane, he put it upon the partially finished roof when, suddenly, the cane slipped into the hollow space between the two walls of the building and rattled all the way down to the foundation.

This writer heard about the rumor and years later, when the teacher's seminary was moved from Addison to River Forest, the faculty homes were dismantled. The writer posted a witness as the walls were taken down to the foundation. What did they find? Absolutely nothing! Unless other evidence still arises, one would assume that Vehse's account was pure speculation. No hollow cane ever existed.

After Stephan's expulsion as bishop of the colonies, there followed a period of chaos, depression, disaster, and deaths. This continued for two years from May 1839 to April 1841. The primary issue that kept stirring up animosities was the question: what is the role of the clergy and what is the role of the laity? The leader of the lay group was Carl Eduard Vehse (1802–1870). He had studied law in Dresden and had become curator of the Saxon state archives. He was a strong supporter of Martin Stephan.

Having become totally disillusioned by the sequence of events, Vehse returned to Germany in December 1839.[27]

After his return, Vehse put all of his notes and animosities together with a strong anti-clerical position. He wrote *Die Stephan'sche Auswanderung nach Amerika* (*The Stephanite Emigration to America*).[28] Vehse's assault was primarily against the clergymen after Stephan was expelled. He believed that the clergy were in doctrinal error because they considered the office of the ministry to be of Old Testament origin, and that they were using the office to exert Levitical rigor. He called it a *Priester Herrschaft* (lordship of the priests).

In his book, Vehse proposed six theses given in summary here as background for the forthcoming Altenburg Debate.

1. All Christians are priests by Baptism through faith.
2. The office of the priesthood is common to all believers. All have like authority.
3. The office of the priesthood has been given to the congregation by God.
4. It is a bastion of the papacy that one certain estate should be made to be a spiritual class ordained of God.
5. It is an accursed saying that a priest is something more than a Christian.
6. The office of preaching is no more than a public service entrusted to someone by the whole congregation.

Conrad Bergendoff summarizes the issue well:

Vehse was beginning to challenge the authority of the hierarchy still represented by Stephan's lieutenants. When his theses received little consideration, the other laymen joined him in a direct "Protest." The Protest constitutes a ringing assertion of rights of the congregation as opposed to synod, episcopacy, a domineering clergy, or any other agency in the Church which would tend to curtail those rights. Hereby the three immigrant, Saxon laymen gave strong utterance to a principle which has assured the autonomy of the local congregation.[29]

In spite of these unresolved tensions, the clergy in Perry County demonstrated deep courage and far-sightedness by purchasing a six-acre plot in Dresden, and with their own hands and tools erected a small log cabin school, 16 feet by 21 feet. The owners and builders were J. F. Buenger, Ottomar Fuerbringer, Theodor Brohm, and C. F. W. Walther. The cloud hanging over the colonies was still dark and foreboding, and the future looked impossible. Nevertheless, this little school was opened for its first classes on December 9, 1839, with eleven students, seven boys and four girls. The youngest was Sarah von Wurmb, almost six years old. Among the seven boys was J. A. F. Wilhelm Mueller, who was the first graduate of this school on October 7, 1847. Later he entered the ministry. This school was the beginning of Concordia Seminary.

After ten years, in 1849 the small school was relocated in St. Louis to a site on Jefferson Avenue. There a new building was constructed and dedicated in 1850. Various additions to the building were made over time. In 1882 all the buildings were demolished and a "new Concordia" was built in 1883, made of imposing red bricks. It stood at the center of St. Louis Lutheranism, with nearby faculty homes, Concordia Publishing House, Holy Cross Lutheran Church, and the former Lutheran Hospital.

Eventually, this building also became too small and another site was obtained in Clayton, a suburb of St. Louis, where the present seventy-two acre campus is located. These Tudor Gothic buildings were dedicated in 1926. Nearly 11,000 pastors have graduated from this school of the prophets since 1847. They have gone on to enter what Jesus calls "fields white unto the harvest" (John 4:35) from one end of the world to the other. What incredible blessings God has bestowed!

Of interest is the fact that the seminary was established almost eight years before the Missouri Synod itself was organized. C. F. W. Walther was the school's leading theological professor for some thirty-seven years (1849–1887). In 1850 he became its president, an office he held until his death in 1887.

However, in the immediate wake of the Stephan debate, the future seemed to hold no such bright spot. Not only were there theological tensions among the immigrants in Perry County, but the physical hardships and living conditions became demoralizing. Their homes and shelters were poorly built, allowing rain and the elements to destroy their personal treasures and possessions. Often the husbands and fathers were ill because they were not used to the hard labor of felling trees, building log cabins, and planting grains and vegetables. With blistered hands and aching shoulders they went to bed at night after eating a meager meal. Many people, both adults and children, succumbed to an early death. Traces of the early cemeteries can still be seen today. It was a devastating period for the immigrants. Haunting and unpleasant questions continued in their minds. Were the colonies with their worship groupings the true church or were they merely a mob? Where was the church? Who were the pastors? They still remembered how they had been rubbed raw between the Scylla of rationalism and the Charybdis of Pietism. If only they could return to their homeland!

THE ALTENBURG DEBATE

In a letter Walther wrote to his brother Otto Hermann on May 4, 1839, he introduced the unanswered questions that were being asked: "Are we pastors or not?"

"Are our calls valid?"

"Do we have a godly call since we quit our German call, due to an erring conscience, and ran away?"

"Would it not be better if they [the laity] dismissed us, try to maintain themselves through a spiritual priesthood and then call new pastors?"

"Do we have the authority to call and to exercise church discipline?"

Many even doubted that the congregations were Christian congregations, that there were any valid calls, and that therefore they could exercise any church discipline.

The clergy were very much aware of the fractured relationships. Some of the congregations even asked for the resignation of their pastor. Walther had his doubts about serving both the Johannesburg and the Dresden congregations. He, too, asked whether it might not be better to return to Germany.[30] E. M. Buerger resigned his pastorate in Seelitz where his wife and child had died. Loeber even debated whether he should return to Germany or remain in America as a layman.

Walther became deeply disturbed by feelings of guilt and could not find peace anywhere.[31] He spoke of the "fearful stains which certainly attach to me." He felt this guilt because he had blindly followed Stephan. An observer wrote: "Some of the candidates walked about loaded down with melancholy, as if mentally disordered."[32]

The darkest hour is often just before dawn. With the people living under extreme physical and emotional problems and contending with burning theological questions, dissatisfaction, and death in their families, the sunrise of the immigration was about to occur. Adolph Marbach (1798?–1860), an attorney who had served in Dresden, Germany with Walther and who had been one of Stephan's supporters, challenged Walther to a debate on the question, "Are we a church or not?" The debate was held on two consecutive weekends (April 15 and 21) in 1841. At the conclusion of the debate Marbach, although not totally convinced of Walther's stand, nevertheless acknowledged Walther's superior theology.

The colonists were most joyful that this haunting issue had once and for all been disposed of.

Georg Schieferdecker, President of the Synod's Western District, summarized the great significance of the Altenburg Debate at its convention in 1856:

> It was shown with convincing clarity that in spite of our mistakes we still had the Lord Jesus, His Word, His true Sacrament, and the Office of the Keys in our midst; that the Lord had also heard His people, His Church. More was hardly needed to take the pressure off our conscience and to revive faith in the hearts of those who had all but despaired. It was the Easter morn of a severely-tried congregation, on which they, as once the disciples, saw the Savior again, whom they believed dead, and in the light of His grace and in the power of His resurrection were filled with joy and hope.
>
> There are many present today who remember the very day with tearful but grateful hearts to a merciful God. … It was as important as the Leipzig disputation of 1519 for the Reformation—and I say this confidently—that this disputation had great significance for the building and establishment of our Lutheran Church here in the West.[33]

In the debate, Walther presented eight theses that became known as the Altenburg Theses. They became the platform on which the Missouri Synod was founded in 1847. They continue to be of great significance not only for that time, but for today as well.

Because of their importance, the theses appear below.

I

The true Church, in the most real and most perfect sense, is the totality (*Gesamtheit*) of all true believers, who from the beginning to the end of the world from among all peoples and tongues have been called and sanctified by the Holy Spirit through the Word. And since God alone knows these true believers (2 Timothy 2:19), the Church is also called invisible. No one belongs to this true church who is not spiritually united with Christ, for it is the spiritual body of Jesus Christ.

II

The name of the true Church belongs also to all those visible companies of men among whom God's Word is purely taught and the holy Sacraments are administered according to the institution of Christ. True, in this Church there are godless men, hypocrites, and heretics, but they are not true members of it, nor do they constitute the Church.

III

The name Church, and in a certain sense, the name true Church, belongs also to those visible companies of men who have united under the confession of a falsified faith and therefore have incurred the guilt of a partial departure from the truth, provided they possess so much of God's Word and the holy Sacraments in purity that children of God may thereby be born. When such companies are called true churches, it is not the intention to state that they are faithful, but only that they are real churches as opposed to all worldly organizations (*Gemeindschaften*).

IV

The name Church is not improperly applied to heterodox companies, but according to the manner of speech of the Word of God itself. It is also as such immaterial that this high name is allowed to such communions, for out of this follows:

1. That members also of such companies may be saved; for without the Church there is no salvation.

V

2. The outward separation of a heterodox company from an orthodox Church is not necessarily a separation from the universal Christian Church nor a relapse into heathenism and does not yet deprive that company of the name Church.

VI

3. Even heterodox companies have church power; even among them the goods of the Church may be validly administered, the ministry established, the Sacraments validly administered, and the keys of the kingdom of heaven exercised.

VII

4. Even heterodox companies are not to be dissolved, but reformed.

VIII

The orthodox Church is chiefly to be judged by the common, orthodox, public confession to which its members acknowledge and confess themselves to be pledged.[34]

These theses have become a benchmark for The Lutheran Church—Missouri Synod throughout its history, and many of the doctrines of church and ministry adhered to by the Synod have their foundation in this 1841 debate. This theme cropped up again in the late 1840s and subsequently emerged as a special constitutional article. The theses were expanded extensively and presented to the 1850 convention of the Missouri Synod. They were officially adopted by the Synod in convention, which resolved to publish the manuscript "in our name and as our unanimous confession." The theses are contained in the volume entitled *Kirche und Amt* (*Church and Ministry*) first published in 1852.[35]

The second part of the volume *Church and Ministry* contains an additional ten theses on the holy ministry or the pastoral office, also presented by Walther to the Synod and adopted by it.

This had become another very controversial issue, particularly between J. A. A. Grabau of the Buffalo Synod and the Missouri Synod position. Grabau espoused a hierarchical position, akin to the authoritarianism of Martin Stephan.

In the theses on the ministry, Walther treads very carefully between the hierarchical position of Grabau and the extreme congregational position, which had been proposed by Vehse. Walther emphasizes that the ministry is a divinely established office, but that it is conferred by God through the congregation and not, as Grabau held, that it is the continuation of the ministerial office without the congregation.[36]

TRINITY, ST. LOUIS

On January 21, 1841, just months before the Altenburg Debate, Otto Hermann Walther, pastor of the group that remained in St. Louis, had died. He was deeply loved by his congregation. His wife was Agnes Buenger, one of the children of Mrs. Christiane Buenger who had remained with her mother in the jail in Bremerhaven. The only child of Otto Hermann and Agnes, Johannes, was only three months old when his father died. Widowed, Agnes later married Ottoma Fuerbringer.

The St. Louis congregation had barely survived the great turmoil and difficulties related to the question of church and ministry at the time of their pastor's death. But in spite of their struggles, the church grew steadily as German Lutherans settled in the area. Worship services were held in Christ Episcopal Church on Broadway and Chestnut.

O. H. Walther had received a salary of $15 per month and rental for lodging. Later when he was married, the congregation decided to gather funds for a wedding gift. Otto Hermann limited their zeal and accepted only two pieces of furniture, a bedstead and a table, so that the congregation would not feel the gift burdensome. Very generously, the congregation paid for their first pastor's funeral which cost $27.95 and agreed to pay his widow $5.00 a month.

C. J. Otto Hanser, later pastor of Trinity congregation, describes O. H. Walther as a "highly gifted and richly blessed preacher … His death doubtless belongs to the darkest ways and leadings of God with this congregation and His Lutheran church at this place."[37]

Otto Hermann's faith was evident in a letter of assurance and comfort he wrote to his brother C. F. W. on November 9, 1840:

> One thing is needful. This also applies to you. You lack only this one thing in which all else is given. Your excerpts concerning the call [into the ministry] avail you nothing if you do not first assure yourself of your call in Him unto His everlasting kingdom of grace. In Him all is done right and all that is crooked [is made] straight.[38]

On February 8, 1841, Trinity congregation called C. F. W. Walther as his brother's successor to the pastorate. Since there was only limited postal service, the call document was personally delivered to Walther in Perry County by the shoemaker, Johann Martin Quast.[39] Walther acknowledged the receipt of the call on February 10, recognized the congregation's desires for an early response, noted his humble appreciation for the undeserved confidence, but ended by saying it was impossible to come to an immediate decision.

But Walther did finally accept the call to Trinity. He met with the congregation in St. Louis on April 26, 1841 and informed them that what previously prevented him from accepting the call had now been removed. That included his partially restored health, the conviction that through the study of the Reformation fathers his call was proper, and everything had been done according to the divine procedure and therefore the pastor called may not decline. Undoubtedly due to the success of the Altenburg Debate, Walther also informed the congregation that any mistakes he had made in connection with the immigration did not constitute sins which would render him unworthy of the office.[40]

On Sunday, May 2, 1841, he delivered his initial sermon. Because of Walther's continued weakness, the congregation graciously conceded that he preach only once on a Sunday and read a sermon at the afternoon service. Services were held in the basement of Christ Episcopal Church.[41]

At about this time an individual by the name of Fr. Sproede arrived on the scene. He had emigrated in 1836 and became a baker in New York. He was a staunch supporter of Stephan and came to Perry County with the New York group just as Stephan was exiled. However, he remained loyal to the former bishop. Sproede was determined to continue harassing Walther, and therefore moved from Perry County to St. Louis. In his support of Stephanism, Sproede called Walther a miserable pietist, a deceiver, and a wolf who did not know true Lutheranism. Finally, after several voters' meetings, Walther was instructed by the congregation to reply to the slanderous attacks. In defense of Walther, the congregation emphasized that the response should contain the following points:

1. Errors were committed in the immigration;
2. Everyone should be encouraged confidently to testify that we are, indeed, Lutherans;
3. It should be declared that the congregation voluntarily chose Walther as their pastor;
4. That Sproede had made a statement to the public which had been filled with falsehoods.

The congregation further added a statement that it cannot be charged of anything if its teachings are correct. It invited all to come and see and hear what was being taught in their church and school. Anyone who doubted that there still was a priestly rule was invited to come and observe the administration and the statues of the parish. It stated further that Walther had not forced himself into the office of pastor of the congregation, but that he was properly released from his former office in Germany and now had been properly and correctly called by the entire congregation.[42]

This did not set well with Sproede. After a violent temper outburst, he returned home, sat in his chair, and suddenly and unexpectedly died.

Still, in spite of this and many other challenges, Trinity Congregation began to grow, strengthened in the love of Christ and in unity. Several of Walther's biographers indicate that this growth was due in some degree to the Altenburg Theses and especially through the preaching of the Gospel and its Reformation theology.

Trinity, as noted earlier, originally conducted its worship services in Christ Episcopal Church. This continued until late fall 1842, when the congregation built its first separate building. When this church was dedicated on December 4, 1842, Walther preached a sermon on Exodus 20:27. At the time of dedication, a debt of $3,300 remained.[43]

It is well to take a look at the congregational constitution that was adopted. Drafted by Walther, the voters adopted it after having scrutinized it on the basis of the Word of God, the testimonies as found in the Lutheran Confessions, and the writings of the Reformation fathers. All these authorities were cited in the voter's assembly. The constitution states, in part:

> We acknowledge all canonical books of the Old and New Testament as God's revealed Word, and the entire Symbolical Books of the Evangelical Lutheran Church as the form and norm derived from God's Word, according to which, since they are taken from God's Word, not only the doctrine in our congregation is to be taught and examined, but also all occurring disputes in doctrine and religion shall be judged and regulated. These are: the three chief symbols, the Unaltered Augsburg Confession, the Apology of the same, the Smalkald Articles, Dr. Luther's Small and Large Catechisms, the Formula of Concord, and the Visitation Articles.
>
> The congregation in its entirety has the highest authority in the administration of the external and internal affairs of church and congregation. No regulation or decision for the congregation or for an individual member as such has any binding force, even if it stems from an individual or from the body of the congregation, if it has not been transacted by the authority of the congregation and done in the name or according to the general or special authority. Whatever is decided or transacted according to the authority given by the congregation by an individual or smaller bodies, may at any time be referred to the congregation as the highest authority for the ultimate decision. The congregation, however, has no authority to order anything or decide anything against God's Word and the symbols of the pure Evangelical Lutheran Church. If it does that then all such decisions and transactions are null and void.[44]

When daughter congregations were organized, they determined to remain a part of their mother church, Trinity, and hence developed the so-called "Union Congregation" or the "*Gesamtgemeinde*" The establishment of the *Gesamtgemeinde* occurred on November 27, 1848. St. Louis was divided into districts instead of congregations. Walther was the head pastor who was supported by the pastors referred to as "vicars" in each of the districts. The voters of the districts met every second month in a united congregational voters' assembly. Each district operated its own treasury as well as a separate administration.

The *Gesamtgemeinde* turned out to be quite an operation and ultimately included four congregations. The first, the Immanuel District, was formed in 1847 with Pastor J. F. Buenger, the former teacher at Trinity, St. Louis, as its pastor. The second, Holy Cross in South St. Louis, formed a separate district in 1858. Nine acres of land were purchased for the church in 1845 for $900. It was located on Trinity's cemetery where quite a number of burials had taken place. By the time worship services began at Holy Cross, Theodor Brohm (1808–1881) was called as pastor and served from 1858 to 1878. Brohm was a member of the Saxon Immigration. He first served Trinity Lutheran Church in New York City. He remained a close personal friend of Walther throughout his life.

Trinity, the original congregation in the *Gesamtgemeinde*, constituted the third district, and the fourth of these member districts of the Union Congregation was Zion, served by E. D. K. Boese. The congregation started as a branch school on November 30, 1858, and became a district in 1860. These four congregations, then, Immanuel, Holy Cross, Trinity, and Zion constituted the *Gesamtgemeinde*.

The main responsibilities of the *Gesamtgemeinde* were:

1. to call and depose pastors and teachers;

2. to exercise church discipline;

3. to accept new members;

4. to establish district boundaries;

5. and to decide other matters that required united action.

The *Gesamtgemeinde* stayed in existence during Walther's entire life. After his death, the question of whether to dissolve it or retain it was discussed in every single voters' meeting, beginning with June 6, 1887, a month after Walther's death. Essentially, it was a disagreement between the pastors of the four congregations and the lay leaders who still honored their revered "*Ober Pfarrer*" or senior pastor. The final decision to dissolve the arrangement was made in the meeting of January 14, 1889. An observer who was present at this final meeting told this writer, "The last meeting was so—"ferocious" is not too strong a word. There were actual threats of fist fights." After this, each congregation was autonomous.

Dr. Edmund Seuel, for many years head of Concordia Publishing House, informed this writer in an interview conducted on March 1, 1951 (deposited at Concordia Historical Institute), that at voters' meetings all the lay voters sat on chairs on the main floor. The officers of each of the district parishes sat on the second elevation, and on the third elevation facing the voters were the pastors of each district, including Walther. Clearly, the clergy had top priority.

What a contrast this was for Walther himself when he occupied the highest position in the voters' assembly! After the difficulties encountered with Martin Stephan, the pastor was not even permitted to attend the voters' meetings. During the first year after the Stephan fiasco, the pastors were not even asked to open the meetings with prayer.

> Finally one of the laymen suggested that the meeting of a Christian congregation ought to be opened with prayer. The chairman was asked to go to the pastor's residence and ask him to write out a proper prayer, which he, the chairman, read regularly at the beginning of the meeting. The voters were afraid that they might become the victims of priest rule.[45]

Trinity's constitution, drafted by Walther, was based strictly on the Scriptures and the Lutheran Confessions as well as on the writings of the orthodox Lutheran church fathers. This constitution was adopted in 1843 and emphasized four points:

1. That it is the will of God that every congregation have its constitution;
2. That God has given His children liberty to arrange all things according to their needs;
3. That for this procedure there is precedence in the Church;
4. That a constitution is particularly necessary in this country where the government does not concern itself with the affairs of the Church.

This constitution became the model for all the congregations organized in the LCMS. It was printed in a separate pamphlet and sold by Concordia Publishing House throughout the Synod. Incidentally, similar *Gesamtgemeinde* policies were also established by the congregations in Fort Wayne, Indiana; Cleveland, Ohio; Chicago, Illinois; and in New London, Wisconsin.[46]

The *Gesamtgemeinde* system modified the traditional way in which Walther had been interpreted as being the father of Missouri's "Congregationalism." Much could be said about the advantage of this system. Today we try to accomplish much of the city-wide church work through councils, para-church organizations, and so on. Erich Allwardt has traced the history of the demise of the *Gesamtgemeinde*.[47] Rather than fostering Congregationalism, he argues that Walther's policy of coordinating districts and amalgamating them into a single parish was actually a violation of the notion of "congregational supremacy."

EDUCATION

It was a Saxon principle, even on the high seas, that the children should be taught without any interruption. As soon as facilities and teachers or pastors were available, elementary schools had been established. J. F. Ferdinand Winter, a thirty-year-old teacher, immigrated on the *Republik*. He established a school in Altenberg, Missouri, serving at first under the crudest conditions in the open air.[48]

In St. Louis rented quarters were obtained for a parish school on Poplar Street, between First and Second. The second floor served as the parsonage for Otto Hermann Walther. The teacher in St. Louis from 1839–1840 was Carl Ludwig Geyer (1812–1892), a participant in the Saxon Immigration. His mother and Walther's mother were sisters. He served in St. Louis only briefly since he was called to teach at Johannesburg, Cape Girardeau County, Missouri, where C. F. W. Walther, his cousin, was pastor. Candidate J. F. Buenger succeeded Geyer, in St. Louis. He was installed on August 2, 1840.

In Walther's biography of Buenger[49] he gave the following information about the school:

> The Schoolroom could really accommodate only fifty pupils at the highest (the teacher's bed and other household goods took a considerable portion of the comparatively small room), but eighty were often present. In that case some sat on the front porch, and many sat crowded closely together on the stairway that led to the parsonage above. The reputation of the school grew to such an extent that even the evangelical Pastor Wall sent his adopted child. The subjects taught were Bible history, catechism, reading, writing, arithmetic, other common branches of learning, and some English.

> The absence of suitable textbooks was a prime difficulty. The German ABC-book consisting of twelve sheets had been issued by the local German paper, *Der Anzeiger des Westens* (*The Western Review*). In religious instruction Luther's Small Catechism was, of course, used. This book was also bought by the non-Lutherans, who did not send their children for the sake of religious instruction, but conformed to the rule that no child was excused from this instruction. Since there was a dearth of hymnbooks, the hymns and other songbooks entitled *Kern geistlicher Lieder* (*The Best of Spiritual Songs*) were used. The New Testament was used at first as a reader. Buenger later ordered a number of tracts from the American Tract Association. The congregation bought a map of the United States.

In his instruction, Buenger followed the rule that all classes had the same subject and the same time. For instance, if reading was the subject, all classes practiced reading. While the beginners were taught, the rest of the classes studied their reading lessons.

Buenger at first succeeded poorly in school discipline. He did not feel like punishing the little children because of much talking, and so they talked to their heart's content. What was to be done? Since he had no school on Wednesday afternoon but on Saturday forenoons, he visited the English schools of the city, to see what they did about discipline, and how they were organized. There he found quiet and orderly classes. He soon learned the secret, namely, that the pupils in these schools were specially exercised and drilled in discipline. He learned various other things, but especially how to rule a large number of children with few words. His discipline improved visibly. Everything was done upon brief commands. Order and quiet reigned in the school.[50]

Christian elementary education was of supreme importance, so "branch schools" were established in Chicago and elsewhere. These later emerged gradually into separate congregations. When Trinity constructed its first separate church building at the end of 1842 across the street from the Buenger home between Third and Fourth on Lombard, the school was placed in the basement. J. F. Buenger, the assistant pastor, and Walther, the pastor, worked in great harmony in their service to St. Louis Lutherans.

From the initial crude elementary school established under every imaginable handicap came secondary schools for both girls and boys. The story has been told well by A. C. Stellhorn in his *Schools of The Lutheran Church Missouri Synod* and by others. St. Louis boasted the "Miller Private English School." A pastor's son, J. Clement Miller was born in Lebanon, Pennsylvania. The school was established in 1855, but due to Miller's severe illness he was forced to abandon it.

Pastor J. W. Albach, formerly of the Ohio Synod, taught English at the Fort Wayne seminary in 1846. Albach was willing to come to St. Louis to teach in the Miller school, but refused to take over the remaining personal debts of Miller spent in establishing this school. It was the financial problem which ended the school in about 1856 or 1857.[51]

When the Miller School was closed, Immanuel Congregation, part of the *Gesamtgemeinde*, established its own school. With Walther's own personal instigation and encouragement at a meeting of August 26, 1857, he urged that the higher classes also be taught. To get this done, Walther recommended that Albach teach these classes beginning in 1857. A new building was erected to provide living quarters for Albach and a classroom. The new unit was dedicated on January 11, 1858 at a cost of $2,600. The school offered a wide range of courses, including Catechism, Bible and church history, as well as mathematics, geography, physics, German and English, geometry, and penmanship. Later even Latin and bookkeeping were added. Walther was pleased with the success of the enterprise. He had inspected the school, known as an Academy, and rendered a glowing account. The school was closed in 1889, two years after Walther's death.

Walther was, indeed, dedicated to schools. He headed these programs even while the Immanuel Academy was still in existence. Walther advocated the establishment of a church-wide Lutheran high school in St. Louis. The original *Gymnasium*, which had been established in conjunction with Concordia Seminary in Perry County, had been moved to Fort Wayne during the turbulent days of the Civil War. The different draft laws between Indiana and Missouri compelled this. Thus the *Gymnasium* was moved to Fort Wayne and the Fort Wayne seminary was brought to St. Louis. The "practical seminary" remained in St. Louis attached to the "theoretical seminary" until 1875, when it moved to Springfield, Illinois.

Walther enunciated very clearly his view of the proper objectives of Christian education on a number of occasions. In an 1859 *Der Lutheraner* article addressed to "Parents Who Are Concerned About the Welfare of their children," he wrote:

> By parents who are concerned about the welfare of their children, we mean such as are concerned above all that their children might become true Christians and have eternal salvation. While this is certainly the first and foremost aim, the proper concern for children includes more, for just as it is not only God's will that we be saved, but also that we serve our neighbor, and become a blessing to the world and the church, so also must parents, the representatives of God, aim not only to secure their children for heaven but to train them to be a blessing for the world and the church.[52]

To underscore the great need for Lutheran higher education for young people, Walther wrote several years later:

> If we German Lutherans in America are not forever to play the role of "hewers of wood and drawers of water" as it is said of the Gibeonites in Canaan (Joshua 9:21), and if we wish to contribute our part to the advancement of the common welfare of our new fatherland according to this special gift God has given us, then the situation

dare not remain as it is. Rather we must establish institutions of higher learning, and offer more than our parish schools, regardless of how highly we value them. Certainly, there are enough American schools whose goal is higher education to which we could send our youth. Unfortunately, our children would lose their irreplaceable treasure of the German language and nature (in the best sense). Worse, they would be subjected to the pressing danger of losing their Lutheran faith. In addition, there are many other great weaknesses from which the American educational system is suffering, for a discussion of which we do not have time at the present. Because of this there are even many Americans who send their children to the imported Jesuit schools. But, as the adage says, we are merely moving out of the rain into the shower.

The conclusion doubtless remains: We German Lutherans need a German institution. Built on the foundation of the pure Word of God, our boys and young men, with typical thoroughness, can be equipped with the necessary training to become technicians and business men. Thus prepared, they may dedicate themselves to the vocation of their choice and study any of the secular branches. They would then be able to serve in any of the common or governmental offices with ability and usefulness. Through such solid education they could serve in any kind of vocation or position. In brief, we are in need of a German Evangelical Lutheran so-called polytechnic or industrial or business school. We shall simply call it a German Evangelical Lutheran high school for citizens, of which many ... existed in our blessed dear old fatherland.[53]

On another occasion, Walther enumerated four reasons for a thorough Christian education:

1. The Christian religion is, humanly speaking, in part a body of learning which exceeds all human knowledge in depth and scope. Its teachings embrace time and eternity, the beginning and the end of the world, God in His nature, attributes, counsel, and works; man, his origin, purpose, and eternal destiny; heaven and earth—in a word, the universe and its ultimate purpose. When a Christian has comprehended the fundamentals of the Christian religion, his spirit is already more enlightened on all questions pertaining to mankind and the mysteries of the world than was that of ancient philosophers.

2. The Christian religion is based on a history written thousands of years ago, namely that of the Old and the New Testaments. There is practi-

cally no field of human knowledge, be it the knowledge of languages, of history, geography, mathematics, nature, science, the art of speech, poetry, logic and the like, that the Christian church does not need to understand and explain its old holy Book; as well as to defend it, or it may use such knowledge for its own purposes. Therefore, it requires especially of its public servants that they be well grounded in general learning.

3. Next, the Christian religion requires a personal examination and study of one's beliefs. It will not tolerate a blind authoritarian faith, based on men. Christ says to all that are His own: "One is your Master, even Christ. Search the Scriptures." St. Paul writes: "Prove all things; hold fast that which is good," And St. John: "Try the spirits whether they are of God." If there is a church that does not demand of its laity to search and prove, but expects the members to depend upon their priests, it is not a true but a false church ... The true church wants no immature but mature—no blind but well-judging members.

4. Again, the Christian religion holds that all gifts and riches of nature be highly regarded as the great gifts and riches of God. Far from discarding any useful knowledge of them or any of the useful arts, the Christian religion beholds the goodness of God shining forth from everyone of them, and believes that they should be used for the service and glorification of God. Far from looking askance at all true progress in learning, she rejoices over every step forward as a precious, invaluable gift of Divine Providence for the government of the world.

The Christian religion, as a religion of true humanity, follows the command of love of the neighbor and even of the enemy as its legal basic law. It demands that the Christian not live unto himself, but wholly in the service of others. It implies that no one should let those gifts lie dormant with which God has endowed his nature from the time of birth but allow them to be awakened for the general welfare, practiced, and used. The church, therefore, considers it a duty to establish all kinds of schools in which the gifts with which the Lord has endowed the spirit of its children are developed and the children prepared to serve the church and the state with their knowledge and skills.[54]

Walther's insistence on teaching the German language must be understood in the context of that time, namely 1866. He was speaking to German immigrants who, like himself, were still German to the core as new immigrants and who used that language as a medium of expression. In the above article, Walther concludes affirmatively:

> Now, you dear Lutheran family heads, who have been blessed by God with temporal good and are desirous of leaving a legacy for your sons that they may rejoice in them even after your death, do not consider too great the sacrifice of money you are asked to bring when you are giving them a good education. Even if you are leaving them several thousand dollars, remember that they are poorer after your death than they would be if today for several hundred dollars you provide a good education. The latter is a capital which bears higher interest than all the gold and silver, farms, homes, and businesses. How many of the fathers among us today regret that they did not receive a better education in their youth! How totally different they would feel if they could usefully serve the world and be independent ... in their own business! Do not permit your children to lament over your graves: Oh, if only my father had permitted me to learn something worthwhile! That would be more useful to me than my entire inheritance![55]

Lutheran education was a priority for Walther from the very beginning. Concordia Seminary was established in 1839 and moved to St. Louis in 1849. Now he was appealing for elementary and secondary Lutheran schools. But this was only one of his priorities.

Another was the on-going controversy with Grabau of the Buffalo Synod regarding the doctrine of church and ministry. In the midst of all this, at the age of thirty-seven Walther was at the center of establishing the Missouri Synod in 1847—certainly a full time task for a lesser person. A eulogist in Europe summed up Walther's educational impact as follows:

> He manifested himself as a true German-American who, as no one before him, worked for the establishment and development of the parish school system in which he was eminently successful. However, he was no enemy or opponent of the public school system. While he earnestly stressed that all members of the congregation, regardless of the size of the sacrifice, ought to permit their children to be instructed in the Christian parish schools, he stressed with equal earnestness that all ought to support the state schools joyfully and defend them against their opponents.[56]

The rapid expansion of the Missouri Synod can be partially ascribed to its elementary and branch school systems. The typical mother congregation established and supported branch schools located at some distance from the outlying areas of the city until the "daughters" became strong enough and developed into new congregations. This may be referred to as the "fission" expansion with cohesion provided through its doctrinal foundation in the Gospel of Jesus Christ as central. Growth and integration seemed natural.

YOUTH WORK AND NEW SOCIETIES

As if juggling three major projects and concerns at one time were not enough, Walther added to his priorities a Young Men's Society, which took root and grew throughout the Synod.

Young people's work stemmed from Walther's pastoral concern. The minutes of Trinity indicate that the first Young Men's Society was organized as early as 1848. It met monthly for the purpose of giving financial aid to Concordia Seminary students. The dues were ten cents per month. The young men regularly supported the young seminarians through gifts of clothing, books, food, and cash. It established a library. The meetings were closed with brief vespers in the church.[57]

For recreation, the society occupied itself with reading and, yes, pistol target practice. At one time the society boasted seventy members. In a sermon celebrating the first anniversary of this society, Walther provided this evaluation:

> I see in your society not merely a human creation, but a work which is of God. I am convinced that the idea which called your society into being a year ago originated not in a human heart, but in the heart of God Himself. I do not doubt for a second that your society is a thorn in the eyes of hell, but a joyous sight in the eyes of heaven, God, and all His holy angels. I consider it not merely an embellishment for our church; it appears to me at the same time as a sunrise, and thereby also a promise of a future which not only now gives sweet perfume, but whose good fruits will begin to ripen in the future.[58]

Between thirty and forty young men's societies were organized elsewhere in the country. An appeal was issued to establish a Synod-wide organization.[59] Such organization, known as the Evangelical Young Men's Society for Missouri, Ohio, and Other States came into being in 1856.[60]

Walther's support and deep interest on behalf of young people's work was recognized throughout the church, with the result that in 1893, only six years after his death, a youth organization named the Walther League was established in his honor.[61]

Walther helped organize two additional societies. The first was the Bible Society organized on April 24, 1853. Other congregations also supported the society and so it came to be called the "German Evangelical Lutheran Bible Society for Missouri, Illinois, and Iowa in St. Louis, Missouri." Its purpose was to distribute German Bibles and New Testaments in acceptable and correct editions and printed on serviceable paper.[62] Only members of Lutheran congregations were eligible to join. The dues were only two cents a month! A "Bible Festival" was conducted annually on September 22, to commemorate the completion of Luther's translation of the New Testament. Other meetings were held every three months. A teacher of the *Gesamtgemeinde* parish school, Otto Ernst, served as the general agent. Incredibly, the St. Louis group alone had 204 members by October 1854 and had distributed 258 complete Bibles and 20 New Testaments. Free copies were available to the poor.

Although the society had planned to publish its own edition, it never achieved this. Instead complete Bibles were purchased from Teubner of Leipzig, Germany. Sales continued to be brisk, and soon almost 1,000 complete texts were sold. The group then devoted a percentage of its funds to reprint the popular *Altenburger Bibelwerk* with study notes, published in 1866. In 1856 the Society had even purchased its own printing press,[63] as Concordia Publishing House was not established until 1869. Walther was president of the Bible Society throughout his lifetime and at the time of his death, when it was dissolved, the funds consisting of several thousand dollars were turned over to Concordia Publishing House.

To overcome the great lack of Luther resources, the American Luther Society was organized on May 10, 1859.[64] It came about in response to an essay encouraging lay people to be much more seriously engaged in reading Luther's writings. The district itself did not want to undertake the project and asked the Synodical President, F. C. D. Wyneken, to serve as the general supervisor of the society. Dues were fifty cents per year. Within one year 1,667 members joined the organization, representing almost one-third of the Lutheran residents of the St. Louis area. They had contributed $969.44.

As early as 1859 the first publication of the society appeared.[65] The first volume of *Luthers Volksbibliothek* (*Luther for the People*), sold 3,500 copies. This volume contained Luther's sermons on the Sacrament of Holy Communion and on worthy participation in the Sacrament.[66] Between 1859, when the first volume appeared, and 1876, thirty volumes were issued in fifteen bindings. During the Civil War, the society was hurt severely because people were afraid to send their money by mail. When Walther returned to the synodical presidency in 1864, he also served as president of the society, but in 1868 Walther, with the concurrence of the district presidents, turned over the entire project and the left over funds to the synodical Committee for Publications.[67] During most of its existence, Theodor Brohm served as editor of the publication. Prices for the complete set of fifteen books were reduced in the 1880s from $7.50 to $6.00 for the cloth edition. The fact that such a venture was attempted, although with limited success, demonstrates the interest or lack thereof that the members of the Synod had in Luther studies. By the time of the transfer to the Publications Committee, the venture seemed not only to be a disappointment, but an actual failure.

Much more successful and significant was the St. Louis edition of *Luther's Works*, sometimes referred to as "Walch II" because it was extensively based on an earlier edition edited by J. G. Walch (1693–1775). The first volume appeared in 1880 and the last in 1910.[68] Walther, who died in 1887, would have rejoiced to see the entire production of twenty-two volumes plus an index on the shelves of pastors' libraries. George Stoeckhardt labored extensively on the first volumes. But the work really did not take off until Albert Friedrich Hoppe took over. Hoppe had been a student of Luther his entire life. Robert Kolb puts it well when he says that the St. Louis edition of Luther was: "Walther's dream, Stoeckhardt's efforts and Hoppe's life and work bestowed upon the American Lutheran Churches, a treasure worth, in Walch's words, more than many thousand pieces of gold and silver."[69]

St. Louiser Volksblatt

In the political and social arena of the greater St. Louis area, the German residents were being undermined. The daily papers, some edited by atheists and former friends of Karl Marx of Europe, had their own specific agenda on how to draw people away from their Christian foundations. Walther was aware of this. He had already started to publish *Der Lutheraner* in September 1844. But this was not enough. Walther had never intended his paper to be political, but rather theological. Prior to the Civil War, there were many Pied Pipers who were attempting to attract people to their non-Christian positions and also to denigrate those who still adhered to biblical and Christian theology.

To counteract the influence of the secular press, Walther and other St. Louis cohorts established an independent publishing company in the

1850s in order to produce a Christian daily newspaper in the German language. The purpose was to engage as many of the German speaking people as possible in a positive Christian way to resolve the political issues which kept cropping up prior to the Civil War.

The greatest problem was to find a competent editor. On March 25, 1856, after the publication had been in progress for some time, Walther wrote to his friend Gustavus Seyffart, who was in New York. Seyffart had been on the faculty of Leipzig University, then came to America to serve on the faculty of the St. Louis Seminary from 1856 to 1859, when he returned to archaeological studies in New York. Walther wrote to him:

> Up until now it has not been possible to find a suitable editor. This paper, which has been in existence for one year, had an editor who wanted to write for the satisfaction of Christian people, but who was not able to achieve this. Therefore the paper has had a precarious existence. The local Christians here hardly felt like identifying themselves with their own creation. In spite of this thousands of dollars were spent in order to keep the ship afloat in the hope of getting a better pilot. But all our efforts to secure the services of a Christian editor remain fruitless. Therefore we resolved to offer the position to one of the pastors of our Synod who serves in Canada. He had testimonies as to his competence for fulfillment of our objectives. But when we offered a written contract we were met with a rejection. So it was evident that this possibility held out no promise of success. Thus I was commissioned to travel to Canada to try to persuade the designated pastor as well as his congregation of the importance and the urgency of this matter.[70]

Walther carried out his commission personally to persuade Pastor Conrad Diehlmann of Rainham, Canada to become the editor. Diehlmann was with the Basel Mission Institute and had served as editor of German periodicals. The trip Walther made to Canada was probably one of the most eventful assignments he ever carried out. To make it easier for the congregation to release their pastor, Walther took young Candidate Hugo Hanser out of the graduating class prematurely so that if Diehlmann accepted the offer as editor, the congregation would not be without a pastor, but would have Hanser as a replacement. This would sweeten the offer for the congregation, in a day of shortages of pastors. Professor Walther and student Hanser arrived in Buffalo in mid-winter of 1856.

Since they were in Buffalo on a Sunday, the two visited Walther's chief critic, J. A. A. Grabau, in his church. No sooner had the pair arrived in the sanctuary when an usher immediately notified Grabau that Walther was present.

> Hardly had they entered the church when a deacon dutifully announced in the sacristy who was there. In the meantime Professor Walther joined with a full voice in the singing of the hymn, to the secret offense of his pupil who did not open his mouth since he was in a heterodox church, not knowing indeed that the hymn was nevertheless orthodox. Grabau entered the pulpit. He began with a hollow voice, "Judge me, oh, Lord," etc. and with a whining voice he related his persecutions which he had endured from the police in Germany and which he was still enduring from those out West. "Avenge me upon mine enemies!"—that was the gist of his litany. To Wohlgemut [Hugo Hanser] he seemed like a mad dog who was being robbed of his prey. On the way home he asked Professor Walther for his verdict, which was to the effect: "He is an empty barrel from which the spirit has fled."[71]

Harsh winter had reached Buffalo at this time and Rainham was many miles away. In this severe cold no one could be found who would take Walther and Hanser by horse and sled to their destination. Finally, a seventeen-year-old lad was willing to do so for a price of $25. A snowstorm suddenly overtook them with snow swirling around them so fiercely that Walther was concerned about the young candidate sitting beside him and from time to time inquired whether he was still alive.

They crossed the Niagara River and discovered that on the Canadian side the snow lay mountain high. It was a deserted and desolate country with the snow falling furiously. The horse sank up to his belly in the snow which was three feet deep. Hanser recorded in his diary:

> The professor sat stiffly upright looking with tearful eyes at the horse as though he could guide it with his looks.... The snowstorm increased in fury, and the snow was so dense that one could hardly see thirty feet. Whistling and howling, the storm hurtled the snow like needles with such force against the travelers, it seemed as though it penetrated to their bare skin. It was almost impossible to open one's eyes and tears were constantly trickling from them. Running against a stump the sleigh overturned, and Wohlgemut [Hanser] felt himself in a wide arch over a declivity landing headfirst in the snow. When he regained his feet and looked about, he saw Professor Walther still pinned under the snow by his traveling trunk, which had fallen on him. After he, too, had scrambled to his feet, they both helped the driver who was still partly imprisoned under the sleigh.[72]

They barely survived by staying overnight with a settler. The next day they started out again and fortunately found a brook totally frozen over, on which they could actually travel at a trot for about fifteen miles. On the following day they finally reached their destination.

Under Walther's persuasion, Conrad Diehlmann accepted the editorship, and the candidate remained as the pastor of the congregation. Diehlmann began his editorial work on April 24, 1856 with the strong approbation of the Western District, in session at this time. But the Diehlmann editorship lasted only a year when he resigned. Thereafter he joined the Wisconsin Synod, indicating that the "Missourians" were too inflexible for him. The editorship was then assumed by Heinrich Boernstein, whose philosophy both politically and theologically was 180 degrees from Walther's. He also was the editor of the *Anzeiger des Westens*. The subscribers were warned by *Der Lutheraner* XII (August 12, 1856) and urged to discontinue their subscriptions to the *St. Louiser Volksblatt*.[73]

Walther called the paper "*Satans Presse*" (Satan's Press) after Boernstein managed to buy the *Volksblatt* in 1857 and used it to deride religion. Walther advised his readers to discontinue their subscriptions a second time. He reported:

> We consider it a duty of our conscience to inform you since we have recommended the above political paper to our readers previously as one which is edited in a Christian spirit. Since September 13, however, the editorship of this paper changed hands, though the new person promised to edit in the same style as the one who started it. The first issues published by the new editor showed the Christian spirit had vanished from it.[74]

Two Devastating Disasters

Two extremely devastating natural disasters hit St. Louis in early May, 1849. The first was the cholera epidemic that silently but suddenly crept up the Mississippi River from New Orleans. It was thought that this Asiatic Cholera, prevalent in India, was brought from Germany and Holland by immigrants to St. Louis and Cincinnati, Ohio. Precautions were taken to get the passengers off their sailing ships and place them on river steamers rather than to confine the frightening and fatal disease. By late December, 1848 a few cholera deaths already were reported.[75]

By 1849 it grew to epidemic proportions in St. Louis. Of a population of 63,471 in 1849, a total of 8,444 died of the disease. Already on May 10,

1849, Walther wrote to Wilhelm Sihler of Fort Wayne that the epidemic had hit St. Louis and that he probably would not be able to attend the forthcoming convention of the Synod in Fort Wayne, scheduled for June 6–16.

Through the mercy of God, Walther's fifth child, Emma Julie, was born on June 27, 1849, and lived. This was only a few days after Walther's mother-in-law, Christiane Buenger, died of the cholera on June 11 and his sister-in-law, Mrs. J. F. Buenger, died on June 21. Seven days later, on June 29, Buenger's son Gotthilf Nathaniel, only fifteen months old, succumbed to the disease as well. Nevertheless, Walther did attend the Fort Wayne Convention in June, rushing back to his people as soon as possible.

Because of the severity of the situation, the St. Louis mayor and city council formed a committee in June with almost unlimited powers to deal with the epidemic. Hospitals were established in the city's six wards with one or more physicians assigned to each. Monday, July 2, was declared a day of fasting and prayer. On July 29, Walther preached a "cholera sermon" on Matthew 7:15–23. He also was named one of the persons responsible for his ward, to "inquire into the condition of the infected neighborhoods and to use such remedies as necessity demands by supplying the poor with medical devices, having medicines made up for them, and using disinfectants."[76] Dr. Louis Bosse, later the chief physician at the time of Walther's death, also worked with several assistants out of his own drug store to mitigate the horrors.

The earliest victim—and there were many from Walther's congregation—was Margaretha Vetter who died on May 9, 1849 at the age of fifteen. The records of Trinity indicate that there were a total of forty-five cholera deaths in 1849. Guenther quotes Lochner in describing the epidemic:

> Soon after our arrival in Fort Wayne came one Job message after another of the far-reaching effects of the cholera in St. Louis. When we returned the cholera was frightful. It went so far that there weren't enough wagons available to transport all the corpses that were present. Day and night the pastors, Walther and Buenger, were visiting the sick and dying. During this time they had many blessed experiences of the victoriousness of faithful Christians over death itself and the formerly lost who repented and returned to Christ. On Wednesday afternoons, Walther conducted a prayer session during that time. I participated in one of them. It was precious.[77]

But two pastors working in St. Louis were not enough so they called on the Rev. George Albert Schieferdecker of Centerville, Illinois, to assist them in this draining work. Schieferdecker recorded in his journals as reported in *Der Lutheraner*:

> With the permission of my parish and that with heart-felt readiness on my part, I went to St. Louis ... [and there] I beheld the pitiable sight of a city, only recently devastated by fire, in which the hearses from morning till night, without ceasing, carried away those who had fallen as a sacrifice to the plague. At that time nearly 200 persons were dying each day, in a city of 60,000, one third, which however, had already fled the city.[78]

On the eleventh Sunday after Trinity in 1849, Walther preached on Luke 18:9–14. At the close of his sermon he observed:

> Ah, my friends, just now when cholera is again wreaking its vengeance of death against us, just now we need the pure teaching of justification so much! It is the best, yes, the only safe preservative and remedy. If you use this means, no fear of death will torture you, and when death finally embraces you with its ice-cold arms, you will not despair but in faith cry out with the publican "God be merciful to me a sinner!" and when your ear and eye and mouth close in death, all the angels in heaven and God himself will open their mouths and say about you— not "this man went down"—but up, yes, up "into his house," into the mansions of heaven.[79]

On New Year's Day 1850, Walther preached a heart-rending sermon on Galatians 3:23–29. He mourned:

> An entire row of graves, among whom our loved ones are sleeping, serves as a memorial written with an indelible pencil upon our memories. Here are parents whose beloved children have been torn from their side, husbands whose wives, as the crowns of their heads, have been torn away, widows who are lying on the ground like torn-off vines, have been robbed of their husbands, here are orphans who lost their father and mother, here are brothers and sisters, friends, who have lost their loved ones.[80]

In the midst of all that came the great destruction of a fire on May 17, 1849 (Ascension Day evening) when 640 buildings and 27 steamships resting at the St. Louis wharf were turned into ashes. The fire started in the steamboat "White Cloud" at 10 P.M.; the cause was not determined. As the ship slowly drifted down the river, it set most of the other ships at the wharf on fire also. Even though the fire fighters had struggled valiantly to prevent the fires from reaching the wooden row-houses and buildings, a commission house caught fire. This spread in a southerly direction until it consumed almost three blocks of buildings. In order to prevent the Old Cathedral from catching fire, the firemen blew up six buildings with gunpowder brought from the arsenal. By the next morning St. Louis had only smoldering ashes as a reminder.

Years later, the Chicago pastors who had also experienced a great fire in the fall of 1871 requested that Walther publish his *"Brand Predigt,"* the "fire sermon" he had preached on Exaudi Sunday, 1849. Two selections from this sermon will bring Walther into better focus, pastoring his flock in the midst of the cholera epidemic and fire:

> A great and terrible disaster has visited our city just at the time when men have publicly ridiculed the Word of God. Hardly had the sound of church bells and Christian prayers for mercy faded away this last Ascension Day when the fire alarms echoed through the streets and avenues of our city. The night suddenly turned to day. In a matter of hours the raging flames reduced to ashes most of the ships in our harbor and many of the busiest and most prosperous streets of St. Louis. Thousands were deprived of their homes and earthly possessions. Many lost their lives. Some were overcome by water and flames while others were miserably crushed to death by collapsing dwellings. The fury of the ravaging elements defied all efforts by the fire fighters. ... Even the human comfort that has ordinarily followed a loss by fire, namely the compensation paid by the insurance companies, amounts to almost nothing due to the magnitude of the loss. Sad to say, many dear members of our congregation are numbered among the heavily stricken who with tears gaze upon the ash-heap to which their homes and possessions have been reduced. ...
>
> The cursing and swearing kindled in hell from tongues of young and old which echoes through the streets and avenues of our city day and night; the excessive eating and drinking taking place in hundreds of cheap bars in our city; the mocking and blaspheming to God's Word and of all that is sacred carried on by news writers and readers great and small, rich and poor; the lechery and adultery that is pandered to, openly and shamelessly, in hundreds of corners of our city; the usury and cheating in the business world; the blood letting and fraud openly practiced by doctors, quacks, and charlatans who press out the last savings of the poor visited by sickness; the injustices, trickery, and perjury that brazenly hides away in practically all courtrooms; the facelessness and favoritism of those in public office and, on the other

hand, the ridicule by the citizens of government authority ordained by God; the money-grasping of the men and the pride and finery of the women and ladies; the gluttony, the Bible distortion, the hypocrisy and false worship of the unbelieving and fanatical clerics; the shameful abuse of political freedoms; the unconscionable neglect of the youth; the frightful desecration of the Lord's day; the mistreatment of the poor slaves and the faithlessness of the hired help—but who cares to recount all these Sodom-like sins of our city?

In short, all these and similar sins have for so long cried to God for vengeance until God finally sent a contagious epidemic, and now also the flame of a destructive fire.[81]

NOTES

[1] C. F. W. Walther, *Kurzer Lebenslauf des weiland ehrwürdigen Pastor Joh. Friedr. Bünger* (St. Louis: Verlag von F. Dette, 1882), 23.

[2] Claus Harms, "Das Sind die 95 Thesen Oder Streitsatze Dr. Luthers," *Theueren Andenkens* (Kyle: Verlag … academischen Buchhandlung, 1817), 27.

[3] Carl S. Meyer, ed., *Moving Frontiers* (St. Louis: Concordia Publishing House, 1964), 68.

[4] H. F. Quitman, *Evangelical Catechism* (Hudson, NY: William E. Norman, 1814), 47–48.

[5] Walther, *Kurzer Lebenslauf des weiland ehrwürdigen Pastor Joh. Friedr. Bünger*, 29.

[6] *Lutheran Observer*, March 8, 1839.

[7] *Lutheran Worship*, 485.

[8] W. G. Polack, *The Story of C. F. W. Walther* (St. Louis: Concordia Publishing House, 1947), 36.

[9] *Concordia Junior Messenger*, 17 (March 1939), 59. Trans. by W. M. Czamanske.

[10] *Concordia Junior Messenger*, 17, 72.

[11] *Concordia Junior Messenger*, 17, 73.

[12] Walter O. Forster, *Zion on the Mississippi* (St. Louis: Concordia Publishing House, 1953), 289.

[13] Forster, *Zion on the Mississippi*, 291.

[14] Forster, *Zion on the Mississippi*, 294.

[15] Forster, *Zion on the Mississippi*, 299–300.

[16] Forster, *Zion on the Mississippi*, 378–79.

[17] Forster, *Zion on the Mississippi*, 385–86.

[18] Forster, *Zion on the Mississippi*, 392.

[19] Forster, *Zion on the Mississippi*, 404.

[20] Forster, *Zion on the Mississippi*, 418.

[21] Forster, *Zion on the Mississippi*, 422.

[22] Walther, *Kurzer Lebenslauf des weiland ehrwürdigen Pastor Joh. Friedr. Bünger*, 29.

[23] A copy of this correspondence is held at Concordia Historical Institute.

[24] Carl Edward Schneider, *The German Church on the American Frontier* (St. Louis: Eden Publishing House, 1939), 104.

[25] J. F. Koestering, *Auswanderung der sächsischen Lutheraner im Jahre 1838* (St. Louis: A. Wiebusch, 1866), 1–18. See Introduction, XXII, for note on Walther's responsibility for Chapter 1.

[26] Carl E. Vehse, *The Stephanite Emigration to America: With Documentation*, Rudolph Fiehler, tr. (Tucson: Marion R. Winkler, 1975), 17; *Die Stephan'sche Auswanderung nach Amerika* , *Mit Actenstücken* (Dresden: Dresdner Wochenblatt, 1840).

[27] Carl S. Meyer, ed., *Letters of C. F. W. Walther* (Philadelphia: Fortress Press, 1969), 47, n. 82.

[28] Vehse, *The Stephanite Emigration to America: With Documentation*, 17.

[29] Conrad Bergendoff, *The Doctrine of Church and Ministry in American Lutheranism* (Philadelphia: Muhlenberg Press, 1966), 67.

[30] Martin Guenther, *Dr. C. F. W. Walther: Lebensbild* (St. Louis: Concordia Publishing House, 1890), 37–38.

[31] Guenther, *Dr. C. F. W. Walther: Lebensbild*, 41.

[32] D. H. Steffens, *Doctor Carl Ferdinand Wilhelm Walther* (Philadelphia: Lutheran Publication Society, 1917), 144.

[33] Presidential Address, quoted by Guenther, *Dr. C. F. W. Walther: Lebensbild*, 46–47; taken from the *Proceedings of the Western District 1856*, The Presidential Address.

[34] Forster, *Zion on the Mississippi*, 523–25. For details, see William J. Schmelder, "The Altenburg Debate," STM Thesis, Concordia Seminary, St. Louis, 1960.

[35] The latest edition is translated by J. T. Mueller (St. Louis: Concordia Publishing House, 1987).

[36] For details, see August R. Suelflow, "C. F. W. Walther on the Office of the Ministry," *The Pieper Lectures*, The Office of the Ministry (Concordia Historical Institute and the Luther Academy, 1997), 42–59.

[37] Steffens, *Doctor Carl Ferdinand Wilhelm Walther*, 176.

[38] Guenther, *Dr. C. F. W. Walther: Lebensbild*, 42–43.

[39] Walther's letter of response is printed out in its entirety in Guenther, *Dr. C. F. W. Walther: Lebensbild*, 48–50.

[40] Guenther, *Dr. C. F. W. Walther: Lebensbild*, 50.

[41] Guenther, *Dr. C. F. W. Walther: Lebensbild*, 50.

[42] Guenther, *Dr. C. F. W. Walther: Lebensbild*, 53–54; also Koestering, 59–62.

[43] *History of the Gesamtgemeinde*, St. Louis, July, 1847, filed at Concordia Historical Institute.

[44] Chr. Otto Kraushaar, *Verfassungsformen der lutherischen Kirche Amerikas* (Gütersloh: C. Bertelsmann, 1911), 126–37; trans. by this author.

[45] Edmund Seuel, Interview with August R. Suelflow, March 1, 1951.

[46] August R. Suelflow, *The Lutheran Parish in an Urbanized America with Special Reference to the Missouri Synod, Fifteenth Yearbook (1958) of the Lutheran Education Association*, River Forest, Illinois, 31.

[47] Erich B. Allwardt, "The St. Louis *Gesamtgemeinde*—Its Demise," *Concordia Historical Institute Quarterly*, 57 (Summer 1984), 61–80.

[48] August C. Stellhorn, *Schools of The Lutheran Church—Missouri Synod* (St. Louis: Concordia Publishing House, 1963), 81–82.

[49] Walther, *Kurzer Lebenslauf des weiland ehrwürdigen Pastor Joh. Friedr. Bünger*, 57–60.

[50] Stellhorn, *Schools of The Lutheran Church—Missouri Synod*, 83–84; citing Walther, *Kurzer Lebenslauf des weiland ehrwürdigen Pastor Joh. Friedr. Bünger*, 58–60.

[51] August C. Stellhorn, "Lutheran Secondary Education in St. Louis," *Lutheran Education*, 84 (March 1949), 406–21.

[52] *Der Lutheraner*, 16 (July 26, 1859), 193; cited by Stellhorn, *Schools of The Lutheran Church—Missouri Synod*, 112–13.

[53] . *Der Lutheraner*, 22 (August 1, 1866), 181–82.

[54] Stellhorn, *Schools of The Lutheran Church—Missouri Synod*, 114–15; original *Der Lutheraner*, 25 (October 1, 1868), 17–19.

[55] *Der Lutheraner*, 22 (August 1, 1866), 182.

[56] Quoted from *Deutsche Volksblatt*, 12 by Die Ev-Luth Freikirche (July 15, 1851), 111.

[57] "Aufforderung Zur Bildung Von Jünglingsvereinen," *Der Lutheraner*, 7 (June 24, 1851), 169.

[58] Cited and translated in Henry E. Simon, "Background and Beginnings of Organized Youth Work in the Missouri Synod," B.D. Thesis, 1944, Concordia Seminary, St. Louis, 6; original text in Walther, *Casual-Predigten und-Reden* (St. Louis: Concordia Publishing House, 1889), 283.

[59] Simon, "Background and Beginnings of Organized Youth Work in the Missouri Synod," 169.

[60] M. P. Estel, "Allen deutsch-ev.-lutherischen Jünglingen zur gefälligen Beachtung," *Der Lutheraner*, 12 (May 20, 1856), 158.

[61] Cf. Jon Pahl, *Hopes and Dreams of All: The International Walther League and Lutheran Youth in American Culture* 1893–1993 (Chicago: Wheat Ridge Ministries, 1993).

[62] *Der Lutheraner*, 10 (November 9, 1853), 41ff; 18 (November 27, 1861), 57ff.

[63] *Der Lutheraner*, 13 (November 18, 1856), 56.

[64] *Proceedings of the Western District*, 1859, 75.

[65] *Der Lutheraner*, 16 (October 18,1859), 38.

[66] *Der Lutheraner*, 16 (December 13, 1859), 70.

[67] *Der Lutheraner*, 25 (September 15, 1868), 15.

[68] See Robert Kolb, "Luther for German Americans: The St. Louis Edition of Luther's Works, 1880–1910," *Concordia Historical Institute Quarterly*, 56 (Fall 1983), 98–108.

[69] Kolb, "Luther for German Americans: The St. Louis Edition of Luther's Works, 1880–1910," *Concordia Historical Institute Quarterly*, 108.

[70] Roy A. Suelflow, ed., *Selected Writings of C. F. W. Walther* (St. Louis: Concordia Publishing House, 1981), 146.

[71] Karl Kretzmann, "An Adventure of Dr. Walther in 1846," *Concordia Historical Institute Quarterly*, 19 (April 1946), 13.

[72] Kretzmann, "An Adventure of Dr. Walther in 1846," *Concordia Historical Institute Quarterly*, 14–15.

[73] August R. Suelflow, "*St. Louis Volksblatt*," *Concordia Historical Institute Quarterly*, 18 (January 1946), 108ff.

[74] *Der Lutheraner*, 14 (September 22, 1857), 22.

[75] James Neal Primm, *Lion of the Valley: St. Louis, 1764–1980* (Boulder, CO: Pruett Publishing Company, 1981), 162.

[76] J. Thomas Scharf, *History of St. Louis City and County*, Vol. 2 (Philadelphia: Louis H. Everts and Co., 1883), 1580–81.

[77] Guenther, *Dr. C. F. W. Walther: Lebensbild*, 79–80.

[78] F. Köstering, "*Ehrengedächtniss des Seligen Pastors Georg Albert Schieferdecker*," *Der Lutheraner*, 48 (September 13, 1892), 151–52.

[79] C. F. W. Walther, *Amerikanisch-Lutherische Evangelien Postille* (St. Louis: Concordia Publishing House, 1870), 278–79, Donald E. Heck, tr., *Old Standard Gospel*, Livermore, IA, mimeographed, 1955.

[80] C. F. W. Walther, *Amerikanisch-Lutherische Epistel Postille* (St. Louis: Concordia Publishing House, 1882), 49.

[81] C. F. W. Walther, "What Our God Is Telling Us," *The Word of His Grace* (Lake Mills, IA: Graphic Publishing Co., 1978), 168, 171.

3

LIGHT FROM ABOVE

The theme for this chapter, "Light from Above," is taken from the seal of Concordia Seminary. In Greek it reads: "*Anothen to phos.*" Walther had the distinction of being the father of both Concordia Seminary, St. Louis and of The Lutheran Church—Missouri Synod. His abilities, energies, and understanding were plunged into both of these institutions whose mission was to bring God's message of forgiveness through Jesus Christ to people of all tongues and nations.

Before Walther, there was neither a Missouri Synod nor a Concordia Seminary. But there was a Scripture-based theology going back to Martin Luther and the Reformation in the sixteenth century. The credit for strongly reintroducing this theology in America belongs to Walther.

It is the purpose of this chapter to focus on Walther as Concordia Seminary's theological instructor for thirty-seven years and its first president for thirty-three years, covering the span from the mid-nineteenth century to the time of his death in 1887.

This story goes back to the log cabin seminary in Perry County, Missouri, opened on December 9, 1839. During its log cabin years, the seminary received moral and financial support from Trinity in Altenburg, Missouri and Trinity in St. Louis, Missouri, two of the larger congregations established by the Saxon immigrants of 1838–1839. During those early years, five men graduated for the pastoral ministry. They are referred to as "the quintuplets": J. A. F. W. Mueller, who graduated in 1847; Franz Julius Biltz and Rudolph Lange, both in 1848; Heinrich Wunder in 1849, and Heinrich Loeber in 1850.

These five log cabin graduates became outstanding leaders of the Synod. Mueller served pastorates in Missouri, Illinois, and Pennsylvania. Biltz served congregations in Missouri and Maryland, and was president of the Western District from 1875 to 1891. Loeber served pastorates in Missouri, Illinois, and Wisconsin. He was co-founder of what today is Concordia University, Mequon, Wisconsin and served as its president from 1885 to 1893. Lange served pastorates in Missouri, Ohio, and Illinois, and also taught at both seminaries at various times. Wunder served

St. Paul's, Chicago, Illinois for sixty-two years, helped organize Concordia, Mequon and served as the first president of the Illinois District from 1875 to 1891. All five were active in missions and education. These committed men made a wonderful beginning by entering various areas of service to the Lord and His people.

The Seminary was already eight years old when the Missouri Synod was officially organized in 1847. The Synod immediately recognized the need for institutions to train future pastors and teachers. Already at its second convention in 1848 the Synod felt that it would be far better if, as a very minimum, the final years of seminary training could be offered in a large city. The convention decided that the entire institution should be moved to St. Louis.[1]

Negotiations for the transfer were difficult at best. Finally the St. Louis and Altenburg congregations signed the document of transfer on October 8, 1849 and June 4, 1850. The document emphasized that pastors and teachers be trained only through the German language with the use of Latin in certain courses. It created two departments, a theological one and a technical one. This left the door open for young people who did not wish to devote themselves full time to professional service in the church to enroll. Professor J. J. Goenner was to be retained as an instructor by the contract.[2] The entire operation, such as it was, was transferred up the Mississippi River amidst ice and debris from Perry County to St. Louis on December 16, 1849.

The new site was provided by Trinity congregation, St. Louis, which had purchased about nine acres on South Jefferson Avenue for a cemetery. It made some of this land available for the construction of a new seminary. The cornerstone was laid as early as November 8, 1849. In his address that day, Walther emphasized that the church must be a patroness of the arts and sciences, learning, and culture. It appears that he gave greater emphasis to the concept of a *Gymnasium* than a Seminary. The church, he said, must cultivate scholarship and the arts so she might more effectively carry out her tasks.[3]

ITS OWN BUILDING

Temporary instruction was conducted in the home of Christiane Buenger, Walther's mother-in-law, before the St. Louis building was even completed. Her home was located on Lombard between Third and Fourth Streets. Classes began there on January 9, 1850. The new seminary building in St. Louis was designed by Martin Stephan, Jr., who had studied architecture in Germany after his return following the immigration difficulties in Perry County. The south wing was so designed that a second wing could be constructed on the north, all dependent upon finances. Ultimately a major unit would be built between them. The south wing consisted of two stories and a basement, forty-two by thirty-six feet, excluding a back porch. Together with a cistern, out-buildings, a pump, and other interior work, the final cost came to $4,236.88. Trinity, St. Louis had provided $2,035.75.[4] What a vision of future expansion!

When the building was completed, Walther and his family moved into the first floor with five rooms. This was the Walther family home for twenty years, from 1850 to 1870. The second floor housed twenty students.

The building was dedicated on June 11, 1850. A large crowd came for the festive occasion. A long road led out from Geyer in Soulard on Broadway down to Jefferson Avenue, a distance of two and one-half miles, and on into the dusty country roads. As they arrived by horse and buggy, visitors saw the name "Concordia" above the lintel of the main entrance. This was the first time the name was used in conjunction with the Seminary. Concordia means "harmony" on the one hand, but also refers to the Lutheran Confessions, hence conveying the meaning of a fellowship based on unity in doctrine.

A special program folder was prepared for the worship service. "A Mighty Fortress" was sung in Latin and an orchestra and choir beautified the service. Herman Fick composed a special hymn for the occasion, sung to the tune of "Wake, Awake, for Night is Flying."[5] Walther's address that day was ingenious. Speaking in Latin, he said that it was the church fathers and the Lutheran theologians who were in reality the ones occupying the chairs of the professors at the new institution. It was they, not the small faculty (Goenner and Walther), who were to train the future pastors.

F. C. D. Wyneken, Synod president, delivered his address in German to the Germans and the members of the church. He emphasized that English learning had its origins in German, even though the Germans were still Gibeonites, "hewers of wood and drawers of water," in America. Wyneken urged the Germans to make this school the seed bed of German culture while at the same time teaching only pure doctrine.[6]

A second identical building, some fifty feet north of the first, was constructed in 1852. This wing was used for student dormitories, classrooms, library, kitchen, and dining room. Walther preached at the cornerstone laying of this wing. The exact date is not known. A few excerpts from his sermon are noteworthy:

What, therefore, must and can be the only true foundation of an institution for the upbringing of the youth? Out of this institution one day should come servants of the church and of the state, the teachers of the schools, and the craftsmen of industry, the publishers, merchants, heads of the home, in short, the heads and leaders in all stations of life. The true foundation of a school cannot be the passing wisdom of the world, but it must be the eternal truth which comes from God and leads to God, namely, the true religion. For without this foundation an institution for the upbringing of the youth is only an arsenal where weapons are forged and assembled not only against the church and the kingdom of God but also against the welfare of the state and the well-being of families. But if true religion is the foundation of a school of higher learning, it will become a fountain that floods city and land and indeed all-temporal social relationships with blessing.… We look upon a school as a structure that must not be built upon the changing, drifting sand of human opinion and systems, but that must be built upon the eternal rock-foundation of the Word of the Almighty.

By all means we shall never forget that even human science and arts are valuable, precious gifts of God, treasures and adornments of humanity. Here they will be sincerely cultivated and fostered according to our ability. But of what value are marble walls with diamond pillars and golden domes when the foundation of the building rests upon hollow, decaying ground?"[7]

In the fall of 1857 another unit was constructed, comprising the center section of the building. It was three stories high, with a porch and tower. The dedication was scheduled for April, 1858 when the Western District would hold its convention at Trinity in St. Louis. But on April 10, just five days before the scheduled event, Professor Biewend died suddenly, and no dedication was ever held.

The first floor of this unit had a large meeting room or Aula, 47 feet wide and 47 feet deep with an 18-foot ceiling (the Baier *Lehrsaal*). This multi-purpose room provided space for a library, chapel and auditorium. The dining hall and washrooms were located in the basement. The second floor contained five studies and living rooms. The third floor consisted of one large bedroom for the students.[8]

In 1871, a third floor was added to the first two wings. The construction of the entire first building covered a span of twenty-one years (first wing in 1850, second in 1852, center in 1857, and third floor in 1871). In this way, the need for additional space was met piece by piece as time passed.

It demonstrated a tremendous amount of foresight to have Concordia College (Seminary) incorporated as early as February 23, 1853. A quotation may be helpful to understand what the founders of the seminary actually had in mind. The name was registered as "Concordia College" whose purpose was to aid "in the dissemination of knowledge, including all branches of academic, scientific, and theological instruction in general, and giving, moreover to suitable persons desiring it, instruction in the creed and tenets of said denomination in particular. ..."[9]

A "NEW" SEMINARY—1883

A monumental achievement in Walther's life was the dedication of the impressive and artistic new seminary building on Jefferson Avenue in 1883. The time preceding this had been difficult. Although the Synodical Conference had discussed the establishment of a "joint seminary," nothing really became of this. It would have eliminated the need to erect a seminary building at all.

At the age of seventy-two, Walther was privileged to dedicate an entirely new Seminary building, that a professor of the Chicago Lutheran Seminary described as "the most complete ecclesiastical structure in the Lutheran Church of America and a noble monument to its evangelical faith."[10]

Discussion had ensued about a new seminary as early as the mid-1870s because of lack of space. Enrollment stood at about 140 to 160 students. Temporary relief came when the "practical" seminary was moved to Springfield, Illinois in 1875. This move temporarily reduced the need for expanded facilities. When other synods, which had sent their students to Concordia, began to build their own seminaries, even more space became available. Nevertheless, the need for a larger facility was apparent.

By 1881, when the Synod met in convention in Fort Wayne, it determined that a new seminary building was necessary. It resolved to erect a new building on the same spot where the old one had stood. The new structure was to be three stories high, measuring 225 × 95 feet, with 63 rooms, 57 of which were for student occupancy. In addition, six washrooms, a library, a reading room, eight classrooms, an auditorium or an Aula, a basement for the boiler rooms (for steam heat), and a *gymnasium* were all included.[11] The regular classrooms could seat 68 students each, and a large classroom held 102 students. The imposing building was described as modern Gothic. "Pressed brick was used in the construction of the building; the trim was Indiana blue stone. The woods used in the building were black walnut, ash, cherry, and other hard woods."[12]

The convention stipulated that the old building was not to be torn down until two-thirds of the funds needed for the construction of the new one were available. It also determined that the 1881–1882 academic year be closed in May, rather than in June, so the old building could be razed. Walther appealed to all congregations, encouraging them to support the new program. Sixteen architects submitted plans for the new building. Among them was C. May, a member of a local congregation, whose plan was finally chosen.

Efforts for funding were successful. The old buildings were torn down. In the interim, the Christian Lange home became a dormitory. Some of the students also lived in Francis Pieper's former home and still others with various families. Classes were conducted in the old Concordia Publishing House building on the second floor, with the first floor serving as a dining hall, to which a kitchen had been added. Two parlors of the Lange home were also used as classrooms.[13]

Guenther gives a good description of the cornerstone laying of the 1883 building in *Der Lutheraner*.[14] The service on October 1, 1882 began at 3:00 P.M. with the congregation singing "A Mighty Fortress," accompanied by brass. Walther gave the primary address. Deeply moved as he entered the pulpit out in the open, he called nostalgic attention to the first cornerstone laying and dedication. He stressed that Christ is the only cornerstone of the church, saying:

> Nearly thirty-three years ago, on November 8, 1849, on this identical spot, the cornerstone was laid of a building which was to receive into its narrow rooms a twofold nursery of future servants of the Evangelical Lutheran Church. That building, safely completed with the help of God in seven months and solemnly dedicated to the Lord on June 11, 1850, was enlarged from time to time. Having served its sacred purpose thirty-two years, it vanished months ago from the ground. Not fiery flames devoured it; neither did floods of water carry it away, nor windstorms overthrow it. We ourselves took it down to make room on this hallowed spot for a new and greater structure. To do this, we were not prompted by the cravings arising in us after great things. Nay, as in the days past to Israel by the prophet Isaiah, so God has called to us by His blessing on our church: "Enlarge the place of thy tent, and let them stretch forth the curtains of thine habitations." The old building could no longer contain the evermore-abundant blessing that was being poured out among us. If we were not, an

unpardonable surfeit, to say to God: "Heavenly Father, restrain Thy blessing upon us," or if we were not, by base ingratitude, to squander God's blessing that has flowed upon us, we had to procure a larger vessel to hold this blessing.[15]

Earlier the students had sung *"Preis und Anbetung"* ("Praise and Prayer"). Following this Guenther read his detailed history of the seminary, printed in *Der Lutheraner*, but because of intermittent rain he omitted reading the names of all the graduates who had entered the ministry. After Guenther's presentation, the students sang *"Lobe den Herren, den mächtigen Koenig der Ehren"* ("Praise to the Lord, the Almighty.")[16]

The ceremonious laying of the cornerstone was conducted by Professor G. Schaller who read the list of the contents of the stone to the audience. Towards the close of the service the Holy Cross Choir, directed by Teacher H. Erck, sang *"Jauchzet Gott, alle Lände"* ("Shout with Joy to God, All Ye Lands"). Three hammer strokes completed the act.

Professor Lange gave a brief English address defining the seminary's position and purpose. A telegram from Pastor J. M. Buehler from far away San Francisco, California was appropriately read. After Stoeckhardt had spoken a prayer, the group sang "Now Thank We All Our God." The service was concluded with the Lord's Prayer.[17]

In mid-April, during the construction, as the roof and windows were being placed, the Lord prevented a disaster. The dinner bell was rung to summon the students for supper. As one of them passed the construction site, suddenly lightning struck and a huge block of stone crashed down three feet in front of him.[18]

THE DEDICATION

The dedication of the Seminary took place on September 9, 1883. The event catapulted Walther out of the bitter days of the predestinarian controversy in which the Synod was deeply embroiled. The months before the dedication were exhilarating for him—a new era was beginning. Walther had seen the seminary grow from a little log cabin in the woods of Perry County to a grand new building 44 years later. In a day when travel was taxing and difficult, he and his wife traveled to Cleveland, Ohio and Port Richmond, New York to visit their daughters and their families. On the national scene, the first direct telephone service was initiated between New York and Chicago on March 24, 1883. This was an exciting time!

The two-day dedication event brought an overwhelming crowd of 20,000 people to St. Louis. Pastors from all over the country traveled hundreds of miles to be present. Participants included the large student body, representing the highest enrollment of any Protestant theological seminary.

Two services were held on the first day (September 9), with Walther preaching in the morning and Pastor C. Gross of Fort Wayne, Vice President of the Synod (1878–1899), speaking in the afternoon. Professor A. Crull also gave a presentation in English at the afternoon service.

On the following day two addresses were presented in Latin for the academic exercises, one by F. Pieper and the other by G. Stoeckhardt. A student from New Zealand, A. W. Meyer, made a presentation in English, and O. Hattstaedt gave an address in German.

In the evening a music festival was held at the Mercantile Library Hall, with presentations by a symphony orchestra and the seminary choir. They sang Haydn's "Te Deum," accompanied by a chorus. It was a joyous event. Just six days after the dedication had taken place, *Der Lutheraner* described the event as follows:

> People had hastened to the festival location in joyful expectation, but no one had surmised that a crowd of 20,000 people (including 160 pastors) would stream together. What heart could fail to beat with festival joy at the sight of so many fellow believers! What mouth could have failed to break out in joyful jubilation? Almost every state of the Union, yes, every major city in our country had sent representatives to the festival. From the upper Mississippi, from Minnesota, from the Gulf of Mexico, from California and from beyond the sea, from Germany, visitors had come for the occasion. All railroads with terminals at St. Louis brought thousands to the festival on special trains, e.g. from Chicago, Milwaukee, Fort Wayne, and Pittsburgh. About 160 pastors came to the celebration, 133 of whom had studied at Concordia Seminary in earlier or more recent times. A number of synods had sent representatives, the Norwegian Synod: President Koren, Pastor Preus, Pastor Ottesen, Professor Stub from Madison; the Wisconsin Synod: President Bading and Professor Graebner; the Minnesota Synod: President Albrecht and Pastor Tirmenstein. The officials of the Missouri Synod were in large part present also.[19]

Pure joy reigned. Thousands of people were reunited physically, and thousands more reestablished bonds of faith and unity in Jesus Christ. People who had never seen each other before or had never become acquainted shared in the joy of this great event and in singing praises to God. This glorious occasion far overshadowed all previous celebrations.

The service of dedication on September 9 was held outdoors in the open sky. It began at 10:00 A.M. with the chanting of Psalm 150 by the students. The congregation then joined in singing the soul-stirring hymn, "Praise the Almighty, My Soul,"[20] accompanied by trumpets and trombones. The words and melody so inspired the audience that they were almost on their feet as they sang:

> "Trust not in princes, they are but mortal;
> Earth-born they are and soon decay.
> Vain are their counsels at life's last portal ...
> Blessed, O blessed are they forever,
> Whose help is from the Lord most high. ..."

The hymn concluded, Walther ascended the rostrum, which had been specially erected for the occasion. Observers reported that even though he was almost seventy-two, he preached with power, freshness, and great enthusiasm. Every word reached the ears of the listeners who waited for the next thought and sentence. This address was one of Walther's most effective oratorical expressions of his position on theological education's proclamation of the Gospel, and it serves as a foundational epitome of all his life and work. It has never been published in English before. The powerful message, so overwhelming and inspiring, is worth quoting at length.[21]

What is it that has brought us together today from far and near by thousands and thousands at this new building? What is it that has caused us to send to the throne of God hymns of praise, thankfulness, and joy? Is it the great size and impressiveness of this new building? Certainly not! It is of course a mighty and beautiful edifice which proclaims the praise of its builder. Like a beautiful bride of a king it rises above all its neighbors, but who among us has not seen even greater, more artistic, more richly adorned buildings? Who among us would therefore have been so foolish to travel hundreds and even thousands of miles and even to cross the ocean only to feast their eyes on the sight of such a building? Is the reason for our present joy perhaps this, that we Lutherans have erected this great and beautiful edifice and believe that we have thereby made a name for ourselves before the world? Far be it from us! For in that case woe unto us! Then this building would only be a permanent witness to our pride, and therefore not a monument of our honor but of our shame.

We can, of course, not deny that today our hearts are surging with joy when we consider that this institution, which was opened 44 years ago in a forest in our little block hut, is today moving into a palace in this metropolis. But as a surviving eye—and ear—witness I can testify that

44 years ago also our little log cabin appeared as a palace to us into which we entered at that time with no less joy than today in this beautiful building. At that time our poverty was so great that even such a tiny log cabin appeared to our eyes as a miracle for which we could only thank God with tears of joy. Therefore, no! No! My brethren. No! Not the size and stateliness of this new building, not the vain glory that we are its builders, is the true and real reason for our joy today, but there is an entirely different one.

Come now, you Lutherans, be convinced that I am only giving expression to the thoughts of your hearts, I beg that you will permit me to show that the true, real reason of our festival joy is none other than this threefold one: The final purpose which this new building only is to serve (the dispensing, not of earthly, but of heavenly wisdom); the circumstances which brought it about and made it necessary; and finally the love which alone built it and adorned it. ...

This house deserves not earthly but heavenly things. The tower which raises up to heaven with its bell does not only adorn this house, but above all demonstrates its character and hour after hour, by day and by night, calls out to those within and without to *Sursum corda*! Lift up your hearts! This is a house for sacred studies! This is a house of prayer! This is a house of God!

In this house young men are to study, not the word of man or human knowledge and wisdom, but God's Word, and nothing but the Word of God, the entire Word of God. ...

In this house the Book of all books is to be explained and interpreted not rationalistically, on the basis of reason, not papistically, on the basis of the writings of the Fathers, not fanatically, on the basis of alleged new revelations, but in an apostolic Christian manner. ...

In this house no new doctrines shall be discovered, but only the old and yet eternally young doctrine of Him. ...

In this house no private opinions and private views of any man shall be taught and recognized, no matter how pious. ...

In this house there shall be represented as divine truth not the peculiar doctrines of some sect, but only those of the true believing Evangelical Lutheran Church of the Unaltered Augsburg Confession. ...

In this house the doctrine of the Reformation is not to be reformed again, but guarded and preserved with incorruptible faithfulness as an inalienable, inviolable treasure. ...

In this house, therefore, after Christ Himself, our only master, and after the holy apostles and prophets, none other than Dr. Martin Luther ... shall be the chief teacher.

In this house ... the King of truth alone is to rule who said: "If you continue in my word, you are my disciples indeed, and you will know the truth, and the truth shall make you free. ..."

In this house living, believing Christians shall be received in order to be prepared as the heralds of Christ's Gospel, the Son of God and the Savior of the world, who will confess with the Holy 12 apostles. ...

In this house, not only the minds of those who are enrolled will be filled with the knowledge of the teachings of divine revelation, but this doctrine will be above all impressed upon their hearts, So that proceeding first out of the school of the Holy Spirit Himself, they will be able to witness to the truth. ...

In this house those enrolled are not only to have an opportunity to pursue their sacred studies in a hallowed place, far removed from the tumult of the world ... where they willingly renounce the lusts, treasures, and honors of this world and concentrate their life, their powers, their souls, solely in the service of Christ and to saving the world until the day of their death. ...

This house is to become an armory of God in which God-fearing young men are to be equipped with the spiritual weapons of soldiers for Christ ...

This house shall be a spiritual fountain from which the waters of eternal life will be directed over hill and dale, so that the spiritual deserts will be transformed into green meadows. ...

In short, this house is to be dedicated solely to the honor of God and the salvation of redeemed sinners.

How? Is not this a great and glorious goal? Is not this sufficient reason for all believing Christians, and especially for us Lutherans, to cause our hearts to beat joyfully, now that we have, with the help of God without any accidents, seen it turn out so well before our eyes? ... "the Lord has done great things for us; whereof we are glad. ..."

When our Synod ... met for the first time thirty-six years ago in the richly blessed city of Chicago, it was but a small, insignificant group of merely twelve poor congregations. The church which in this country was still calling itself Evangelical Lutheran was in a state of deep deterioration. The teaching of our church was unknown territory to her. The few pastors who still knew something of it and wanted to hold fast to it were looked upon as narrow-minded; it was hoped that they would soon die out. The Confessions of our church were hardly known even by name; they were looked upon as aged documents and obsolete, stemming from an earlier unenlightened age. Instead of the doctrines of Luther, the doctrines of Zwingli and well-known rationalism prevailed in the church, amazingly intertwined with the "enthusiasts" [*Schwärmer*] in converting people. ... In short, the so-called Lutheran church in our land was at that time dead, the laughing-stock of the sects who, similarly to hungry birds of the night, divided the carcass among themselves.

When our Synod took to the field at that time with the unheard of watchword "God's Word and Luther's doctrine pure shall to eternity endure," it was not only the anti-Christian papacy, not only the syncretistic, unionistic evangelical fellowship, not only the fanatical sects but especially all the elements of the so-called Lutheran church in this country which attacked our Synod with the greatest bitterness as a new "old Lutheran" sect, which would lead to ruin, confidently prophesied as a strange plant and an un-American intruder an early inglorious end. ...

And what happened? Even the evil-intended proposals of our enemies did not succeed. When congregations saw that the pastors of our Synod were not proclaiming a new doctrine, but preached nothing else than what the congregations had learned in their beloved small catechism of Luther; when the congregations saw that the pastors of our Synod were bringing them the highest which any preacher can bring, namely the certainty of the grace of God and their salvation; when the congregations saw that the pastors of our Synod were not desirous of exercising priestly authority over them, but in contrast sought to lead them to the knowledge of their glorious liberty as Christians and of their sacred rights as congregations ... when the congregations saw that the pastors of our Synod would rather suffer hunger and distress, rather insult, persecution, and banishment than to depart from even one letter of "God's Word and Luther's Doctrine," then note—one congregation after the other entered into our synodical union. ...

The precious books of our church, the confessional writings together with the writings of Luther, rescued from the dust, carried from house to house, came to the forefront and were eagerly read and studied by our people. The genuine Lutheran faith and the Lutheran way of life spread like a prairie fire across the land; God blessed us with a unity of faith and a joy of faith with inner brotherly love, which at times even seemed to turn us back to the days of Luther. Wherever a tiny Lutheran church, like a fruit tree, even in the lonesome prairies, grew, there also a Lutheran school building sprung up like a young plant. The old pure hymns, filled with the power of faith and the fervor of love, as they were sung by our forefathers, gave music with their old sweet manner. In short, a true Lutheran church, of whom one had sung funeral dirges everywhere, came back to life, rose from the grave, and planted the flag of victory of the pure Gospel over a thousand different places of our great union of states.

Already for years, from all sides, came the Macedonian call ... "Come over and help us." And now an even mightier stream of Lutheran immigrants also of our German language is poured out over our land and is settling it, so that new congregations come into existence almost weekly, congregations which in large part desire teachers for church and school, particularly from us. ... Everywhere doors are opened to us to enter with the joyous news of the free grace of God in Christ for all sinners. Although hundreds of laborers have already been sent out from our institutions into the great harvest, pleas for such laborers have not decreased, but are ever increasing so that finally our hearts were saddened since we could no longer fulfill most of these requests. And so it happened that the great number of students could no longer find room in our seminary building. A larger new building became an urgent necessity.

Therefore I ask you ... isn't all of this today a cause for great joy? Or what? Does a farmer become angry and bemoan the fact he has been so blessed that he has brought in his harvest and feels compelled to dismantle his barns which have gotten too small, and to build bigger? But no! He rejoices and lifts up his hands in fervent thanksgiving to God, the gracious giver. Look please, we do not have any reason to grumble and to complain that we, through God's showering blessings found ourselves compelled to begin an expensive construction; so we too have cause today and, from our inner hearts, raise our hands humbly to God and thank Him. Up till now we have received each applicant for enrollment with renewed concern rather than with joy; beginning today, we can throw open the wide, well-lighted rooms of this our new Concordia, and joyfully greet every new student: "Welcome! Come in, O blessed of the Lord!" Isn't this great joy?

But, there is one more factor which has filled us with such great joy today: It is the love which alone has erected this building and adorned it.

No magnanimous millionaires have built this noble building and offered them to our poor church as a gift. No ruler has imposed any educational taxes by law so that anyone was forced to bring unwilling sacrifices. No one who is not a Lutheran was approached by us and pressured to contribute a single dime ... Not a single person has been urged through unevangelical pressure on his conscience to bring his gift. No one has been deceitfully and falsely promised that he could gain a rich measure of indulgence for his sins by liberal gifts, and, as the saying goes, "build a step toward heaven." No one's gift was obtained by arousing his sense of pride by means of hypocritical flattery. We Lutherans detest the principle that the end justifies the means. According to the apostolic principle, "The Lord loves a cheerful giver," all that was done among us was that a friendly appeal was made. The crying need of innumerable children of our church was portrayed in vivid colors. They are wandering about this land to which they immigrated in spiritual wilderness as sheep without a shepherd, without the servants of the comforting Gospel and end up in spiritual starvation. Above all, we were shown the love of Christ, the Good Shepherd who seeks the lost, who shed His blood for all people, who desires that all people are saved, even the lonely children of our church who have yet to be called to Him. ... Thousands of hearts and hands were joyfully opened without delay in our beloved congregations. Dwellers in the country and in the city, the poor and the rich, men and women, young women and young men, even orphans and widows competed with one another to help that this edifice might be erected and most beautifully adorned.

So I make bold, my brothers and sisters in the Lord (God knows that I do not do it to flatter you, but for the glory of Him whose Word, grace and Spirit has worked this in you)—I say, therefore I make bold to declare openly here: This house has been built with God's help and so beautifully adorned by your love, which is a fruit of your faith. O beautiful, precious building! For what would it be without the love of those who built it, even though it were built entirely of gold, silver and precious stones? It would be a house from which God would withhold His face, into which He would not want to enter. For "God is love." However, the large gifts of love of those among us who are richly blessed in earthly goods and the tiny precious mites lovingly contributed by our poor, widows, and orphans, convert every piece of wood in this building into shining gold in the eyes of God, every stone in its walls into glistening diamonds. Even if this building should sooner or later fall, as all human work, nevertheless, may it serve as a memorial to the love of believing Lutheran Christians as it will stand forever, yes, forever, before God's eyes.

Mind you dear ones, all blessings and success of all works of love come solely from the Lord. Therefore, let us implore Him once more today as we implored Him 44 years ago when the simple log hut finally stood before us, completed:

> "Enter in! Enter in!
> Consecrate this house, O Jesus!"[22]

Ah, yes, Lord, not because of our weak, impure, imperfect love, but on account of your burning, pure, eternal, perfect love, we pray:

Accept this house which we are herewith turning over to You. It is not to be our house, but Your, yes, Your house. Take it into Your gracious omnipotent protection; be and remain in it the real master. Bless both teachers and students in it. Bless in it both the heavenly and the earthly bread. Let an ever-richer blessing go forth from this house into city and country, in the huts and the palaces, for time and for eternity. Bless our beloved Synod and all her congregations whose love has erected this house. Bless the dear brethren who in never failing love have born the heavy burden of seeing this work to completion on our behalf. Bless the builders who planned and erected this building, and the workmen who labored on it. Bless this land and its government, under whose earthly protection this house now stands. Bless this city, which has willingly and kindly received it into its bosom. Bless finally also our celebration today for the strengthening of our faith, for the igniting of our love and for the quickening of our hope.

Thanks, praise, honor and glory be to Your great name, here in time and here after from eternity to eternity. Amen! Amen!

This was the Concordia Seminary that was used by the Synod until the present campus in Clayton was dedicated on June 13, 1926.

THE FACULTY

Sixteen men served as the full time faculty at the seminary during the course of Walther's life. It has been generally held that Walther himself, as president of the institution, hand-picked the men who served with him. While this may have been the case with a few, it was not true of all. It is known that Walther was extremely anxious to engage Gustavus Seyffarth, H. M. Baumstark, Eduard Preuss, and Georg Stoeckhardt. It is uncertain whether others were his choice. For Walther it was the faculty that constituted the seminary.

Walther thought very highly of German education and scholarship during the early years of the seminary. He sought faculty members with excellent German university training and was always looking for scholarship in the classroom and in publications. Although several faculty members were graduates of the Altenburg and St. Louis institutions, most of the seminary professors at this time had studied at Erlangen, Berlin, Heidelberg, Paris, Oslo, Goettingen, and Leipzig, Walther's alma mater. But after two faculty members defected to the Roman Catholic Church in 1869 and 1872, and following the extremely troublesome predestinarian controversy, Walther's mind was totally changed and he then chose promising young men trained in America. They came from various provinces of Germany. Only a few were Saxons; all were well-trained and men of ability. The following were members of the seminary faculty during Walther's presidency.

J. J. Goenner (1807–1864) served as a professor from 1843 to 1857. Goenner moved with the nine students from Perry County to St. Louis. He taught Old and New Testament languages until he was given a leave of absence in 1857 in order to edit the *Altenburger Bibelwerk*.

Adolph Biewend (1816–1858) was on the seminary faculty from 1850 to 1858. Biewend, who also taught English and philosophy as a member of the Pennsylvania Ministerium, was a professor at Columbian College, Washington, D.C. Walther had looked to him to assist with language transition, but his untimely death at forty-one shattered this hope. He left behind a widow and seven young children. The Western District Convention in 1858 resolved to pay the widow his salary, even after his successor would be called. Out of this emerged the first "Widow and Orphan Society" and ultimately the present Worker Benefit Plans. As will be discussed in more detail later, Biewend and his son rescued Walther on one occasion from drowning in the Mississippi River. In gratitude Walther presented him with an engraved cup which was later donated to the Concordia Historical Institute.

Alexander Saxer (?–1872) served as a professor between 1856 and 1861. During the Civil War, the seminary was temporarily closed from April 26 to early September, 1861, and almost everyone left. Only Saxer stayed behind with Walther in the seminary buildings.

Gustavus Seyffarth (1796–1885) served on the faculty from 1856 to 1859. He held two doctorates, one in philosophy and one in theology, and taught at the University of Leipzig before coming to America. Upon acceptance of his call to the seminary, he informed the Synod that he would serve without salary. After a two-year leave of absence in 1859 to continue research in Egyptian hieroglyphics, he did not return because of differences with Walther on the issue of slavery.

Georg Schick (1831–1915) was a professor from 1856 to 1863. He studied at Erlangen, Berlin, Heidelberg, and Paris. Schick came to America in 1854 and joined the Missouri Synod the same year. He served as a pastor in Chicago, Illinois before coming to the seminary to teach ancient languages; he moved to Fort Wayne when the seminary was moved there.

Lauritz Larsen (1833–1915) had a relatively short stay on the faculty, 1859–1861. He had studied at the University of Oslo, Norway, where he received excellent theological training under professors who instilled in him a superior doctrinal background and deep evangelical fervor. He left the seminary when the Civil War broke out and went on to become a significant leader in the Norwegian Synod. Later Larsen became president of Luther College, now in Decorah, Iowa. His specialties were Norwegian and exegesis.

Rudolph Lange (1825–1892) served as a professor for two tenures, 1858–1861 and 1878–1892. He graduated from the seminary in Altenburg, Missouri in 1848, taught English and philosophy, moved to Fort Wayne because of the Civil War, returned to the St. Louis faculty in 1878, and simultaneously assisted extensively with *Lehre und Wehre*. Lange became editor of the *St. Louis Theological Monthly* in 1881 during the predestinarian controversy.

Friedrich August Craemer (1812–1891) taught from 1861 to 1875, when he transferred to Springfield, Illinois. Like many of the other professors, Craemer had a career rich in experiences. He studied in Erlangen, was a Loehe emissary, established the mission colony of Frankenmuth, Michigan in 1845, served as tutor at Oxford University, and was highly revered by the Chippewa Indians for his work among them. He was a faithful friend of Walther, and students lovingly referred to him as "Papa Craemer."

Ernst August Brauer (1819–1896) served from 1863 to 1872. He studied at Göttingen, was a Loehe emissary, and settled in Addison, Illinois in 1847 as a pastor. At the seminary he taught isagogics, symbolics, catechetics, psychology, and logic. Brauer helped edit *Der Lutheraner* and was on the staff of *Lehre und Wehre*.

Johann Michael Gottlieb Schaller (1819–1887) served as a professor between 1872 and 1887. He studied at Nürnberg and Erlangen, came to America as an emissary of Loehe in 1848, and joined the Missouri Synod in 1849. He was assistant pastor of Trinity, St. Louis and president of the Western District, 1857–1863, before coming to the seminary.

F. A. Schmidt (1837–1928) was a faculty member from 1872 to 1876. He graduated from Concordia Seminary, St. Louis in 1853 and taught at Luther College, Decorah, Iowa, 1861–1872. Totally conversant in English and Norwegian, Schmidt taught English, Norwegian, homiletics, encyclopedia, and methodology. He left the St. Louis Seminary in 1876 to serve Luther College at Decorah, Iowa until 1886, and various other Norwegian seminaries for the remainder of his life. Walther referred to him as his "own hands."

Martin Guenther (1831–1893) served as a professor from 1873 to 1893. He graduated from St. Louis Seminary in 1853; served parishes in Wisconsin; and came to the Seminary to teach primarily comparative religions and church history. As a member of the Saxon Immigration, he was totally familiar with the history of Concordia Seminary and with Walther. Guenther wrote numerous editorials for publications; he was the first editor of *Homiletisches Magazin* and the master biographer of Walther.

Francis Pieper (1852–1931), who graduated from the St. Louis Seminary in 1875, served as professor there from 1878 to 1931. He held brief pastorates before going on to teach dogmatics and related subjects. He was Walther's successor as president of the seminary and also became president of the Missouri Synod, 1899–1911. He is perhaps best known for his writing of *Christian Dogmatics*.

Karl Georg Stoeckhardt (1842–1913) was on the faculty between 1878 and 1913. He had served as a private tutor in exegesis at Erlangen and pastor at Planitz, 1873–1876. In 1878, he was called to be pastor at Holy Cross, St. Louis, and simultaneously taught exegesis at the seminary part-time, until he became a full-time professor in 1887. Stoeckhardt ministered to Walther in his dying days. On one occasion Stoeckhardt, with his strong Saxon brogue, asked a class how best he could travel to a designated place. The students responded that he should see the "ticket agent." Stoeckhardt responded, in Saxon German, "I don't know the '*Dicke Oetjen*'" (the "fat *Oetjen*," who he presumed was a student). His publications on Bible history and exegesis have been used with deepest appreciation.

Two other faculty members caused Walther deep consternation and distress when both of them, at different times, left the Lutheran Church to become Roman Catholics. The first was Hermann Baumstark, a graduate of Leipzig University, whom Walther met on his trip to Germany in 1860. Baumstark then enrolled at the St. Louis Seminary where he graduated in 1861. After serving two congregations in Illinois, he was appointed to the pro-seminary in 1864. Everything seemed to go well. Baumstark had a vast background and knowledge of church history, Latin, geography, and German. He also taught courses in Hebrew and dogmatics, and published articles in several synodical publications until 1869.

Baumstark's earlier statement of faith in the first chapter of his *Church History* was totally acceptable to Walther, though it is a decided contrast to his later belief.[23]

Five years after he was appointed to the faculty, Baumstark announced on September 12, 1869 that he had joined the Roman Catholic Church. Though Walther and other faculty colleagues tried to dissuade and counsel him, nothing ever changed his mind.[24]

What put the capstone on Walther's immense disappointment in the early 1870s was the fact that Baumstark's successor, Eduard Preuss (1834–1904) who had joined the faculty in 1869, also defected to Romanism in 1871. Preuss had been highly acclaimed as a great student of Luther and of Lutheran theology. At the synodical convention, as was still customary at that time, Preuss was elected to the faculty by the delegates.[25] Before his arrival in America, Preuss had served in Berlin in various educational institutions. Although the immense pain from the Baumstark experience was still burning, Walther praised the new European university graduate as "a man of eminent scholarship, a teaching ability without comparison, so far as men can judge, of a believing heart and of deep, genuine Lutheran understanding. ..."[26] Walther wrote to Schwan on May 27, 1869: "Now we finally have a Missourian scholar (*Gelehrten*)."

Indeed, Walther did get a scholar. But the scholar changed his mind radically on crucial doctrinal issues. Preuss showed his Lutheran erudition in producing three different works.[27]

As in the case of Baumstark, Walther reported this defection to the church. Starting with deep confidence in German scholarship, the defection of two faculty members to Romanism was more than either Walther or the Synod was willing to accept. After Preuss was re-baptized in the Roman Catholic Church on January 22, 1872, he served that church by doing editorial work. His wife, however, remained a staunch member of the Lutheran Church. Her husband had made the children promise that they would see to it that their mother would be taken to the church regularly for worship.

These were the men who served on the Concordia Seminary faculty during C. F. W. Walther's presidency from 1850 to his death in 1887. It appears that those he personally selected as faculty members may well have turned out to be his greatest disappointments. He was looking for academic excellence and, to his dismay, two became Roman Catholics and one his most serious and unplaced opponent in doctrinal dissension. Yet those who remained with him—Pieper and others—each contributed significantly to the life, growth, and theological stance of the Synod. May their names remain blessed, as Walther's, in the life of the seminary!

BAIER'S *Compendium*

For years Walther had been encouraged and pressured by his friends and even President H. C. Schwan to produce a new dogmatics text. His time, however, was so taken up with teaching, correspondence, presenting essays, and presidential responsibilities, that he simply was unable to pursue the task.

Instead of writing an entirely new text, Walther expanded on the dogmatics textbook which was in use at the time, namely J. W. Baier's *Compendium*.[28] Walther emphasized especially the doctrines of justification, the person of Christ, law and gospel, the sacraments, the Lord's Supper, ministry, election, faith, church, civil government, creation, and the nature of theology. In a letter of 1865 to President Schwan, Walther expressed his burden in writing a new dogmatics textbook:

> I have unfortunately permitted myself to be persuaded to try to come up with a dogmatics for our time out of the dogmatics of our fathers that I can get hold of. I am always brooding over the form that I should observe. Therefore I have decided that as far as the analysis of the whole is concerned, I must proceed synthetically, not analytically. It was clear to me long ago and it becomes clearer to me all the time, that the choice of the analytical form, used since Calix, was a mistake that produced a lot of unhealthy theology. I don't want to try to write a system, but a *Loci Theologici*. Though I have almost no hope of finishing the work, I can start it. I couldn't think of carrying on such work undisturbed.[29]

Walther's concern was to provide doctrinal continuity from the Reformation to the present. He wanted every user and particularly the seminarians to become totally acquainted with the age of Luther and the elaborations that were necessary as time went on. Unfortunately, Walther did not translate the Latin text into German.

During the last months while he was still working on the *Compendium*, Walther declined all invitations, meetings, and the like. In his letter to F. Sievers on May 22, 1879, he declined an invitation to speak at the Northern District convention. He then continued that the work was extremely difficult and that he would incorporate more of his doctrinal lectures with Baier. That summer he accepted only one district convention essay, which undoubtedly was extremely important to him because it was the newly organized Iowa District. Here he presented a valuable essay on how the congregation and the Synod link together.

Walther based his new edition on Baier's 1701 edition. According to a reviewer in *Lehre und Wehre*,[30] the volumes brought together the best of Gerhard, the ingenuity of Dannhauer, and the clear logic of Quenstedt. Contemporary issues such as "open questions," criticisms of the Reformation theology, and particularly issues dealing with the Word of God are presented pro and con but always showing what was in harmony with the Scriptures and the Lutheran Confessions.

Walther's bound text became available in buckram and half leather and sold at $3.50 per copy. There were four volumes in all. Some even were issued in an interleaved edition which the students could use in class for their notes. The previous dogmatics textbook used at the seminary was Christian Loeber's *Evangelisch-Lutherische Dogmatik*, which Walther had edited in 1872, and the Preuss/Baier edition of 1864.

COLLABORATION AND RECRUITMENT

Prior to the Civil War, the Norwegian immigrants were among Walther's early friends. It was in 1855 that the Norwegian Synod, which had been organized just two years earlier, was casting about for an institution where its theological students could be trained. In their search the Norwegians commissioned Pastors Jacob Aall Ottesen and Nils Brandt to visit three seminaries: the first was St. Louis, Missouri, the second Columbus, Ohio, and the third Buffalo, New York.

Walther was very happy when they selected Concordia Seminary, St. Louis, even though it was still an infant institution. The plan was to establish a professorship in St. Louis while the students could attend at the same cost as the "natives." Professor Lauritz Larsen came to St. Louis to teach on November 1, 1859. He brought eleven students along with him. But the association was short-lived because of the outbreak of the Civil War in 1861. The work was not resumed until Professor F. A. Schmidt from Decorah, Iowa filled the position in 1872. He remained until 1876, when he was called back to the Norwegian Synod and a theological school was being established in Madison, Wisconsin.

Dr. S. C. Ylvisaker of St. Paul, Minnesota, writing about "The Missouri Synod and the Norwegians"[31] quotes H. Halvorson in *Synodens Festskrift of 1903*. He describes Walther:

> It may certainly with justice be called an extraordinarily bountiful, magnanimous help which the Missouri Synod has accorded our church-body during the period of about twenty-five years that our students have enjoyed the instruction at its excellent schools. Dr. Walther's Luther-lectures and his both stirring and inspiring presentation of pastoral theology will never be forgotten by the many who had him as their teacher. Our Norwegian students there received a spiritual capital which, in the case of so many of them, has brought the greatest returns for themselves and the congregations to which they were sent, and for Synod and the Church as a whole. They learned to grasp the distinction between Law and Gospel as they had not learned it hitherto; they learned to understand what true Christianity and true Lutheranism is, and not only to understand it, but—and this was of infinitely greater value—they were brought into a personal and close relation to the Lord Jesus, and they learned obedience toward His Word both as to what they should believe and what they should do. Just as Dr. Martin Luther would know nothing unto salvation save God's Christ alone, and just as he would accept no other doctrine save that alone which was firmly grounded in the Holy Scriptures ... thus it was in the case of Dr. Walther also, and thus it became in the case of so many of those who were privileged to sit daily at his feet and hear him speak. ...

> But this is certain, that Dr. Walther, by his thoroughly Christian character, by his great humility, by his personality patterned after the image of Christ, by his rich and productive mind, by his intimate acquaintance with the works of Luther, by his clearness and firmness in confession, by his thoroughly Christian and truly churchly and Lutheran viewpoint, has, both in and through his excellent writings and in and through his many faithful disciples, planted a seed among us Norwegian Lutherans which to this day has borne blessed fruit for the knowledge of the truth, God's revealed truth, for its propagation,

its preservation and establishment in the present generation, and will bear blessed fruit in future generations. His memory will live and shine in the firmament of the Church of God with a luster probably still more glorious in future days, and he will remain a teacher for all time to come. ..."[32]

During this period of time the Missouri Synod also made other friends. Under Walther's leadership, colloquies were held with other Lutheran synods. Following the colloquy with the Wisconsin Synod in 1869, Walther had hoped that cooperation could be established also in academic matters. The plan was that a Wisconsin Synod professor would join the faculty in St. Louis, and that the Missouri Synod would send a professor and students to the Wisconsin Synod institution in Watertown, Wisconsin. Wisconsin would pay the same student fees for room and board as members of the Missouri Synod, and it would send a theological professor elected by the Wisconsin Synod and ratified by the Missouri Synod.[33] Although the Wisconsin Synod never was able to place a faculty member in St. Louis, the Missouri Synod placed F. W. Stellhorn, a nephew of Walther, into the Wisconsin seminary.[34] Between 1869 and 1870, seven of the 147 students in St. Louis were from the Wisconsin Synod. The peak was reached when fifteen Wisconsin Synod students were enrolled in the 1873–1874 academic year.[35]

Similar arrangements were made with the Minnesota and Illinois Synods following the colloquies. At its peak, the Illinois Synod sent three or four students at one time. Guenther reports that at the beginning of the 1873 academic year there were a total of 200 students: 86 in the Theoretical Department, including 20 from the Norwegian Synod and 10 from the Wisconsin Synod; and 82 in the Practical Department, including 16 from the Norwegian Synod, four from the Wisconsin Synod, three from the Illinois Synod, and one from the Minnesota Synod. The remaining 32 were college students.[36]

In 1878, Concordia Seminary was searching for a new faculty member. F. A. Schmidt had expressed an interest in returning to St. Louis, where he had served as professor for the Norwegian students from 1872–1876. When Francis Pieper received the call instead of Schmidt, tradition has it that the latter felt profoundly rejected. When the Norwegians wanted to keep him as a teacher in 1876, Walther, impressed with Schmidt, called him his "own hands." In deep respect to the Norwegian Synod, Walther wrote President U. V. Koren that he would not object to their calling Schmidt to their new seminary because the "Missourians" were the servants of the Norwegians and that their wishes should come first. Less than three years later, however, Schmidt would brutally attack Walther in the predestinarian controversy.

It was thought that perhaps Walther was responsible for personally selecting Pieper, although some believed that Walther favored Schmidt. Elections at this time were conducted by the convention of the Synod and Schmidt had not been nominated. Walther stated in extensive correspondence with Theo. Ruhland of Planitz, Saxony that he would have preferred George Stoeckhardt who was serving a congregation of the Lutheran Free Church of Germany. On May 23, 1878, Walther wrote to Th. Ruhland:

> I received your letter ... when I returned from the synodical session in which the election of a newly-created Concordia professorship took place. That session was very painful for me since our dear Stoeckhardt was not even nominated. ... Yesterday they elected a young man who studied at Concordia. Although he was sent from Wisconsin, he has become a favorite with the Missourians. His name is Francis Pieper. In our Synod there is an almost invincible aversion to all Germans because of Dr. Seyffarth, Lic. Preuss, and Baumstark—with all of whom things went badly.[37]

Perhaps we need to rely on a report which appeared in the *Lutheran Witness*:[38]

> Among the names that were presented for nomination, was also that of Professor F. A. Schmidt, but he was not nominated, because the Synod held it uncharitable to deprive the Norwegian Synod of his services. Professor Schmidt had intimated that he would accept the call, if he could be made the Synod's choice. That he felt rather disappointed when this did not come about is natural. Now someone among his friends or enemies informed Professor Schmidt that Dr. Walther had prevented his nomination by putting on such a face and shrugging up his shoulders in such a manner, when Professor Schmidt's name was mentioned, as to indicate he would not like Schmidt as a colleague. Though there is not a word of truth in this, Schmidt took it for granted and—now comes the worst feature—took it also as an affronting challenge of his [Schmidt's] orthodoxy, which he was bound to avenge. ... We reasoned with him there, and not knowing the facts, we begged him for the sake of the Church, even if Walther should have done something out of the way, not to act in a rancorous spirit, but to consider that God had given him more knowledge and talents than others, to employ these in the maintenance of harmony and peace in the Church, and not to destroy his own usefulness, that our Professors

should not make the whole Church suffer for the infirmities they find with their brethren. But he had his mind fixed.[39]

In a postcard written to President Heinrich Wunder of the Illinois District, a member of the electoral college, Schmidt had indeed expressed his willingness to leave the Norwegian Seminary and come to St. Louis.[40]

This whole matter has continued to remain a mystery. Did Walther want Schmidt or Stoeckhardt? Was the election of Pieper the cause of Schmidt's criticism of Walther's 1877 Western District essay on predestination? Subsequent chapters will take up this discussion.

Meanwhile as Concordia Seminary pursued relationships with other bodies at home, in Germany, Friedrich Brunn, Theodor Harms, and J. K. Wilhelm Loehe carried on as some of the greatest recruiters for students for the Seminary. Between 1842 and 1872, J. K. W. Loehe of Neuendettelsau, Bavaria was responsible for sending about 200 young men to serve as pastors, teachers, students and candidates for American pastorates. This certainly was significant recruitment!

Walther had met Friedrich Brunn in Germany in 1860 and they had become good friends. Brunn left the state church and expressed his intended purpose that he would recruit and train students for the Missouri Synod ministry. On April 12, 1861, the very day when Fort Sumter in Charleston Harbor was attacked, Brunn received four young men for ministry in America. Three years later, the Synod gratefully acknowledged Brunn, and encouraged him to erect a special building in Steeden, Germany for his school. Supported with American funds, the new building was dedicated on July 23, 1865. Eventually, Brunn sent approximately 235 students to America. The Franco-Prussian War, 1870–1871, and even earlier the Austro-Prussian War in 1866 put a crimp on Brunn's work. When Brunn became seriously ill in 1878, the institution was closed because it did not have sufficient students.

Theodor Harms in Hermannsburg opened his school in 1866, hoping to provide four years of training for his German recruits before sending them to a seminary in America. In all he sent 69 young men to this country, the last one in 1885.[41]

Walther's fervent prayer for all the students was, "May God give us a pious ministry!"[42] He loved the students. In his twentieth evening lecture on Law and Gospel, delivered February 27, 1885, he counseled them on the way candidates should accept their first call:

When a Lutheran ministerial candidate is finally given an assignment where he is to conduct his office as a Lutheran preacher, that place should be to him the most precious and beautiful on earth. He should not want to exchange it for any kingdom; it should be to him a little paradise, whether it be urban or rural, whether open prairie or virgin forest, whether a well-established community or sparsely settled. The holy angels with great joy come down from heaven to serve those who shall inherit salvation (Hebrews 1:14). How eagerly ought we pursue our fellow sinners so that we may bring them to salvation, too.[43]

Walther was awarded an honorary Doctor of Divinity degree on January 25, 1878. It was bestowed by the Ohio Synod and Capital University—a clear indication of the close relationship that existed before the predestinarian controversy. A big celebration was held in the Aula of the Seminary to observe the event.

Walther had been offered a similar degree earlier in 1855 by Goettingen University, but declined it because of doctrinal differences. In correspondence of that time, he stated that if he had accepted this, he would appear to be "a crowned donkey."[44]

LIFE AT THE SEMINARY

A large, beautiful campus and new buildings do not make a seminary. It takes faculty and students—those who teach and those who learn. Walther loved the students and respected the faculty. He regularly invited students to his home for Sunday dinner. This included among others, his nephews, Theodor Buenger and Ludwig Fuerbringer, as well as W. Mueller, Carl Craemer, and many others. His home was always open to students and special guests who came for conferences and conventions or just sought lodging.

Some enrollment figures may be of interest. Usable figures do not become available until the 1854/1855 academic year when the *Gymnasium* was still attached to the seminary. That year there were nine students and 36 under-graduates for a total of 45. That number decreased the following year to 42, rose to 48 in 1856–57, and stood at 88 in 1859–60. No figures are available during the early years of the Civil War. But in 1862–63, the enrollment dropped to 30. In 1864–65 and in the late 1860s, enrollment stood at about 40. In 1870–71 the total enrollment increased to 147. In 1874–75 there were 145 students. The "practical" branch of the Seminary moved to Springfield, Illinois, in 1875. By 1877–78 the enrollment was only 90. The following academic year there were 85 students, and in 1879–80 there were 96. There was a slight increase in 1882–83. During the construction of the new seminary the enrollment increased steadily.[45]

Although the language of the day remained German, classroom lectures were usually given in Latin. Several faculty colleagues were well-versed in English, Norwegian, and especially Hebrew, Greek, and Latin, which was the language of the important textbooks available.

The courses offered by the seminary during Walther's presidency were very similar to those of today. There was special emphasis on systematic (doctrinal) and exegetical theology, isagogics, hermeneutics, philosophy, church history, ancient languages, Norwegian, English, symbolics, catechetics, homiletics, psychology, and more.

In those uncomplicated days, "House Rules" were adopted in 1860. Students arranged among themselves common tasks such as sweeping the classrooms, providing water from the pump for the washroom, making beds, and helping in the house, yard, and garden. Chopping wood for fuel was also essential.[46]

A valuable history of the Seminary by Guenther provides excerpts that are of special interest.[47] The history speaks of a wide range of student activities. There were athletic or recreational activities, including games on the playground and the use of athletic equipment, small gardens which were tended by each student for beautifying the grounds, swimming in the Mississippi a mile away ("under supervision of an instructor"), and Sunday morning church attendance. The cost per academic year averaged about $85. This included eating in the dining room, wood for fuel and light, necessary books, and clothing. A financial aid system was available for second year men whose academic records warranted it.[48]

As early as June 1858, the students formed a literary society. The group of twelve observed their first anniversary on the banks of the Mississippi. A portion of a speech delivered that day gives an indication of the use of English at that time: "Hail to thee, thou glorious morning sun of a beautiful day, whose rays greet us so delightfully. ..."[49] Other societies with various purposes were subsequently founded among the student body.

The most devastating blow Walther received during his presidency at the seminary came on October 20, 1881. Otto F. Hattstaedt wrote of his student days as follows:

> The only sad experience we had was when in October, 1881, a student slashed his throat with a razor. He was missed for three days, when finally his body was found under the staircase of the central portion of the seminary, close to the dining hall. Could a greater sorrow befall Dr. Walther than this deplorable occurrence? But it had this good

effect on us students, that we prayed instantly that God would preserve us from the temptations of Satan.[50]

Walther reported to Pastor H. G. Sauer of Fort Wayne that a troubled student had committed suicide. At first the Seminary family felt that he had suffered a burst blood vessel (*Blutsturtz*) as a result of a possible stroke. But later they learned that the student had taken his life by slashing his throat. Walther, who was severely shaken by the incident, wrote:

> What terrible lamentation (*Jammer*) has filled our institution you can well imagine. I well realize how deeply this information will shake you, since you personally had given such fatherly love and had accepted this unfortunate man as a father. … May God have mercy on us.

Walther signed the letter "lying in dust."[51]

THE CIVIL WAR

Twenty years earlier, Walther and the seminary had experienced the bitterness and carnage of the Civil War (1861–1865). During this time it was difficult to maintain a quiet equilibrium among the faculty and the students. While Fort Sumter in the Charleston, South Carolina harbor was under attack on April 12, 1861, Walther and the area clergymen and lay delegates were in Altenburg, Missouri attending the sessions of the Western District from April 11–17. A pastoral conference followed the convention. With military movements increasing, Walther closed the seminary and sent all the students home on April 26, 1861.

Prior to that time some of the students had formed "half a company" under the direction of seminarian Captain Styrk Sjursen Reque (1836–1910), a Norwegian who had served in the military before his enrollment. Reque graduated in 1865. Seminarian August Crull was appointed a lieutenant. Though they exercised with broomsticks instead of rifles, the force was not needed and was never called into action.

The arsenal in St. Louis was located less than a mile from the seminary. As the federal forces were planning to move against the Confederate troops occupying most of Missouri, rioting and skirmishes took place in the streets of St. Louis. On one such occasion, a clash between the Union forces and Confederate captives who were marched through the street got out of hand when someone threw a rock. Before it was all over, there were twenty-eight people who had been killed. Bitter partisan warfare was to follow.

For part of the war, the faculty moved to safer havens outside of the city. Mrs. Walther and the children took refuge in Jefferson County where they spent most of May 1861. Others sought refuge farther away. Only Walther and Saxer remained in the building "living there alone and solitary like two eccentrics in the attic."[52] A plan had been devised already in 1860 to merge the two seminaries and to have a separate *Gymnasium* and a seminary. The plan was quickly implemented in 1861. One of the primary reasons for the change was that the state of Indiana did not excuse men studying for the pastoral ministry from military service while Missouri did. Thus the entire Fort Wayne Seminary was moved to St. Louis while the St. Louis *Gymnasium* was moved to Fort Wayne. This ushered in the period of time when Walther served as president of both the "theoretical" and the "practical" seminaries, which continued until 1875.

During the war, Walther wrote to his friends and also to his "precious Emilie" from the Seminary to her place of refuge at Sandy Creek, Missouri on May 10, 1861:

> I have just heard that the battle has begun here, but at quite a distance from the college. The arsenal and the Marine Hospital are manned by only a handful. Almost all soldiers have moved out into the camp of the Missouri State troops and have begun their activities. Thus you can see how the dear God has graciously taken care of me. What will happen next, no mortal man can know. But we can be confident and sure that God will continue to rule and protect. Therefore do not be alarmed because of me! Without God's will not even a sparrow falls from the roof, nor a hair from our head: Why then should we fear? I am where God himself has placed me. ...[53]

By June 6, 1861 Walther's family returned to their seminary home. The seminary was re-opened once more in 1861 when it appeared that grave dangers were no longer threatening St. Louis, although over 1000 skirmishes and battles were fought in the state of Missouri. Toward the end of August and early September, Walther urged the students to return to the seminary, but only 36 came back for that school year by September 1. This included the students who were transferred from Fort Wayne.

Prayers of gratitude were spoken when the war was officially over, with Lee's surrender to Grant on April 9, 1865 under the terms forged at the Appomattox Courthouse.

However, even after the war Walther was faced with a severe personal dilemma. The state of Missouri adopted a new constitution in early 1865 which demanded a loyalty oath of those holding public office, including the clergy. The oath required that those signing had never supported the Southern cause. The punishment for failing to subscribe was severe.

Walther signed it with reservations. Two years later the law was declared unconstitutional by the United States Supreme Court.[54] Walther became a naturalized citizen in 1847 and deeply appreciated the freedom he experienced in America, especially the freedom of worship and conscience.

An allegation which deeply disturbed Walther during the Civil War was that the Confederate flag had been raised over the Seminary cupola. The difficulties of the war were bad enough. The bottom line is that Walther vigorously denied this had ever been the case.

The *Lutherischer Kirchenfreund* accused the seminary of having flown the Confederate flag. In *Der Lutheraner*, Walther published an item called "Florilegium."[55] Under that title he wrote: "That is the stench of a bouquet coming out of a deranged garden of the *Lutherischer Kirchenfreund*." Walther continued:

> Here the *Kirchenfreund* makes use of its unionistic honesty; it creates untruths. In its own self-defense, it finds this to be a necessity … if a small or white lie isn't effective against "Missouri," then the *Kirchenfreund* comes up with a giant fistful of lies and, with supreme unionistic love, bangs it over Missouri's head.

This false story has been printed as fact elsewhere, even as recently in such prominent works as Werner Elert's *Morphologie des Luthertums*.[56] Yet in his 1870 rebuttal, Walther once and for all stated:

> On our part we have nothing against it when … the fabricator of the fable of the rebel flag dreamed such insane rubbish, and refreshes his soul with such fantasies. But, we do when he so unabashedly publishes such a fable in his *Kirchenfreund* and trots it off to market as truth in the evil anticipation of having fellow American citizens hate us. Perhaps [we can expect] a correction when we take this scrawling and herewith declare it a reprehensible lie and brand him as a lying calumniator, who ought not to have any further credibility among upright people. The truth is that during the period of war, at no time ever did we fly the rebel flag. Instead, repeatedly, the Union flag was decked out over our college in St. Louis.[57]

It was only the "Light from above" that permitted Walther to continue in his work at the Seminary and permitted the Seminary, through all its challenges, setbacks, and renewed purpose, to carry on. The Seminary was afflicted with tragedies among its student body, the ricocheting bullets and skirmishes of the Civil War, faculty defections, theological controversy, and more. In spite of all of this, the number of students trained by Walther at the Seminary during his lifetime included 230 "theoretical" candidates for the holy ministry and 265 "practical" for a total of 495, almost 500 of God's gifts to the church. At the time of Walther's death there were 931 pastors in the entire Synod. This means that 50 percent of all clergymen at that time were trained under Walther's presidency.[58] As this era in Missouri Synod history came to an end, it was clear that the "Light from above" prevailed!

NOTES

[1] *Proceedings*, Missouri Synod, 1848, 17.

[2] *Proceedings*, Missouri Synod, 1850, 18ff.

[3] "Rede bei Gelegenheit ...," *Der Lutheraner*, 6:21 (June 1850), 161–63.

[4] *Proceedings*, Missouri Synod, 1850, p. 15–16.

[5] *Lutheran Worship*, 177.

[6] R. Lange, "Einweihung des deutschen ev.-luth. Concordia-Collegiums bei St. Louis, MO.," *Der Lutheraner*, 6:23 (July 9, 1850), 179–80.

[7] C. F. W. Walther, *The Word of His Grace (ELS Translation Committee*; Lake Mills, IA: Graphic Publishing Co., 1978), 114–19; original text in Walther, *Casual-Predigten und-Reden* (St. Louis: Concordia Publishing House, 1889), 324ff.

[8] Martin Guenther, "Geschichte des Concordia Seminary," *Der Lutheraner*, 38:24 (December 15, 1882), 186.

[9] English translation in *Synodalhandbuch* (St. Louis: Concordia Publishing House, 1924), 105–7.

[10] George H. Gerberding, *Life and Letters of W. A. Passavant, D. D.* (Greenvale, PA: The Young Lutheran Company, 1906), 389.

[11] The 57 student rooms were to be 12 × 16 feet, the remaining 6 rooms 16 × 16 feet, the 8 classrooms were 23 × 37 feet and 24 × 30 feet, the auditorium or Aula 65 × 30 feet. *Proceedings*, Missouri Synod, 1881, 46–50.

[12] Meyer quoted from the *St. Louis Globe-Democrat*, published in the *Lutheran Witness*, 2 (October 7, 1883), 79–80. See C. S. Meyer, *Log Cabin to Luther Tower* (St. Louis: Concordia Publishing House, 1965), 79–80.

[13] Guenther, *Der Lutheraner*, 39:6 (March 15, 1883), 44.

[14] Guenther, *Der Lutheraner*, 38:20 (October 15, 1882), 156.

[15] Th. Engelder, ed., *Walther and the Church* (St. Louis: Concordia Publishing House, 1938), 7–8.

[16] *Lutheran Worship*, 444.

[17] Guenther, *Der Lutheraner*, 38:20 (October 15, 1882), 156.

[18] A similar incident occurred in 1975 when this writer and his wife saw lightning shear off a huge stone from the top of Luther Tower at Concordia Seminary, St. Louis.

[19] C. F. W. Walther, "Rede, gehalten bei Eröffnung der feierlichen Einweihung des neuen Concordia Seminar Gebäudes zu St. Louis am 9, September 1883." *Der Lutheraner*, 39:18 (September 15, 1883), 137–38.

[20] *Lutheran Worship*, 445.

[21] Christian Hochstetter, *Die Geschichte der Evangelisch-lutherische Missouri-Synod in Nord-Amerika, und ihrer Lehrköpfe von der sächsischen Auswanderung im Jahre 1838 an bis zum Jahre 1884* (Dresden: Heinrich L. Naumann, 1885), 447–58.

[22] Part of a poem written by O. H. Walther for the dedication of the log cabin in Perry County, Missouri. For full text of poem, cf. Guenther, *Der Lutheraner*, 38:20 (October 15, 1882), 155–56.

[23] H. M. Baumstark, *Geschichte der christlichen Kirche* (St. Louis: August Wiebusch and Son, 1867).

[24] In 1870, Baumstark and his brother told the story of their way to Rome in *Unsere Wege zur katholischen Kirche* ("Our Journey to the Catholic Church") (Freiburg im Breisgau, 1870). Later Baumstark did editorial work for a Catholic newspaper. Ludwig E. Fuerbringer, *Persons and Events* (St. Louis: Concordia Publishing House, 1947), especially chapter 11, 157ff.

[25] *Proceedings*, Missouri Synod, 1869, 86–87.

[26] Walther to Sievers, March 22, 1869; printed in Ludwig Fuerbringer, ed., *Briefe von C. F. W. Walther … an seine Freunde, Synodalgenossen, und Familienglieder* (St. Louis: Concordia Publishing House, 1915), Vol. 2, 155–57.

[27] *Die Römische Lehre von der unbefleckten Empfängniss aus den Quellen dargestellt und aus Gottes Wort widerlegt* (Berlin: Gustav Schlawitz, 1865). This monograph opposed the Roman Catholic doctrine of the immaculate conception. The second book was even more significant for the Lutherans. Julius A. Friedrich translated this book entitled *The Justification of the Sinner Before God on the Basis of Holy Scripture*, 2nd ed. (Chicago: F. Allermann, 1934). The original edition on the doctrine of justification was entitled *Die Rechtfertigung des Sünders vor Gott aus der Heiligen Schrift* (Berlin: Gustav Schlawitz, 1871). The third volume was a new edition of Johann Wilhelm Baier's *Compendium Theologiae Positivae* (Berlin: Gustav Schlawitz, 1864).

[28] J. W. Baier (1647–1695) had studied at Jena where he became a professor of theology. Later he served as general superintendent and chief court preacher at Weimar. He was orthodox and pledged himself to the Lutheran Confessions. His Latin dogmatics appeared in thirteen editions between 1686 and 1750.

[29] Fuerbringer, *Walthers Briefe*, Vol. 1, 210.

[30] *Lehre und Wehre*, 25:8 (August 1879), 242–43.

[31] S. C. Ylvisaker, "The Missouri Synod and the Norwegians," *Ebenezer*, 2nd ed. (St. Louis: Concordia Publishing House, 1922), 264ff.

[32] Ylvisaker, "The Missouri Synod and the Norwegians," *Ebenezer*, 271–72.

[33] Carl S. Meyer, "Intersynodical Unity Fostered through Cooperation in Education, 1859–1874," *Concordia Historical Institute Quarterly*, 29:1 (Spring 1956), 50–66.

[34] Stellhorn was married to Walther's niece, and later sided with Schmidt and Allwardt, Schmidt's brother-in-law, against Walther in the Missouri Predestinarian controversy.

[35] Meyer, "Intersynodical Unity Fostered through Cooperation in Education, 1859–1874," 62.

[36] Guenther, *Der Lutheraner* 39:2 (January 15, 1883), 112.

[37] Letter from Walther to Th. Ruhland, Saxony, Germany, May 23, 1878; translated in Roy A. Suelflow, tr., *Correspondence of C. F. W. Walther* (St. Louis: Concordia Seminary, 1980), 79–80.

[38] *Lutheran Witness*, 1 (June 21, 1882), 4.

[39] See Meyer, *Log Cabin to Luther Tower*, 70.

[40] Francis Pieper, "Erklärung auf eine in No. 7 von 'Altes und Neues' enthaltene Herausforderung," *Lehre und Wehre*, 27 (1881), 504. Also Fuerbringer, *Persons and Events*, 153, 173.

[41] "Editorial Comments," *Concordia Historical Institute Quarterly* 39:2 (July 1966), 95.

[42] Ylvisaker, "The Missouri Synod and the Norwegians," *Ebenezer*, 32.

[43] C. F. W. Walther, *The Proper Distinction between Law and Gospel*, trans. by Herbert J. A. Bouman (St. Louis: Concordia Publishing House, 1981), 108–9.

[44] Letter from Walther to G. A. Schieferdecker, July 21, 1855; partially cited in Martin Guenther, *Dr. C. F. W. Walther: Lebensbild* (St. Louis: Concordia Publishing House, 1890), 129.

[45] Meyer, *Log Cabin to Luther Tower*, 303–4.

[46] *Programm des Ev.-Luth. Concordia-Collegiums der Synode von Missouri, Ohio, u. A. St. zu St. Louis, Missouri* (St. Louis: Aug. Wiebusch u. Sohn, 1860).

[47] Guenther's history of the seminary was published serially in *Der Lutheraner*. The installments were 38:20 (October 15, 1883), 12; 39:6 (March 15, 1883), 43–44.

[48] Letter from Walther to Puhl, December 15, 1883; transcription by Werner K. Wadewitz at Concordia Historical Institute.

[49] Otto F. Hattstaedt, "First Literary Society Among the Missouri Synod Institutions," *Concordia Historical Institute Quarterly*, 17:1 (April 1944), 11–4.

[50] Otto F. Hattstaedt, "Reminiscences of the Seminary at St. Louis, 1881–1884," *Concordia Historical Institute Quarterly*, 14:1 (April 1941), 10.

[51] Walther to H. Sauer, October 20, 1881. transcription by Werner K. Wadewitz at Concordia Historical Institute.

[52] Letter from Walther to Pastor J. M. Buehler, May 21, 1861; translation in Roy A. Suelflow, ed., *Selected Writings of C. F. W. Walther* (St. Louis: Concordia Publishing House, 1981), 149ff.

[53] Letter from Walther to his wife, May 10, 1861; in Fuerbringer, *Walthers Briefe*, Vol. 1, 164.

[54] For details on this and the war, see August R. Suelflow "Walther the American" in Arthur H. Drevlow, ed., *C. F. W. Walther: The American Luther* (Mankato, MN: Walther Press, 1987), 13–35.

[55] C. F. W. Walther, "Florilegium," *Der Lutheraner*, 26:11 (February 1, 1870), 84.

[56] Werner Elert, *Morphologie des Luthertums* (München: Beck, 1931), Vol. 2, 277.

[57] Walther "Florilegium," *Der Lutheraner*, 26:11 (February 1, 1870), 84. For more on this, see August R. Suelflow, "Walther the American," in *C. F. W. Walther: The American Luther*, 33.

[58] Meyer, *Log Cabin to Luther Tower*, 304–8, and *Statistical Yearbook*, 1937, 152.

4

In Unity of Faith and Spirit

The Lutheran Church—Missouri Synod owes an enormous debt of gratitude to C. F. W. Walther as one of its founding fathers. As a teacher of the Word and the Confessions, he always proclaimed the theology of the cross—we are justified by faith in Christ without the deeds of the Law. Walther's preaching radically changed the minds and hearts of many, as they came to faith in Christ.

Isolated and insulated settlements were found almost everywhere in the Midwest following the Louisiana Purchase in 1804. Travel routes into the Midwest included going directly by wagon (some even by wheelbarrow) as they passed from Virginia through the Cumberland Gap to the places they selected to settle. Others left by boat and entered the Gulf of Mexico, coming up the Mississippi River into the central part of the United States. Still others used the Great Lakes and canals to get to Illinois and Wisconsin. Immigrants and those resettling from the Atlantic colonies were coming into the Midwest in increasing numbers.

Among these were the Saxon immigrants of 1839, who settled in St. Louis and Perry County, Missouri. Through the combined efforts of Friedrich Wyneken of Indiana and the workers (*Sendlinge*—the sent ones) sent by Wilhelm Loehe of Germany, the Gospel was brought to an enormous number of German settlers in Ohio, Indiana, and Michigan. J. A. A. Grabau arrived in New York in 1839 with the "Old Lutheran" immigrants from Prussia. They traveled by way of rivers and canals and eventually settled in Buffalo, New York and in southern Wisconsin. Most of these immigrant families were quite separated and isolated from Lutheran pastors. This created a vexing problem not only for the few traveling missionaries who were there, such as Wyneken, but also to those in the German homeland who were touched by the plight of the people who had settled in America.

From this background we can trace the beginnings and the 1847 establishment of what is now The Lutheran Church—Missouri Synod. The LCMS emerged from a set of complex issues that included doctrine, language barriers, geographical distances, and lack of theological literature (including Bibles, catechisms, and the Lutheran Confessions). People were hard pressed to define what it meant to be a Lutheran in America under the existing conditions. Loehe had established a pastoral training school in Fort Wayne with one of his emissaries, Wilhelm Sihler, as the head. The Saxons, on the other hand, had established a training school for pastors in Missouri. This is the "stuff" that led to the organization of the Synod.

Even before the Altenburg debate in Perry County over the question of church and ministry in April of 1841, Georg Albert Schieferdecker applied for membership in the old Pennsylvania Ministerium, which had been organized in 1748 under the leadership of H. M. Muhlenberg. To this body Schieferdecker recounted the experiences of the Saxons in Perry County, Missouri and concluded:

> In order now, to take all the necessary steps which are required according to God's order, I am herewith applying for placement through the Lutheran Pennsylvania Synod as a candidate for the Holy Ministry or for a teaching position in an elementary or higher institution. … I would naturally, gladly subject myself to examination of your honorable Synod.[1]

Instead of accepting the "candidate," President Demme advised Schieferdecker that it was necessary for him to appear personally before that Ministerium in order to be admitted. As an alternative, Demme encouraged Schieferdecker to join one of the existing western synods of the church. Would other Saxon pastors have followed suit if Schieferdecker had been accepted?

FORMATION OF THE MISSOURI SYNOD

It was an epoch-making meeting when the Loehe missionaries of the Ohio Synod and F. C. D. Wyneken met on September 18, 1845 in Cleveland, Ohio to discuss the difficulties which they perceived as members of the Ohio Synod, organized in 1818. Among the problems they identified were the lack of confessional theology, professional laxity, and the rapid rate of Americanization including a precipitous change from German to English at the Ohio Synod's seminary at Columbus, Ohio, established in 1830. Actually, this first meeting expressed its dissension with much of the Lutheranism that existed in America at this time.

At this meeting, the former Ohioans determined to leave the Ohio Synod and asked whether any of the Saxons in Missouri would be interested in joining them in order to draft a constitution for a new church body.

How did they become acquainted with the Saxons? Of course there had been connections with Loehe and the men whom he had sent. A major link was developed on September 1, 1844, when the first issue of *Der Lutheraner* was produced, edited by Walther and supported by Trinity Congregation, St. Louis. Limited by the amount of money available to circulate such a paper, it was handed on from one to another. Most were deeply impressed, and thus the publication became a glue or catalyst which formed a solid basis for a new synod. Hochstetter observes correctly:

> In the midst of all the theological confusion, sectarian and Lutheran and otherwise, Walther's [*Der*] *Lutheraner* was like a great trumpet call. Its motto was "God's Word and Luther's doctrine will never disappear."[2]

The first inducement for the publication was Walther's severe illness in the middle of 1844. When it appeared that he would recover, he prayed that the Lord would grant him the strength and the means to write and to publish a periodical in which the Lutheran Church might be shown in its true light. During his illness he was grieved that the Lutherans were being grossly disparaged, particularly by the Methodists and the Baptists.

At the suggestion of the Ohio Synod men who had met in Cleveland, a second significant meeting was held looking toward the organization of the Missouri Synod. Walther had invited these men to come to St. Louis. The meeting took place in May 1846. The sessions were largely held in "Grandma" Buenger's house on Lombard Street. The Loehe pastors (formerly of the Ohio Synod) were represented by Wilhelm Sihler, Adam Ernst, and Friedrich Lochner. The Saxons outnumbered them with Walther, Loeber, Keyl, Grueber, Schieferdecker, and Fuerbringer. Lochner gave a detailed description of the meeting as well as an excellent drawing of Trinity church and the Buenger home. His purpose in coming to St. Louis was actually two-fold: 1) to explore the possibility of joining the Saxons in forming a new synod, and 2) in his own words, "to seek a helpmate in the home of Pastor Walther."[3]

Wilhelm Sihler of Fort Wayne, who had participated in the first meeting in Cleveland, now came to St. Louis to meet with the Saxons. His description of the Walthers, hosts of the St. Louis meeting, is priceless. At that time the Walthers were still living on the first floor of the Grandma Buenger home across the street from their church. In his autobiography Sihler wrote:

Pastor Walther welcomed us heartily to his home, and his good wife was most cordial. Walther impressed us most of all. Pastor Walther … and his worthy wife, nee Buenger, hosted us excellently with her Saxon cooking, frying, and baking ability.

Walther made a deep impression upon us all. He was not yet thirty-five years old, but he seemed facially to have been aged considerably, probably through the many and difficult battles he had to engage in after Stephan had been deposed. His thoughts and words, on the other hand, were filled with spirit and life. … He was the enlivening and formative influence, outlining principles for an orthodox, that is, Lutheran organization of congregations or a synod.[4]

These words of Sihler are extremely interesting because he had envisioned a different type of synodical constitution than Walther's. Two years before the organization of the Synod, Sihler presented his concept of the proposed organization, envisioning a synod with permanent delegates, rather than the annual meetings which Walther envisioned consisting of *ad hoc* delegates. Sihler had envisioned considerable centralization of authority. It is interesting to observe that Sihler's initial articles appeared in the *Lutherische Kirchenzeitung*. Later Walther reprinted some of these first installments in *Der Lutheraner* of December 13, 1845. Sihler felt that when one can no longer depend upon the state or a state church, the new organization needed more administrative and supervisory power. Walther countered with his "advisory body." The Synod in the process of formation did indeed have choices.

Walther was the host at this meeting in which the basic framework of the new synod was worked out. Lochner says that the group spent an entire week framing the constitution. Some of the sessions were held with the voters of Trinity. Of special importance, Lochner recalled:

At this time several meetings were held with the St. Louis congregation, in which their pastors presented the plan for consideration. I, being wholly inexperienced, occasionally opened my eyes wide in astonishment when I saw that the congregation did not at once acquiesce, but questioned this and that item; indeed, several members disputed sharply with the pastors [Walther and Buenger]. These men, however, entered into their doubts and objections with such calm and consideration as if the congregation were made up of none but scholarly theologians. …

But I remained a week longer, for on Pentecost Monday I was to marry Pastor Walther's sister-in-law [Lydia Buenger, sister of

Walther's wife Emilie], to whom I had become engaged on Sunday Exaudi.[5]

After the St. Louis meeting, the group agreed to meet in Fort Wayne again on July 2–8 at St. Paul's Church. This was a much larger meeting because it included the Loehe missionaries, the Franconians of Michigan, the Saxons, and others. Walther and Loeber traveled from St. Louis by steamer, down the Mississippi and up the Ohio River. After that it was a canal boat on the Miami and Erie Canals. Craemer had traveled by water with the last leg on the Wabash Canal. At the tiny village of Junction, at the juncture of the two canals, Craemer met Walther, as well as Loeber and his young son. This brought Craemer and Walther face-to-face for the first time; they remained close friends for the rest of their lives. Craemer described the meeting with Walther as follows:

> It did not take long, when a slender man with a prominent nose and fiery eyes stepped out of the door of the small inn, followed by a mild-looking tall man and a young student, who at once came aboard our boat. Of course, the former was Walther and the other the venerable Pastor Loeber and his son. The joy of a happy meeting was great on both sides and soon, while we were riding along the canal, easily and undisturbed, all were engaged in eager conversation. Thus I met Walther. It meant much to me to know personally and more closely the man who I, by his [Der] Lutheraner, had already been recognized as a pillar of real biblical Lutheran truth.[6]

THE CONSTITUTION

Of special interest is the constitution that was adopted in 1847.[7] By 1854, seven years later, the constitution was greatly revised.[8] Over the years, only a few further revisions have been made to the constitution, but no changes were ever made in Article II. It is an unalterable paragraph and speaks to all members of the Synod. Article II states:

Conditions under which union with the Synod may take place and fellowship with it can continue:

1. Acceptance of Holy Scripture of the Old and the New Testaments as the written Word of God and the only rule and norm of faith and life.

2. Acceptance of all symbolical books of the Evangelical Lutheran Church (to wit: the three Ecumenical Symbols, the unaltered Augsburg Confession, its Apology, the Smalcald Articles, the Large

and Small Catechism of Luther, and the Formula of Concord) as the pure, unadulterated statement and exposition of the divine Word.[9]

Perhaps none of the constitutional paragraphs have created such enormous problems of understanding and interpretation as the present Article VII. (Originally this appeared in Article IV, A, 9.) There is no question that this article was inserted at the insistence of Trinity, St. Louis. Walther had devoted three voters' meetings to discuss the entire Constitution. In the background the lay people were still afraid of centralization, of clergy authority, and of a loss of congregational autonomy.

It is somewhat amazing that the 1846 draft of the constitution did not contain even a seminal concept of Article VII enunciating congregational autonomy, which the St. Louis Trinity voters had examined so critically earlier in the year.

The development and acceptance of Article VII has been based on assumptions and possibly even some misinterpretation. After the first three preliminary meetings looking towards the organization of The Lutheran Church—Missouri Synod, Trinity in St. Louis proposed an amendment to include the famous Article VII in the Synodical Constitution. The congregation even threatened that it would not join the Synod unless it accepted the amendment. From this point on, the story becomes even more interesting. After spending three voters' meetings reviewing the proposed constitution at the meeting in St. Louis in May 1846, the congregation was not satisfied. The proposed amendment contained the concept of Article VII regarding congregational autonomy. Trinity adopted its proposed amendment at its voters' meeting on February 22, 1847 and proposed that the following be inserted in the Synodical Constitution:

> The Synod is only an advisory body; therefore none of its resolutions, as such, have any binding power on the individual congregations. Such binding authority is attained by a synodical resolution only when the individual congregation has reviewed it and has voluntarily adopted it through a formal congregational resolution. Should a congregation find a synodical resolution not in accordance with the Word of God, or unsuited to its conditions, it has the right to reject the resolution.[10]

The amendment was adopted by the delegates at the organizing convention in 1847. In addition, however, it needed acceptance also from the Synodical congregations. The adopted amendment contained the following terminology:

Synod is in respect to the self-government (*Selbstregierung*) of the individual congregations only an advisory body. Therefore no resolution of the former, when it imposes anything on the individual congregation as a synodical resolution, has binding force for the latter. Such a synodical resolution has binding force only when the individual congregation through a formal congregational resolution has voluntarily adopted and confirmed it. Should a congregation find a synodical resolution not in conformity with the Word of God or unsuited (*ungeeignet*) for its circumstances, it has the right to disregard, that is to reject, it.[11]

The matter did not end here. Undoubtedly Walther concurred with the proposed amendment of 1847.[12] What was the problem? All member congregations were required to approve the amendment. The same 1847 convention had to deal with other constitutional amendments; in 1848 two more were proposed and in 1849 one more. Of the three proposed in 1847, contrary to popular Synod history, all amendments failed to be approved by the congregations. This was finally announced in 1850.[13]

In retrospect, it seems strange that the member congregations that were to ratify the amendment did not do so. Of the six amendments proposed between 1847–1849, four were declined and only two were approved. Trinity's amendment, consequently, was not approved nor added to the constitution.

A favorite myth in synodical history is that the so-called "autonomy" paragraph has been a part of the Synod's constitution ever since the founding of the Synod in 1847.

Apparently Walther had also assumed that the paragraph would be approved by the congregations and consequently delivered his frequently quoted 1848 presidential address when the paragraph was not even a part of the constitution.[14] A quote from that address may be helpful, especially to emphasize that the Synod was not a "law-giver," but rather an instrument through which the member congregations could carry out joint activities. Walther said:

According to the constitution under which our synodical union exists, we have merely the power to advise one another, we have only the power of the Word, and of convincing. According to our constitution we have no right to formulate decrees, to pass laws and regulations, and to make a judicial decision, to which our congregations would have to submit unconditionally in any matter involving the imposing of something upon them. Our constitution by no means makes us a consistory [many had experienced this European form of church government], by no means a supreme court of our congregations. It rather grants them the most perfect liberty in everything, excepting nothing but the Word of God, faith, and charity. According to our constitution we are not above our congregations, but in them and at their side.[15]

In 1853 the constitution of the Synod received a major overhaul. This constitution reinstated the 1847 text of the "congregational autonomy" article. It simply became a part of the new constitution which was adopted in 1854. It appeared as Article IV, paragraph 9. In addition, the 1854 version is not at all the same as the present Article VII. A comparison of the two versions will demonstrate a significant difference.[16] The controversial section deals with what has been translated as "inexpedient." The original word (*ungeeignet*) should really be translated as "unsuited," not "inexpedient."

A SOLID FOUNDATION

At issue regarding the Synod's Constitution during Walther's time was the fear of a potential recurrence of Stephanism or the exercise of human authority over the local congregation. The present Article VII must be studied in conjunction with the constitutional Articles II, III, and VI.

During Walther's lifetime, there is only one incident when the question of Synod's authority came under attack. This happened at the 1860 convention when a delegate, referring to the "advisory clause," questioned whether the Synod had the authority to move the Fort Wayne seminary to St. Louis without having the resolution ratified by member congregations. Almost impatiently, the convention replied that the Synod certainly had the authority to adopt the relocation of its seminaries, since it had absolutely no bearing on the autonomy of the local congregation nor did it affect the principle of self-government in any way. To satisfy the questioner, however, the congregations were urged to register their reactions to the synodical vice-president by mail.[17] The vice-president never bothered to report at the subsequent convention whether he had received any ballots. In contrast to that single incident, the present wording of Article VII, adopted in 1920, has resulted in a large number of inquiries for interpretation.

Articles II and VIII.C of the constitution form an interesting platform from which to study Walther. Article II was of importance and provided a kind of centrifugal force for the Missouri Synod from its beginning, helping to develop it as a non-geographical body, different from many other synods. This was at a time when the Lutheran Confessions were barely known or were simply ignored. To Walther the Lutheran Symbols were of the utmost importance and provided cohesive glue.

Pastor John Adam Ernst, a member of the Ohio Synod and Loehe's first missionary, earlier had asked Walther for his ideas pertaining to a synodical constitution. In his reply of August 21, 1845, Walther stated:

> I wish that the Synod [would] organize itself, in addition to the Word of God, on the basis of all the symbols of our church, and if possible, include also the Saxon Visitation Articles. However, I shall not insist on the latter, glorious, concise confession.[18]

Walther initially did include the Saxon Visitation Articles (SVA) in the confessional corpus. These Articles had been drafted in 1592 as a document for the parish and pastoral visitation in the church of Saxony.[19] Trinity, St. Louis adopted the SVA as part of its confessional corpus in its constitution. Yet, although Walther valued the Articles, he did not insist that others accept them confessionally.

This is also partially true of the Formula of Concord. A pamphlet containing the text of the proposed synodical constitution published by Weber and Olshausen, St. Louis in 1846, has an interesting footnote. It states that even though the Formula had resolved the controversy following Luther's death, and although it was not adopted by all the Lutheran churches in Europe, nevertheless it was of utmost importance to the church in America because the Formula enunciated precise and binding formulations and a defense of pure doctrine against Calvinism. It would be extremely irresponsible and unconscionable not to pledge oneself to it.

The article subscribing to the Lutheran Confessions and identifying Holy Scripture as the written Word of God took courage in 1847. The Confessions had been virtually forgotten. This was partly because of the language problem, since the corpus was not translated in its entirety into English until 1851. On the other hand, although the Lutheran clergy in America were largely English-speaking, they had a passing acquaintance with the Augsburg Confession.

A second factor in the neglect of the Confessions was that liberalism was in the air. This was the period of time in Lutheranism in America when Samuel S. Schmucker was most anxious to get Lutheran pastors and congregations to accept a greatly modified doctrinal statement, the famous Definite Synodical Platform of 1855. Schmucker had hoped that by rewriting the Augsburg Confession in a Reformed tone, American Lutherans might more readily accept it.[20]

In view of these developments, Article II was bucking the mainstream of Lutheranism. Walther was so committed to the Lutheran Confessions that the confessional platform became fixed and still appears in the LCMS constitution as Article II today. This is one of the reasons that Missouri stood alone in its confession.

For some, the interpretation of Article VIII-C has created problems. The article in Paragraph C merely states in today's constitution, "All matters of doctrine and conscience shall be decided only by the Word of God." The original 1847 constitution included it in paragraph 8 of Article III. Walther also echoed this in his *Form of a Christian Congregation*, which he presented to the Western District in 1862 and published in 1863. In the sixteenth thesis Walther said:

> Matters of doctrine and of conscience are to be resolved unanimously (*Einstimmigkeit*) according to God's Word and the Confession of the church (Isaiah 8:20). Adiaphora, however, that is, matters which God's Word neither commands nor forbids, are to be decided according to the principles of love and fairness, after a previous deliberation, in a Christian order by a majority of votes (1 Corinthians 14:40; 16:14; Colossians 2:5). Should anything in the congregation be decided and established contrary to God's Word, such a decision and establishment is null and void and should be declared rescinded as such.[21]

UNANIMITY IN THE WORD

The word *Einstimmigkeit* is intriguing as one reviews the Synod's reaction to doctrinal problems it faced during Walther's life. Did this mean a unanimous vote? No, it did not. It would be better translated as "unanimity" rather than "unanimous," because the term implies unity and singleness of mind. The German original also uses the word *durch* which means "through." It is better to translate this constitutional paragraph with the words: "Matters of doctrine and conscience are decided through the Word." The Word consequently is the only authority by which the Synod determines matters of doctrine and conscience. Nothing but God's Word itself could formulate doctrinal statements.

During Walther's lifetime, matters of doctrine could be defined only by the official voice of the Synod's convention and then only as the resolution pertained to matters of doctrine under dispute. There was no other commission, faculty, or other instrument to define doctrine. Two test cases are particularly of value in understanding this article.[22]

The Synod experienced an internal controversy on chiliasm (millennialism) as early as 1857. After years of discussion with Pastor G. A. Schieferdecker, who had introduced the doctrine of chiliasm in his congregation, the convention discussed the issue in twelve sessions. President Wyneken was in the chair. All the convention delegates were on their knees engaged in prayer before a vote was taken. Immediately after the vote, the secretary recorded that one pastor had not given his assent to the formulation. The vote opposed to the paragraph on chiliasm was cast by G. A. Schieferdecker, president of the Western District and a registered voting pastor.[23] In spite of this, the secretary recorded that the paragraph was adopted with *Einstimmigkeit*.

This underscores the fact that the *Einstimmigkeit* did not mean a unanimous vote, but much rather a vote expressing unanimity. As Schieferdecker was leaving the convention after he was informed that he was no longer in fellowship, he asked whether he could rejoin if he ever changed his mind. President Wyneken assured him that he could. In 1875 he was readmitted to the Synod.[24]

There was a second time during Walther's life when this article was applied at a Synod convention. This was during the disruptive "predestinarian controversy." Walther's "Thirteen Theses," based almost exclusively on the "Thorough Declaration" of the Formula of Concord, were being discussed. Previously they had been published in *Der Lutheraner*. After much discussion, the "Thirteen Theses" were brought to a vote at the 1881 convention. The theses had been read before they were presented for adoption. During that time someone asked what would happen to those who disagreed with these "theses." The convention answered that it maintained the hope that they would ultimately assent or agree to them. But if they felt there was no agreement between these theses and the Word of God and the Confessions, patience would have to be exercised. Consciences were not to be oppressed. It was stated that the Synod sought unity, rather than to continue with two opposing factions.[25]

Then came the vote. Only six negative votes were registered. Again, it was not a unanimous vote, but adopted with unanimity. It is significant that even though the two doctrinal statements regarding chiliasm and predestination were not adopted unanimously, no one suggested that they should have been. The Synod assumed, without further ado, that its convention formulations on these issues had been resolved according to the Word of God and in harmony with the Confessions.

Two important statements are reflected in the minutes of 1881:

1. That it was entirely possible that a minority could, conceivably, proclaim and confess the truth, while the majority would be trapped in error. By declaring this as a possibility, the convention undoubtedly echoed Luther's pronouncement that councils can err. The convention, however, responded that the proof of such an event would have to be based upon God's Word and the church's Confessions.

2. While the Synod was profoundly grateful that each of its district presidents adhered to the Theses, it admitted that it would be a totally different situation if there were presidents who sided with the opponents. By the grace of God, the minutes state, without a single exception, they were faithful and firm to a single man on the Theses. In view of this, the Synod was assured of the total confidence that the presidents, as the shepherds of pure doctrine, would exercise the responsibilities of their office according to the Word of God.[26]

THE OFFICE OF THE PRESIDENT

In the constitution, the office of the president was considered as the primary cog or linchpin in the Synod. He was the one person who represented the Synod in virtually everything. This was at a time when there was only a limited number of committees, boards, and commissions. There was also but a single vice-president. Walther served in the capacity of president for the first term from 1847 to 1854. In this capacity he was required to visit all parishes of the Synod during a three-year period (conventions were held annually). Although he was to ordain and install all pastors, this responsibility could be delegated. The major responsibility during those first years was to render counsel and advice upon request. This created a heavy correspondence in the absence of the telephone, fax, and e-mail. By 1850 he was also granted the right to suspend a pastor temporarily.[27]

With the division into four districts in 1854, many of the presidential responsibilities were transferred to the district presidents to the extent that they applied to a district. The Synodical presidency remained largely a supervisory office, especially over the district officers, attending district conventions and some pastoral conferences. The president also retained his responsibility as a "visitor." Because Wyneken, who had served as president from 1850 to 1864, declined reelection, Walther was reelected to a second term. Wyneken served Synod as a full-time president from 1859 to 1863, whereas Walther never did, always maintaining responsibilities at the Seminary and in the St. Louis *Gesamtgemeinde*. H. C. Schwan, Walther's successor in 1878, also served as a full-time president from 1881 until his retirement in 1899 at the age of eighty.

It is not surprising that Walther, in both his official and unofficial correspondence, often complained that he was overburdened with work. His responsibilities at the Seminary were far-reaching, he was the head pastor of the four congregations constituting the *Gesamtgemeinde* (joint congregation), and from 1864 to 1878 he was president of the Synod. Already at the 1874 convention Walther had asked not to be reelected. To persuade him to change his mind, the convention decided to reduce his work load by no longer requiring him to preach at the opening services of each of the six district conventions, to shorten his Seminary teaching responsibilities to a six-month period (November 1–April 30); and to provide him with two synodical vice presidents to assist him. In spite of this, Walther continued to teach from early September to June.

Walther's successor, H. C. Schwan, became Synod president in 1878. Commenting on the unity of the Synod in his 1884 presidential address, he stated:

> What has kept us together until now was not our Constitution, as good as it is, not the personality of those who bear the highest synodical offices. No, it was something radically different, something which God Himself has given us. This was the unity of spirit and faith. We remain together outwardly because we are one inwardly. Because of this, districts, congregations, and individuals can never be careful enough in whatever they are doing to maintain the bond of unity. Even though they may have the best intentions in undertaking certain items, if these are not properly thought through, and are not properly considered on the backdrop of love to others and with due respect to the welfare and furtherance of the whole [this unity cannot be maintained]. As long as we by God's grace remain one in heart and soul through the Word and faith, our bond of fellowship at the continued existence of the Synod will not be seriously challenged. If this [spirit] is ever lost, then no constitution will coerce those who rebel, and the resulting cooperation will be of no value.[28]

Other officers who served during Walther's presidency were a secretary and a treasurer, the latter a layman. The commissions or committees created were: A "Commission on Colloquies" (*Pruefungskommission*), which was established in the first synodical convention in 1847. This commission was responsible both for the "practical" and "theoretical" seminary graduates. Boards of control for the educational institutions of the Synod (*Aufsichtsbehoerden*) were established in 1848, one for St. Louis and one for Fort Wayne. An Electoral College (*Wahlkollegium*) was also established in 1848. This "college" was responsible for the elections of all professorships at the synodical institutions. As early as 1847 a Commission for Heathen Missions (*Heidenmissionskommission*) was responsible for the Synod's Native American mission work. To supervise the work of *Der Lutheraner*, a "Publications Committee for Official Journals" was established in 1847. The "Immigrant Missions" commission came into being in 1869 when this work was undertaken. The Board of Directors of Concordia Publishing House had its beginnings in 1849 and assumed its present responsibilities in 1869.

In 1887, the year of Walther's death, President Schwan reported that the Synod had 60 traveling missionaries, 70 pastors who were serving mission congregations and a total of approximately 450 preaching stations. This work was placed under a "Home Mission Commission" established in 1878 when the districts and congregations alone were no longer able to coordinate such a tremendous missionary outreach. During Walther's lifetime a commission on Jewish missions was established in 1884 and a commission on English missions in 1887.

As president of the Synod, Walther was constrained to write a letter of financial appeal to the members of the Synod in January 1875. Due to the Civil War, the entire country was faced with "secondary post-war depression" in early 1874 and ending in 1879. Rapid price deflation had reached a state of panic in 1873. To complicate matters, the railroad made it possible for land settlers to move west and the Synod's coffers were depleted. In the midst of this situation, Walther appealed to all the congregations of the Synod. The Synod itself had grown rapidly, and the congregations on the frontier were still weak and often poor. Building additions were needed at synodical institutions in Addison, Illinois, Fort Wayne, Indiana, and Springfield, Illinois. In October 1874, the Synod convention met in Fort Wayne and approved new construction at all three schools. In what was perhaps the strongest appeal for financial support he had ever issued, Walther called for support:

> God Himself has given us these great opportunities to train pastors and teachers. ... In view of this, it is my first petition which requires haste. Elect members of your congregation who will be able to go

from house to house in order to obtain contributions for these constructions. May each one give according to his ability and with a willing heart, in gratitude to the precious Word of God. ... When you have collected a small sum, send it to your district treasurer and tell him in what period of time and how it is to be used. Please note, this is not something concerning pastors, but it is your business. ... Our institutions are not institutions of pastors, and the educational institutions are not the property of pastors, they are actually your property. Each member of the congregation is a co-owner.

Truly, the current expenses of the Synod are increasing each year as more teachers are being trained in our remarkable schools—the growth is quite impressive. But even though our Synod has grown larger, our congregations, because they are too poor or too new, have not been supporting this as well. Our synodical treasury will send a financial report to you, but that will follow later. We have not received enough support in our synodical treasury to cover the current expenditures. Our treasurer—and do not be surprised at this—had to borrow thousands and even on high interest in order to pay all the teachers [professors] at our synodical institutions. ... Dearly beloved brothers, please think of our synodical treasury *with greater concern* [italics in original]. Without that, our synodical household will not be able to live. I for my person would gratefully be satisfied with less, but there are several professors in our institutions who have large families and cannot subsist during these very costly times. The best would be if all of our congregations would regularly send small offerings. These can accomplish great things.

So there you have it, I have poured out my entire heart. Do not be angry because of this, but consider that the Synod is your spiritual house, and you are the stewards of that house—we pastors and teachers are only caretakers. Be concerned about this then that your earthly house will not be suffering but much more that the blessings will be yours through the promises of our Christ. Luke 6:38. ...

I have begged in an unembarrassed way, but I am not ashamed of that for two reasons: First because I know that you are very willing to do something for God's kingdom, as many of your pastors indicate they have been too hesitant to come again and again to ask for your love.

Secondly, because I'm not asking for myself but on behalf of our dear Lord Jesus—I am begging—who Himself was poor on earth, but now above in heaven is the Lord of lords and of all riches, who, however rules His church on earth through His Word, through faith ... until

He will finally crown us with the crown of eternal life ... for the sake of our eternal Savior. Amen.[29]

To further emphasize the lack of funds, Walther wrote to Theodor Ruhland of Saxony shortly after writing his financial appeal to the Synod:

> So many people are out of work; in the West there is a dire need because the grasshoppers have destroyed crops last summer; in the North there have been many snowstorms and we in the northern part of the South still daily have to heat our homes so we don't freeze. Even though the convention has approved construction in Addison, Fort Wayne, and Springfield, there is so little money available today that it would be laughable to start construction on that basis. ... Our treasury is often embarrassed. We're sorry that there hasn't been any more money for the work in Germany. ... We're placed into some severe doubts about the future.[30]

In October 1876, Walther wrote: "We are still in desperate financial trouble more so than at anytime during the entire period since the Synod was founded."[31] Nevertheless, Walther did send Friedrich Brunn $300 to share with his co-worker in Europe. Brunn, at the time, also had the full responsibility to care for the physical illness of Alfred Grubert, former Leipzig missionary in India. Shortly thereafter Grubert died. In the same October letter, Walther suggested to Brunn that the amount he sent should also be available "for our beloved patient, so that you, Brunn, in your poverty will not be embarrassed with the financial care of your patient."[32]

MISSION OUTREACH

We have already mentioned the vast prairies, woods, valleys, mountains, and waters to which immigrants were pouring forth from overseas and the colonial east. Some have compared this westward migration following both the Revolutionary and the Civil Wars to a great *Völkerwanderung*, migration of nations. These expansionist periods were crucial for the churches, not only to establish contact with their own members, but also to reach out to those who had lost their church connections. An emphasis on "home missions" (*Innere Mission*) was the priority of all ethnic Lutherans (Germans, Swedes, Norwegians, and later Danes), who witnessed their countrymen coming over in massive numbers. But that period, too, was followed by an outreach to the rest of the globe. Walther had a heartfelt concern and a wide-ranging vision for mission outreach and for reclaiming the lost.

Wilhelm Loehe had the immense foresight to prepare a map of the United States which illustrated the location of German Lutheran congregations. He made it available to the German emigrants leaving their homeland so that they could locate existing German Lutheran settlements. The map is most impressive because it even identified where the various synods were located. In a magnificent way it demonstrates the love and concern Loehe had for immigrants to prevent them from settling wildly and helter-skelter. The map served a two-fold purpose. First, it assisted the traveling missionaries who, like Wyneken, were struggling in the forests and swamps to find the isolated German settlements. Secondly, it enabled the German immigrants to determine where they wanted to settle.

It was also Loehe who in 1845 thought of bringing the Gospel to the Chippewa Indians in Michigan. He made church extension support available to the settlements in the Saginaw Valley and provided them with liturgical resources to bring the Gospel to various stations. The Synod inherited these mission stations in 1847.

Paul Heerboth quotes Richard A. Jesse, formerly dean of students at Concordia Seminary, St. Louis, as saying: "The birth of the Missouri Synod was due to a God-guided catastrophic cataclysm."[33] God's providence over political, social, and religious history describes not only Missouri's founding but also the emergence of its mission outreach.

The synodical *Reiseprediger*, traveling missionaries, used organized congregations, especially in the chief centers of the country—the larger cities—as the hubs from which mission work was carried out. From there they could use one of several different methods of outreach.

The "fission" type of expansion began with a branch school or schools, whereby the original congregation divided itself. First, a branch school was organized. After it prospered, occasional worship services were held, and eventually a new congregation was born. Particularly outstanding in this type of mission expansion were Pastors H. Wunder in Chicago, C. F. W. Walther in St. Louis, H. C. Schwan in Cleveland and F. A. Craemer in Frankenmuth, Michigan. Sometimes these branch schools and full-fledged congregations decided to remain together. The St. Louis *Gesamtgemeinde*—a union of congregations—formed a single administrative unit and pastoral ministry. Sometimes, such congregations were hesitant to separate completely from the mother congregation. Hence they carried out specific projects jointly.

A second procedure to reach out to unchurched settlements may be called the "leap frog" method. Under this process the organized congregation called an assistant pastor whom they actually did not need in their own parish. Areas 50 to 100 miles away from the parish were considered their mission field. An assistant pastor therefore virtually became a traveling missionary and radiated out into distant settlements to bring the Gospel to isolated settlers. When one of these settlements decided to organize a congregation, the traveling missionary frequently was called to serve them as their pastor. Then a new traveling missionary was called and the process went on into new areas. This is one of the reasons why the Missouri Synod did not need a home mission board until 1878. The congregations assumed the responsibility of outreach. Such work continued until the peak of German immigration to America was reached in 1882.

Walther served as an informal mission executive of the Synod. This was mainly because he served both as synodical and seminary president. He received countless letters asking him to propose candidates for a new situation or to evaluate pastors for a specific congregation. He even offered, when requested, to propose mission strategies.

A few quotations from Walther's sermons effectively demonstrate the "life and death" perspective within which he viewed mission work. Consequently, he felt an urgent need to preach the Gospel wherever and whenever opportunities arose. He offered prayers and support for Native American and heathen missions. The theme of his sermon on Epiphany, 1845 was "Jesus Came into the World Also to Save All Heathen." He stated in this sermon:

> "Go ye therefore and teach all nations" ... A Christian is obligated not only to respond to God, but to preach the Gospel to all his brothers and sisters. According to the flesh, are not all poor and miserable heathen our brothers and sisters? Hasn't the same God created us and them? Don't we all have the same father in Adam and the same mother in Eve? Are they not flesh like our flesh, blood of our blood, and bone of our bone? Are Christians actually able [to] quietly watch as millions of their brothers and sisters are living without God, without light, without grace, without comfort in suffering, without hope in death, in sins, in blindness, under God's wrath without grace, and, [tormented by] inexpressible doubts within and without, are going on to their death without seeing the light? They are lost according to body and soul now and forever. If somebody would be falling into a body of water, wouldn't it be brotherly love to reach out his hand and save him from drowning ... ? Now millions of our brothers are

drowning in the flood of eternal death without [anyone] giving one penny to come to their rescue![34]

Note how eloquently and impressively Walther described missions to the Native Americans as he preached on Matthew 2:1–12:

Woe to those citizens of these states who do not wish to do anything to bring the comfort of the Gospel to the unfortunate heathen aborigines of this western land and [see to it that] its blessing be brought to them! We are living on their hills and on their grounds; we pasture our herds on their prairies; we cut our wood in their forests; we travel on their streams and rivers: How we will be shocked before God's judgment throne when on the last day they accuse us before God and we hear the words from their mouths: There stand our enemies; they drove us out of the earthly fatherland which we owned, but the way to their Father's house, O God, they have not shared with us. They have taken away our temporal property and fortune; they have spilled our blood and have irritated our souls, but the eternal wealth which you have entrusted to them, they have not only trod under foot, but they have begrudged this to us. Lord, revenge, revenge, what they have grudgingly not given us.[35]

Walther preached several different sermons on Isaiah 60:1–6. This was a text that sparked him to proclaim the Gospel to the entire world. A few quotations from these sermons reveal his great missionary zeal, as he emphasizes that every Christian is a missionary:

Every believing Christian should be a missionary and has the responsibility to do everything possible according to his call and his duty, to bring the great treasure of saving knowledge which is already his ... Now let us look into central and eastern Asia, into the interior of Africa, to Australia and the countless islands of the Pacific and you will notice that the largest and to a great degree the most beautiful areas of the globe are located right there in the night of heathenism. Even in our new beautiful fatherland there are more than 100,000 heathen inhabitants, and in Europe when the Gospel has been proclaimed for a millennium ... Of about a thousand million inhabitants of the earth, there are probably about six hundred million—two thirds—who are still without the light of the Gospel.[36]

The results of unbelief? Walther identified them in the same sermon:

They are sinners like we are, and their hearts are bent on evil from youth up. They have no power to resist the sin. They live in all the sins and repulsiveness, parents are murdering their children and sell them into slavery, the children murder their old, no longer useful parents. Murder, uncouthness, thievery, lying are the most abhorrent idols that are popular with them.[37]

Another sermon based on Isaiah 60:1–6 emphasized the worldwide dimension of mission work. We might call this "globalization" today:

> Where are the boundaries of the kingdom of Jesus Christ? What ruler on earth has such wide and broad parameters in his kingdom, other than the king whose life was ended so shamefully on the cross? Where is the land of this world which does not have subordinates who have given themselves, through Baptism, and pledged themselves to the bloodstained manner of their eternal Savior? Yes, the voice of the Gospel has gone out with power to all the lands, and its sound to the ends of the earth! It has pushed into the impenetrable forests of Africa, it has reached to the icy heights of the distant northern areas, it has been heard in the islands of the Pacific, it has even made a path through the doorways to America which Satan had for so long barred shut with the mighty beams of the ocean; Jesus Christ is the only king, who, as prophesied in Scripture, rules right in the midst of his enemies. There is no language or speech in which the name Jesus is not known; the differences of the lands, nations, and colors have fallen away. Everywhere it is acknowledged that Jesus Christ the Lord, the glory of God the Father is known. Untold Caesars, kings, dukes, and lords have laid down their scepters, their crowns, and their purple before the shepherd's staff of the Good Shepherd and humbly prayed at the foot of the cross.[38]

The power of the Gospel in the name of Jesus conquers everything. Evangelism and mission outreach are completely interwoven in the fabric of Walther's life and theology. Walther's own words and life readily dispel the myth that he was a theologian who was not interested in missions. Countless other sermon quotations could be added to underscore his intense concern for mission work.[39]

Walther also emphasized the congregation's obligation to carry on mission work. According to him, each individual congregation is a mission society:

> A congregation should be zealous to spread the written Word of God. 1 Thessalonians 5:27: "I charge you by the Lord that this epistle be read unto all the holy brethren." Colossians 4:16: "And when the epistle is read among you, cause that it be read also in the church of the Laodiceans and that you likewise read the epistle from Laodicea."[40]

Walther also stressed that it is the congregation's responsibility to carry the Gospel forward: "A congregation should do its share that the Gospel may be brought to those sitting in darkness and the shadow of death, [namely] to the wretched heathen and Jews."[41]

Walther's essay on "Duties of an Evangelical Lutheran Synod," presented at the first convention of the newly-created Iowa District in 1879, is an excellent blueprint for congregational responsibilities. Particularly significant for missions is Thesis 6,C:

> [T]ake an enthusiastic and, as much as possible, active part in all God-pleasing organizations dedicated to the spread of Christ's kingdom in the world. ... That is the duty of every synod, including our own. It is to join the ranks of that great army of laborers in the harvest field of Christ. For the harvest has long been "dead ripe"; it is only a matter of reaping that harvest. In other words, it should cooperate with every organization of both home and foreign missions for the spreading of the Holy Scriptures.[42]

In the same essay Walther urged congregations to be mindful of and to prepare adequately for the seed of the Gospel to be transmitted to all descendants: "Therefore this congregation and every individual Christian is to be a seed from which new Christians and congregations can ever again grow. That is why the Apostle says so emphatically that the church is the mother of us all [Galatians 4:26]."[43]

Already in the earliest constitution of the Synod, one of the six reasons for its establishment was for "the joint extension of the kingdom of God and the establishment and the promotion of special church enterprises. ..."[44]

Home missions became a primary focus of the Synod. Congregations and missions were planted everywhere. In 1884 Walther wrote a letter to Daniel Landsmann, a missionary to the Jewish people in New York. Part of the letter was written in Hebrew. Walther quoted Micah 2:13, "God will open the way for them and lead them out of exile. They will break out of the city gates and go free. Their king, the LORD himself, will lead them out." He further refers to Ezekiel 34:23, prophesying Israel's great king: "I will give them a king like my servant David to be their one shepherd, and he will take care of them." In the letter Walther encouraged Landsmann as follows:

> Even if our power is so small, the news of Christ the crucified and arisen is powerful enough even to awaken even the dead. ... On this approaching festival of Easter triumph, may the Lord send you renewed courage and renewed joy for this marvelous work to which

you have been called and constantly strengthen you in faith in your election, and thereby cheer you, that from your life streams of living water may flow (John 7:38).... Use these few lines to note them as a witness that, when you are engaged in heated battle against the devil's bulwark, we are behind you, kneeling and raising our praying hands to the Lord. ... Greetings also to your faithful wife and all who through your faithful service have been won as our brothers from Israel.[45]

Immigrant missions were particularly close to Walther because they were under the direction of Stephanus Keyl, his son-in-law. The work, which started locally in New York, became a synodical effort in 1869. Keyl touched the lives of most of the Lutheran immigrants who came through New York. He assisted them in resettling and aided them in various other ways, even financially. During the 20-year period from 1885 to 1905, Keyl cared for 79,843 German and 5,342 Scandinavian immigrants in the *Pilgerhaus* (pilgrim house) reception center in New York. The outreach was enormous.[46]

Home missionaries were the great heroes who sacrificed everything for the sake of missions, including their families and personal well-being. The strength and outreach of the Synod became stronger and stronger because of their sacrificial work. In Minnesota alone one circuit rider simultaneously served 42 preaching stations and 500 families! North Dakota asked for a physically robust and theologically conservative trained pastor for one of its congregations, someone who could withstand the harsh winter blizzards!

The work continued in all directions. Beginning in the 1860s, Walther whole-heartedly supported English missions. He also encouraged the continuation of African-American missions, which had been started by the Synodical Conference in 1877.

In addition to his great concern for mission work, Walther also felt a compelling need to support social ministries. Lutheran Hospital in St. Louis, for example, was founded in 1858 at a time when hospitals were often considered "pest houses" for the dying. The Orphan's Home in Des Peres, just outside of St. Louis, was organized in 1868 to care for orphans and the elderly. Although it was J. F. Buenger, Walther's brother-in-law, who was the catalyst for founding these institutions, Walther stood firmly at Buenger's side with encouragement and support. In *The Proper Form*, Walther emphasized:

Congregations shall also provide food, clothing, habitation and all other necessities for the poor, the widows, orphans, aged, and invalids, which they themselves cannot procure and [for which] they have no relatives who first of all owe them these things. ... A congregation shall see to it that its members in their sickness are not without the necessary help, daily and nightly nursing, and comfort. ... The congregation shall also care for those who suffer distress through special calamities like fire, famine, scarcity, robbery, and so forth.[47]

The numerical growth of the Synod was enormous during Walther's lifetime. In 1847, there were 19 pastors, 30 member congregations, and 4,099 baptized members. Forty years later, at the time of Walther's death in 1887, there were a total of 931 pastors, 678 member congregations, and another 746 which were affiliated but had not joined, and 544 preaching stations for a total of 1,968. The baptized membership stood at 459,376.[48]

The world in which Walther lived, preached, taught, and encouraged was considerably different than the world today. Now local, state, and federal governments through their various agencies supply many of the services that were once the responsibility of the local congregations. According to Scripture, however, the ultimate responsibility always rests with Christians, who band together in order to accomplish as much as possible in sharing the Gospel and reflecting Christ's love.

THE HISTORIAN

Walther wrote two biographies of fellow pastors during his lifetime. The first was of his brother-in-law J. F. Buenger (1810–1882), titled *Kurzer Lebenslauf des weiland ehrwürdigen Pastor Joh. Friedr. Bünger.*[49] The second was of C. J. H. Fick (1822–1885).[50] In writing these biographies, Walther paid tribute to close friends and co-workers. He portrayed these men— one a pastor and social service worker, the other a pastor and writer—as witnesses of Christ. The biographies were intended to instruct and edify their readers.

On the subject of writing a history of the Missouri Synod, Walther expressed himself in a letter to J. C. W. Lindemann in 1876, paraphrasing Tobit 12:11: "The advice and secrets of kings and princes should be kept secret, but God's work should be praised gloriously."[51] Walther went on to say that those who participated in the Synod's history "ought not to die off without having written a history of our Synod." Then he cautioned:

Aside from that, however, I regard it partly too difficult, partly too dangerous a thing that a history of our Synod should be published as long as its founders are still living. To be sure, it should be written during their lifetime, but it should not be published.[52]

Several attempts were made to write about some aspects of the history of the Missouri Synod during Walther's lifetime. His own contributions in the biographies of Buenger and Fick point in that direction. Several histories of the Saxon Immigration had also been written earlier, most of which were highly subjective.

An important contribution in this area was made by Christian Hochstetter (1828–1905), who wrote a comprehensive history of the Missouri Synod.[53] It was published in 1885, two years before Walther's death. The book continues to be the most reliable source available from that time.[54] Hochstetter had been a pastor in the Buffalo Synod, but joined the Missouri Synod in 1867 when his theological convictions shifted. Walther received a copy of the volume from Hochstetter and read it immediately, though with great trepidation because he was so personally involved with the Synod's history. In a letter to the author of the book, dated July 31, 1885, Walther expressed his great satisfaction with the history:

Now after I have completed reading with great interest and joy your history of our synod, and its doctrinal controversies, I am compelled to express my deepest and most sincere appreciation to you for the great service which you have rendered by it not only to our synod, but above all to the cause of truth. At first, I grant you, I dreaded to read your splendid book, because I myself occur in it so often. I was afraid of my own evil heart, which is so greatly prone to ascribe a little also to myself for what God has done to me out of incomprehensible mercy and for [how] he has used me as his most unworthy instrument. Finally, however, after God allowed me again and again to feel my incompetence for all good and my damnableness, I overcame my dread. …

[Y]ou allowed the facts to speak, facts which simply cannot be gainsayed. … When I was reading your book it struck me more vividly than ever before, that next to God's incomprehensible mercy in making us poor sinners a memorial of His free grace, the true cause of our success is the conviction (given us by God) under all circumstances to remain with His truth and the heritage of the Reformation and not to sacrifice one iota of it, even if (because of that) everything erected would be brought to ruin again. That this conviction was also mine and remained mine to this hour, I cannot deny for the sake of God's

honor, who gave it to me. Cursed be every thought that seeks to claim
for itself what belongs to God, but far be it, too, out of false modesty
to deny what God has done in us.[55]

NOTES

[1] Letter from Schieferdecker to Karl R. Demme, President of the Pennsylvania
Ministerium, postmarked August 13, 1840 in the archives of Krauth Memorial
Library, Philadelphia, PA.

[2] Hochstetter, *Geschichte* … (Dresden: Heinrich J. Naumann, 1885), 148–49. See also
August R. Suelflow, "Congregational Autonomy," *Concordia Journal*, 3:6 (November
1977), 261ff.

[3] Friedrich Lochner, "F. Lochner's Report on His First Contacts with the Saxon,"
Concordia Historical Institute Quarterly, 7:3 (October 1934), 79.

[4] Wilhelm Sihler, *Lebenslauf von W. Sihler … auf mehrfaches Begehren von ihm Selber
beschrieben*, Vol 2 [no publication information available], 52–53.

[5] Lochner, "F. Lochner's Report on His First Contacts with the Saxon," *Concordia
Historical Institute Quarterly*, 80–81.

[6] Martin Guenther, *Dr. C. F. W. Walther: Lebensbild* (St. Louis: Concordia Publishing
House, 1890), 72; translated by W. G. Polack, *Building of a Great Church* (St. Louis:
Concordia Publishing House, 1941), 68–69, 72.

[7] See Roy A. Suelflow translation: "Our First Synodical Constitution," *Concordia
Historical Institute Quarterly*, 16:1 (April 1943), 1–18.

[8] Its translation appears in Carl S. Meyer, ed., *Moving Frontiers* (St. Louis: Concordia
Publishing House, 1964), 149–61.

[9] Meyer, *Moving Frontiers*, 149–50.

[10] Trinity, St. Louis, Minutes, February 22, 1847. Held at Concordia Historical
Institute.

[11] See Meyer, *Moving Frontiers*, 151.

[12] *Proceedings*, Missouri Synod, 1847, 6.

[13] *Proceedings*, Missouri Synod, 1847, 15.

[14] For the text of Walther's address see Paul F. Koehneke, tr., "Dr. Walther's First
Presidential Address," *Concordia Journal*, 2:5 (September 1976), 200f.

[15] Paul F. Koehneke, tr., "Dr. Walther's First Presidential Address," *Concordia
Historical Institute Quarterly*, 33:1 (April 1960), 13.

[16] *Handbook of the LCMS* (St. Louis: LCMS, 1995), 11.

[17] *Proceedings*, Missouri Synod, 1860, 62.

[18] Ludwig Fuerbringer, *Walthers Briefe* (St. Louis: Concordia Publishing House,
1915), Vol. 1, 16; also Meyer, *Moving Frontiers*, 143 for other aspects of this letter
in translation.

[19] See *Concordia Triglotta* (St. Louis: Concordia Publishing House, 1921), 1150ff.

[20] E. Clifford Nelson, ed., *The Lutherans in North America* (Philadelphia: Fortress
Press, 1975), 222–23. A comparison of the Augsburg Confession of 1530 and the
Definite Synodical Platform can be seen here.

[21] C. F. W. Walther, *The Form of a Christian Congregation*, trans. J. T. Mueller (St. Louis: Concordia Publishing House, 1963), 56–57.

[22] In Francis Pieper, *Christian Dogmatics* (St. Louis: Concordia Publishing House, 1953), 3:430. Francis Pieper stated that a vote on matters of doctrine serves only the purpose of establishing whether all now understand the teaching of the divine Word and agree to it. Most emphatically it does not approve a new doctrinal statement by majority vote. See also August R. Suelflow, "Remembering Zion," *Concordia Journal*, 1:4 October (1975), 159ff.

[23] *Proceedings*, Missouri Synod, 1857, 29.

[24] August R. Suelflow, "The Life and Work of Georg A. Schieferdecker," BD thesis, Concordia Seminary, St. Louis, 1947.

[25] *Proceedings*, Missouri Synod, 1881, 35–36.

[26] *Proceedings*, Missouri Synod, 1881, 44.

[27] *Proceedings*, Missouri Synod, 1850, 15.

[28] *Proceedings*, Missouri Synod, 1884, 29–30.

[29] Open letter from Walther to Members of Synodical Congregations, January 12, 1875; full translation by C. S. Meyer, ed., *Walther Speaks to the Church* (St. Louis: Concordia Publishing House, 1973), 32–34.

[30] Letter from Walther to Th. Ruhland, May 5, 1875; transcription by Werner K. Wadewitz at Concordia Historical Institute.

[31] Letter from Walther to Friedrich Brunn, October 8, 1876; transcription by W. K. Wadewitz at Concordia Historical Institute.

[32] Hans Zorn, "Carl Manthey-Zorn in India and His Coming to America, II," *Concordia Historical Institute Quarterly*, 33:2 (July 1960), 59.

[33] *Concordia Historical Institute Quarterly*, 67:3 (Fall 1994), 103.

[34] C. F. W. Walther, *Lutherische Brosamen—Predigten und Reden, seit 1847 …* (St. Louis: M. C. Barthel, 1876), 33ff.

[35] Walther, *Lutherische Brosamen—Predigten und Reden, seit 1847 …*, 48–49.

[36] Walther, *Lutherische Brosamen—Predigten und Reden, seit 1847 …*, 51, 53–54.

[37] Walther, *Lutherische Brosamen—Predigten und Reden, seit 1847 …*, 53–54.

[38] C. F. W. Walther, *Amerikanisch-Lutherische Epistel Postille* (St. Louis: Concordia Publishing House, 1882), 62ff.

[39] See especially C. F. W. Walther, *Goldkoerner* (Zwickau: Johannes Hermann, 1901), 72–93, esp. 91ff.

[40] Walther, *The Form of a Christian Congregation*, Thesis 64, 185.

[41] Walther cites Matthew 28:18–20 in *The Form of a Christian Congregation*, Thesis 65, 185–86.

[42] C. F. W. Walther, *Essays for the Church*, Volume 2, (St. Louis: Concordia Publishing House, 1992), 62.

[43] Walther, *Essays for the Church*, Volume 2, 62.

[44] Meyer, *Moving Frontiers*, 149.

[45] Letter from Walther to Daniel Landsmann, April 6, 1884; transcription by W. K. Wadewitz at Concordia Historical Institute.

46 See Theodore S. Keyl, "The Life and Activities of Pastor Stephanus Keyl," *Concordia Historical Institute Quarterly*, 22:2 (July 1949), 65ff.

47 Walther, *The Form of a Christian Congregation*, Theses 34–35, 147–48, 151.

48 *Statistical Yearbook*, 1937 (St. Louis: Concordia Publishing House, 1937), 150–52.

49 St. Louis: Verlag von F. Dette, 1882.

50 *Der Lutheraner*, Vol. 42, Nos. 14 (July 15, 1886) to 18 (September 15, 1886).

51 Letter from Walther to J. C. W. Lindemann, August 8, 1876; for full translation see Roy A. Suelflow, ed., *Selected Writings of C. F. W. Walther* (St. Louis: Concordia Publishing House, 1981), 133–134. Tobit is from the Apocrypha of the Old Testament.

52 Letter from Walther to J. C. W. Lindemann, August 8, 1876.

53 The 480-page volume is entitled *Die Geschichte der Ev.-luth. Missouri Synode* [*The History of the Missouri Synod*] (Dresden: Heinrich J. Naumann, 1885).

54 Georg Stoeckhardt, who had spent most of his life in Europe and was not born into the Missouri Synod, said in reviewing Hochstetter's book:

> The writer has a special gift of God for writing history. He has not imagined anything out of his own head. But as a reliable writer of history, he used the synodical reports, *Der Lutheraner*, *Lehre und Wehre*, and other authentic sources. The entire history in its total work is based upon many sources, and is a correct presentation of the history of the Missouri Synod as its title states. This book presents a living picture to which it adheres to this day of the outward development of the Missouri Synod as also of its doctrinal position in various doctrinal controversies (*Lehre und Wehre*, 31:7–8 [July–August 1885], 243–45.

55 Letter from Walther to Hochstetter, July 31, 1885; transcription by W. K. Wadewitz at Concordia Historical Institute.

5

WE BELIEVE, TEACH, AND CONFESS

Although Lutheranism in America can be traced all the way back to the New Amsterdam (New York) settlements beginning in the 1630s, a number of factors caused it to be quite fragmented. Geographical distances, lack of Lutheran publications and modern communications, differences in their European background and training, the time and place of arrival of the immigrants, and the transition from German, Norwegian, Swedish, and Danish to English all contributed to this fragmentation.

The process of moving from periods of Orthodoxy centered in the Book of Concord to Pietism with its emphasis on a special lifestyle and finally to Rationalism affected Lutherans. Theological divergences developed as the emphases changed. As northern and central European immigration to America reached its peak in the 1880s and 1890s, this grand potpourri had resulted in geographical, theological, and linguistic diversity among Lutherans in America.

When Walther arrived in America in 1839, virtually all of the above factors were already at work. The literature of the time reflects this, as do the accounts of the beginning of Lutheran seminary education with the opening of Gettysburg in 1826 and others shortly thereafter. Moreover, one can see the development of American Lutheran church books (hymnals, agendas, catechisms) as well as the establishment of publishing houses.

As varying backgrounds left their imprint, so did the new situation in America. The social and political environment, travel conditions from canals and rivers to the railroads, the formation of major cities surrounded by farming communities—all these factors had a tremendous impact on the clergymen, the theology professors, and the leaders of the church. Picture all the varying shades and hues of the spectrum in theology, in geography, and in rural and urban influences. Walther was exposed to all these mixtures during his early years in America. Whether he should turn left or right or go forward or backward was not always an easy question.

This chapter will deal with the published theological literature that Walther produced. We can classify it in several categories: 1) justification by faith, 2) to God alone all glory, 3) Law and Gospel, 4) church and ministry, 5) election of grace, and 6) Scripture and the Lutheran Confessions.

JUSTIFICATION BY FAITH

In the corpus of Walther's writings, justification of sinful human beings emerges as his central theme. Walther's emphasis on justification overshadows all other church doctrines. For Walther, every aspect of theology, regardless of its content, is based on justification by faith. This is the hub of the wheel of doctrine. Everything centers on faith in Christ, "which the Holy Spirit works in [people] through the Word of the Gospel."[1] Only this can bring the peace of God, Christian freedom, sanctification, and the confidence of eternal life. Man does not contribute anything. God through the Holy Spirit in Christ does everything.

In this respect Walther becomes the master teacher of doctrine. Some systematicians are inclined to teach one doctrine after another as though they were unrelated to each other. In this approach, doctrines, often referred to as *loci* (common places of theology), tend to lose their center, their driving force. In contrast, Walther saw all the passages of Christian doctrine interwoven, with justification recurring through all and interconnecting with them. Forgiveness of sins, to repeat the metaphor, is the hub and all other doctrines are the spokes. And how did Walther know that justification was the center of all theology? Through Scripture, God's revelation and "love letter" to each generation.

To understand Walther's theology, it is necessary to dig deeply into the doctrine of justification which both Martin Luther and Martin Chemnitz had proclaimed in all of their doctrinal writings. Walther did not merely consider it one of the doctrines, but the primary doctrine, without which none of the other doctrines find a place in theology. But man is always in opposition to it. Thus the "theology of glory" has evolved where man thinks that his salvation depends upon himself. In fact, human beings contribute absolutely nothing.

Justification through faith in Christ is central. It is the one doctrine by which the church stands or falls. The church rises upon this doctrine or it falls wretchedly. It is central to all understanding of Scripture, the Confessions, and Walther's teachings and preaching. It is the great and joyful teaching of God's message to all people. This, too, is what comforts us as we go through life, knowing that we are redeemed children of God.[2]

Justification was thoroughly discussed by Walther at the Western District convention held in Addison, Illinois in May 1859. The theme of the presentation was: "That the Evangelical Lutheran Church Alone Has Been Entrusted with the Pure Doctrine of Justification."

Walther describes the doctrine of justification as a difficult doctrine to accept, especially when people feel that they mastered it long ago. Yet the doctrine is understood only through the work and operation of the Holy Spirit. Walther asserted that it is easy to lose this doctrine and its message for several reasons:

1. Vulgar rationalism and Pelagian supernaturalism flatly reject it;
2. Philosophical assumptions are superimposed and thus reintroduce ancient heresies;
3. Unionistic activities suggest that the doctrine is no longer of such great importance;
4. Enthusiastic stimulation of feelings through all sorts of new regulations that downplay the means of grace;
5. An over-emphasis on the visibility of the church, on ceremonies, rules, constitution, tradition, etc. may easily becloud justification by faith.[3]

Walther concluded this essay by cautioning:

In order to let all our work be thus and always permeated by the doctrine of justification, it is above all necessary that our own heart become very firm in it, and it will become so only under temptation. That is why a pastor who avoids the cross and seeks an easy life will never teach this doctrine properly.

The so-called "awakened" Christians who come into our congregations are usually not satisfied when we preach the Gospel so sweetly and comfortingly to poor sinners. But that should not lead us astray. If they think that we thereby make people lazy and slow to good works, it is certainly because they have not yet fully realized their own sinful wretchedness, for otherwise they would know that the assurance of the forgiveness of all sins, and it alone, makes the love of Christ burn brightly in us and [makes it] impossible for us to go on living in the works of the flesh and without [doing] truly good works.[4]

William H. Cooper, writing on "C. F. W. Walther's Pen," commented on Walther's views on justification:

This, too [Walther's 1859 essay], was published and, while briefer than the report of 1862, it is an illuminating revelation of the author's intelligent and loyal adherence to the great doctrine of justification by faith. We learn from this declaration that Dr. Walther regarded the doctrine as the indispensable key to the right understanding and the right practice of the Christian religion. In this paper Walther appeals to pastors to make a direct study of St. Paul's Epistles and recommends Luther's writings to the laity.[5]

Another way of summarizing Walther on justification appeared in an article entitled "The 'Bright Torch' in Walther's Thought and Action." It offers an insight into justification as the center of doctrine, as well as the center of Walther's life and ministry. Following are some excerpts:

> Walther agreed with Luther that the doctrine of justification can not be mastered. "We are always to be pupils; it is always master."

> Walther pointed out that Protestants in general formally endorse this doctrine; yet many of its noted preachers were "sour Law preachers." Their sermons often caused impenitent sinners to feel secure because they were diligent in church attendance, contributed to missions, or had a pious demeanor.

> Those who make "strict orthodoxy" their goal, Walther noted, are apt to stray from the truth of salvation for the sinner by the grace of God through acceptance of the promises in Jesus. They concentrate on opposing "reputed heresy," "all that has the appearance of laxity," and "ecclesiasticism."

> Thus they lose sight of the center of Christianity, he said. Pure doctrine is a matter of relationship, of harmony "with the article of justification before God by grace alone through faith in Jesus." One who understands this doctrine will teach others correctly.[6]

The Apology to the Augsburg Confession, IV, paragraph 2 states: "The Lutheran Confessions call justification by faith 'the chief topic of Christian doctrine.'"Again, this speaks of the center of everything. For Walther this was at all times and under all circumstances, in times of peace and in times of controversy, the most important doctrine. Justification never is on an equal plane with other doctrines. If there are compartments into which all doctrines can be placed, justification is not in one of them—it is in a class all by itself. All others flow from it.[7]

Like Luther, Walther also had a *Turmerlebnis* (conversion experience) which he described in his biography of his brother-in-law, Johann F. Buenger. Walther was in great fear and trembled before an angry God because of his sin and his soul was in anguish because he did not know a loving heavenly Father. Together Buenger and Walther had tried everything possible to right themselves with God, including legalism, pietism, and subjectivism of every kind. The harder he had tried with his fellow students at Leipzig, the greater his failure seemed to be. In despair, Walther was urged to write Martin Stephan of Dresden (see chapter 1) for comfort. Walther later described this experience:

> As the writer [Walther] finally received an answer [from Stephan], he did not open the letter until he had prayed fervently to God that He would spare him not to receive a false comfort. However, after he had read the letter, he felt that he suddenly had been placed in heaven out of hell. The repeated prayers of fear and pain had now been transformed into tears of true heavenly joy. He could not resist, but he had to go to Jesus. Stephan had shown him that the repentance [Busse] taught by the Law, which he sought, had already long taken place; that he was missing absolutely nothing other than the faith [in Christ] … so the peace of God entered in. And so he received the living absolution as a sinner with a broken heart.[8]

This experience greatly influenced the rest of Walther's life. In joy he now saw Jesus Christ as his Savior. From this point on, this doctrine of forgiveness of sins through Christ's death became the heart and soul of everything Walther preached, taught, and wrote. One can determine whether a doctrine is true or false only by exploring how it harmonizes with the article of justification. This, Walther believed, makes it so important to study and review the Lutheran Confessions again and again because they testify to Christ as Savior.

Walther's statements at the first meeting of the Synodical Conference in 1872 are significant:

> When we speak of justification, we speak of the Christian religion, for the doctrine of the Christian religion is none other than God's revelation concerning the way in which sinners are justified before God and saved through the redemption made by Christ Jesus. All other religions teach other ways that are supposed to lead to heaven; only the Christian religion points out a different way to heaven by its doctrine of justification. This indeed is a way the world has never heard nor known, namely, the counsel of salvation that was hidden in the mind of God before the foundation of the world was laid.[9]

Walther developed an excellent comparison to emphasize that this doctrine cannot be tampered with. It would be like a little child who does not know the purpose of a watch and therefore regards this little wheel or that little pin as unnecessary and removes it. Walther further compared the doctrine to a pile of stones from which one dare not take away some without greatly disturbing the entire stack. He stated emphatically:

> Upon this article our salvation rests, and therefore it is absolutely necessary for every Christian. If anyone would not rightly know and believe this doctrine, it would not do him any good if he knew correctly other doctrines, as, for instance, those of the Holy Trinity, of the person of Christ and the like.[10]

Understanding his emphasis on justification enables one to understand Walther's theology in every one of his essays and books. He based his authority on the Holy Scriptures as summarized in the Lutheran Confessions. Consequently, this matter was of such great importance to him. In *The True Visible Church*, Walther clearly stated his views:

> The Evangelical Lutheran Church assigns to every doctrine of Scripture the rank and significance which it is given in God's Word itself. As the foundation, core, and guiding star of all teaching it regards the doctrine of Christ or of justification.[11]

Walther also observed that the doctrine of justification can not only be beclouded, but it can gradually disappear altogether. It is this doctrine that Martin Luther recovered and that Martin Chemnitz and Johann Gerhard reinforced when there were constant threats against the emphases on justification. Walther suggested measures to be taken to reawaken consciousness of justification:

> Just as monastic living, crusades, and things like that were formerly substituted for the Gospel, so today [the substitutes are the] mourner's bench, camp and class meetings, temperance, and anti-smoking unions. So, for example, whoever puts his pipe away is regarded as converted; whoever doesn't must be of the devil. That is how this sweet Gospel, in which heaven is revealed with all its glory, is perverted into Law, and miserable trifles that are of no concern whatever to God are adorned with the precious words of Scripture, thereby plaguing poor souls unto death, [only] to plunge with them into the abyss of hell. And we ourselves often still have great respect for such false saints. Simple Christians hardly ever dare to speak out against their wretched rubbish and instead to boast of the righteousness of Christ obtained in Holy Baptism. May God help [us] to improve![12]

It may be of interest to observe that Walther was a heavy smoker. He had roughly a dozen long-stemmed pipes with big porcelain bowls standing at his desk. At times he filled his new bowl with tobacco and even took the soggy dregs of the previous pipe and put them on top of the new pipe bowl. One wonders whether he was ever challenged to give up smoking. The records are silent.

Another quotation from Walther's 1859 essay on "Justification" will help to deepen our understanding of this doctrine.

> So far as the art of making the doctrine of justification the focus of all our pastoral work is concerned, it will no doubt want to claim us as its students forever. There are many pastors who indeed know how to preach marvelously about justification, but the rest of their pastoral work is a legalistic procedure. This doctrine should so dominate a pastor's whole mindset that it not only makes him gentle toward every poor sinner and discourages him from using any other means to hearten him, but also gives him the weapons to drive out Satan from everyone he meets, as was the case with Luther, since all our hope for accomplishing anything stems from this doctrine. If we do not succeed in this, then it is our fault if the work of renewal does not go forward in our congregations.

> Law and Gospel must necessarily go hand in hand. Over against secure and public worldlings we must preach the Law as if there were no Gospel, so that it proclaims only God's wrath over sin and brings them no comfort—nothing but the verdict of curse and damnation. But the moment they realize that God means business with His Law, then they need the Gospel, which offers no advice but this: "Believe on the Lord Jesus Christ!" And does not require [one] first to do and become this and that in order to be a child of God.[13]

SOLI DEO GLORIA

While justification of the sinner through Christ was the central doctrine of his theology, Walther also left a distinctive legacy on the question whether a church or religion always gives all glory to God—never to men. This is referred to as *Soli Deo Gloria*. Walther's Western District essays delivered between 1873 and 1886 covered this theme under the title, "The Doctrine of the Lutheran Church Alone Gives All Glory to God, an Irrefutable Proof that Its Doctrine Alone Is True."

The series was well-planned, but the controversy on election of grace—or predestination—interrupted it. Consequently, during the controversy, Walther intermittently discussed this issue in 1877, 1879, 1880, and 1886, in a total of eleven topical presentations.

Walther used the thesis form in these presentations. He substantiated his views with ample references to Scripture, often using the original Hebrew or Greek to underscore the meaning. Walther also cited the Lutheran Confessions, using them as a standard, insuring that what he was saying was in agreement with the Lutheran Symbols. In addition, he presented quotations from Luther—always rejoicing in harmony with Luther—and from the Reformation church fathers.

Although he edited Baier's *Compendium*, Walther never wrote a dogmatics textbook as did Francis Pieper. The closest Walther ever came to producing a systematics textbook was the series of his presentations to the Western District on *Soli Deo Gloria*. Here one can see how well Walther remained abreast of what was going on in the Christian churches throughout the world. He was familiar with the foremost teachers. If he agreed with them, he confirmed what they had written, but if he disagreed, he indicated where they had been wrong and why.

In a sense, one might say Walther was a "popularizer." He took the profound message of God in Scripture and presented it so that people could understand it and integrate it into their daily lives. He fine-honed theology to the "real life" of the church. Never an ivory tower theologian, Walther was fascinating in his sermons as he addressed contemporary situations. He knew what people were thinking and saying, and since he knew his theology, he could relate it to their daily lives.

But what did Walther say about *Soli Deo Gloria?* He stated that only a church that gives all glory to God alone in everything it does can be considered correct in its doctrine. In contrast, when the church's workers and congregations attribute accomplishments and successes to themselves, that church fails Walther's test. In his series of essays, Walther asserted that it is an irrefutable proof that a church's doctrine and theology are correct and true when they give all glory to God alone.

Orthodoxism, pietism, and rationalism all became man-centered in their theology. Pieper speaks of this as an *Ich Theologie* (self-theology). Others speak of this as the "theology of glory" which is man-centered, in contrast to the "theology of the cross" which is Christ-centered. Inversion from God to man occurs when what we believe, teach, and confess is based on such things as the latest research man may have accomplished, on personal experiences, or on feelings.

Walther's anthropology is completely and totally biblical. He taught that Adam and Eve were created perfect in the garden. But their falling into sin and wanting to be equal to God destroyed their relationship to their Creator, who expelled them from paradise.

When tempted by Satan, we still feel that somewhere or somehow we can become equal with God. We ask, "Did God really mean what He said?" We begin to question the manner in which God has revealed Himself. Consider how much of our personal beliefs are centered in ourselves or other mortals, not in God. At times we may put our confidence into a visible church, a pastor, a teacher, or even a friend. When we reflect on Walther and the immigration to America, it is apparent that the immigrants had put their trust and focus on their leader, Martin Stephan.

Like Luther, Walther firmly believed, taught, and confessed "the just shall live by faith." This leaves no room for self-centered theology, no boasting, no good works, no self-righteousness, no pietism, no legalism, nor anything except faith in Christ. We are justified—made righteous, declared holy, friends of God—and made members of God's holy family, the church. Through Christ we have become "fellow citizens with God's people and members of God's family." How comforting it was for Walther to read: "We are no longer strangers and foreigners, but fellow citizens of the saints" (Ephesians 2:19–22).

Walther's messages reiterate that God is at work in us through the Holy Spirit. He is cleansing our sins through Jesus Christ, our Lord and Savior. Just as it was for Luther, so Walther saw sin and grace in terms of Galatians 2:16: "Knowing that a man is not justified by the works of the Law but by faith in Jesus Christ, even we have believed in Christ Jesus, that we might be justified by faith in Christ and not by the works of the Law; for by the works of the Law no flesh will be justified."

Walther affirmed that one can always tell whether a religion is false, misleads its adherents, and destroys salvation. It does so when man is expected to contribute to or earn his own salvation. Such a religion does not give glory to God alone. Walther stated distinctly that:

> Everything has already been done; you are already redeemed; you have already been made righteous before God; you have already been saved. You therefore do not have to do anything to redeem yourself; you do not have to reconcile God to yourself; you do not have to earn your salvation. Only believe that Christ, the Son of God, has done all this in your stead; and by means of this faith you are a participant in this salvation. Being saved by faith means [being] saved through the righteousness of Another, namely Christ, whose righteousness becomes man's personal possession. In that the Lutheran Church ascribes the reconciliation and redemption of all men to God alone,

and totally denies man's participation or cooperation in this, it also in this teaching gives all glory to God alone.[14]

As long as we continue to feel that we must merit our salvation, we rob God of His glory. Sometimes we also believe, Walther reminds us, that by attending church we work up some merit so that God loves us a bit more. It is then that we mistake what worship is; it is not man-centered, but it is God serving us. He is the subject and the center of our worship. He comes to us with His Word and sacraments, and showers us with His righteousness and forgiveness. That is the heart and soul of the Gospel. God is giving and keeps on giving to us. Walther repeatedly warned that we are not to rob God of His glory:

> Man is required to do nothing, absolutely nothing, to become righteous before God; he is only to believe, that is, to appropriate by faith the righteousness that is acceptable before God. That is the correct doctrine. Remember: God did not create man as a *tabula rasa* [clean slate] and then watch and wait to see what would become of him. Man was not neutral after creation, but perfect. God Himself said: "It was very good" [Genesis 1:31]. God had created man with innate righteousness, a holy will, clear understanding, enlightened intellect, pure love for God and the neighbor. Man was not first to become righteous, but God had made him righteous at his creation. What will God now do after man has so horribly wasted it and now lies filthy, torn, and ragged in his blood in the mud? Will He call to him: "Rise, you dead one, you sick one, you sinner, you reprobate and become a better man"? No, certainly not! God creates everything, so He also recreates for man the righteousness which He had created in Adam but which man in Adam had lost. Upon this grace the human race is to rely in faith.[15]

The illustrations Walther used are easy to understand. When he presented his position on reconciliation, redemption, and justification, he emphasized that faith is not the condition under which we are justified but much rather the means by which we become partakers of justification. He illustrated:

> The situation is about the same with a beggar. Would he not be surprised if we said: "I'll give you something, but only with the provision that you extend your hand and take it"? He wishes nothing more fervently than that we give him the gift. That he would extend his hand to take it is self-evident. This is the only way he can receive it. One can see the doctrine of justification correctly only when one consid-

ers faith as merely the hand with which one appropriates the offered justification.[16]

In his essay Walther also came to grips with Lutheran preaching and teaching. Is it too easy in the Lutheran church to hear about this justification in which God does it all through Christ? Walther responded:

The accusation that we Lutheran pastors announce the forgiveness of sins to all, regardless whether people repent or not, is unfounded. We pastors cannot search hearts. Forgiveness has been wrought also for the unrepentant. Only unbelief keeps justification from being effective in their case. It is therefore not that God views our faith, nor that He elected us because we believe, since He has elected us only by His grace. Thus our Lutheran Church proves also in this respect to be the true one, since it teaches that it is God alone who justifies us. Justification is not something that occurs in our heart, but it occurs in God. Sanctification occurs in us. Justification is a judicial act of God, in which He absolves the sinner from guilt and punishment and declares him justified.[17]

Justification was the center of Walther's theology. He was not averse to addressing the contemporary theologies, particularly within the Christian church, that were so prevalent during his time and also in our own "Post-Modern" age. Walther vehemently denied that man has any ability whatsoever to come to faith or make a decision for Christ. Man does not even have the ability to choose between heaven or hell. Even that robs God of His glory. Walther spoke of man's inability to turn to God:

They forget that one has to be alive in order to possess and make use of any powers at all. Just look at a stick or a stone and imagine one could breathe all sorts of powers into it—the stone would not even care about such powers, things would remain just the way they always were. Powers presuppose something that can use powers. Thus man would already have to be converted in order to convert himself. He would have to be awake in order to wake himself. He would have to be renewed in order to renew himself. That is obviously nonsense. No, when man is far enough along to make use of the powers of grace, then he is already converted. Then God has already decided for him, given him a new heart and regeneration by the Holy Spirit. Then he is already awakened in the biblical sense.

We stress "in the biblical sense," because the word "awakening" is often greatly misunderstood. Pietists think of it as a middle ground, where a person is no longer completely dead spiritually, but not exactly alive either. That is a lot of foolishness, for there is no middle ground between life and death. Either someone is still dead in sin, or he is awakened out of that death. If he is awakened, then he is alive; and if alive, then he is a new, spiritual, converted person. Consequently, Scripture does not distinguish between conversion, awakening, and regeneration. In one instance, it describes this great, mysterious work of grace one way; in another instance another way.[18]

LAW AND GOSPEL

Walther was extremely anxious to lecture on the distinction between Law and Gospel. He prepared convention essays on this subject twice. The first was for the newly-created Iowa District in 1880. Walther was unable to attend this convention personally, but he prepared thirteen theses on the subject. In his absence, Francis Pieper delivered an essay on the basis of these theses. Walther expanded on them during the "Luther Hour" lectures which he gave in the *Aula* or Baier *Lehrsaal* of the St. Louis seminary from September 12, 1884 to November 6, 1885. Walther's *The Proper Distinction between Law and Gospel* (known simply as *Law and Gospel*) and C. P. Krauth's *The Conservative Reformation and Its Theology* are considered to be two of the greatest Lutheran theological books produced in America.

Although these lectures were delivered in the 1880s, every student at Concordia Seminary, St. Louis is still required today to read *Law and Gospel*. Many consider this one of the greatest theological legacies Walther left to his church. Here Walther opens up an understanding of the Bible. To be able to make the necessary distinction between the Law on the one hand and the Gospel on the other, Walther called "the highest art in Christianity." So many of the errors that are made with respect to an understanding and application of Holy Scripture come through a confusion of Law and Gospel.

Law and Gospel was originally published in a German edition in 1897. The stenographic notes for that volume were taken by a student, Th. Claus. The first English translation was rendered by W. H. T. Dau (1864–1944), a former member of the St. Louis seminary faculty. At the time of the preparation of this edition, he served as president of Valparaiso University, Valparaiso, Indiana. Concordia Publishing House published a new edition of Dau's translation, the fourteenth printing, in 1986.

In his seventh evening lecture in 1884, Walther discussed thesis three and emphasized the importance of distinguishing between Law and Gospel in one's studies of Scripture:

If you will consider that it is only in the school of the Holy Spirit and of genuine Christian experience that the proper distinction between Law and Gospel is learned, you can easily perceive how it is possible that a person may be a graduate of all schools in existence and yet not have acquired this art.[19]

A week later, Walther explained that a deep knowledge of the Bible does not alone enable one to distinguish between Law and Gospel:

However, while the historical-grammatical meaning of Scripture can readily be opened up by anyone who understands its language, it is impossible without the Holy Spirit for anyone to understand the Holy Scriptures unto his salvation, no matter how great a linguist, how famous a philologist, how keen a logician he may be. ... Now, the primary requisite for a salutary knowledge of the Holy Scriptures is the correct understanding of the distinction between Law and Gospel.[20]

When discussing thesis four, Walther continued in the same vein:

The matter of paramount importance, of course, will always be this, that you have experienced this distinction upon yourself. I am not referring to those among you who have never been in anguish over their sins, who consider themselves orthodox because they have been reared in Christian homes. I am referring to those who are concerned about their salvation. There will be moments when such of you will imagine that you are God's children. Again, there will be times when you think your sins have not been forgiven you. If on such occasions you desire genuine peace, it can come to you only through the knowledge of the distinction between Law and Gospel.[21]

Towards the end of this series, when he presented the twenty-fifth and final thesis, Walther made the observation that the Gospel must at all times have predominance over the Law.

True, we have to preach the Law, only, however, as a preparation for the Gospel. The ultimate aim in our preaching of the Law must be to preach the Gospel. Whoever does not adopt this aim is not a true minister of the Gospel.[22]

When you preach, do not be stingy with the Gospel; bring its consolations to all, even to the greatest sinners. When they are terrified by the wrath of God and hell, they are fully prepared to receive the Gospel. True, this goes against our reason; we think it strange that such knaves are to be comforted immediately; we imagine they ought to be made to suffer much greater agony in their conscience. Fanatics adopt the method in dealing with alarmed sinners; but a genuine Bible theologian resolves to preach the Gospel and faith in Jesus Christ to a person whom God has prepared for such preaching by His Law.[23]

How wonderful it would be if we could have heard him make this excellent comparison:

> Now, do not merely listen to this statement of the apostle [1 Corinthians 15:3—that Christ died for our sins] but think of the time when you will be the pastor of a congregation, and make a vow to God that you will adopt the apostle's method, that you will not stand in your pulpit sad-faced, as if you were bidding men to come to a funeral, but like men that go wooing a bride or announcing a wedding. If you do not mingle Law with the Gospel you will always mount your pulpit with joy. People will notice that you are filled with joy because you are bringing the blessed message of joy to your congregation.[24]

The distinction was of utmost importance to Walther not only in proclaiming the Gospel, but in applying it to the lives of people. According to Walther, Gospel preaching can never be overdone:

> Now, the preacher may come to the conclusion that he has preached too much Gospel to them and must adopt a different policy; he must hush the Gospel for a while and preach nothing but the Law, and conditions will improve. But he is mistaken; the people do not change, except that they become very angry with their minister for not permitting them to do what they very much like to do. ... He resolves to give these people hell and damnation next Sunday. ... Neither does God love service rendered under coercion. Preachers who have succeeded in abolishing certain evils by the preaching of the Law must not think that they have achieved something great. Even the most corrupt congregation can be improved, however, by nothing else than the preaching of the Gospel in all its sweetness.[25]

In his theses on Law and Gospel, Walther pointed out that there were twenty-one ways in which they are not properly divided, or are confused. Because this can happen so easily, he urged that they be studied and reviewed by pastors repeatedly.

CHURCH AND MINISTRY

The following pages take up the literature Walther produced on the doctrine of church and ministry, which is another spoke in the wheel of doctrine. It is perhaps the most widely discussed and controversial subject in the church today. Because it is such a timely topic, Walther's views are extremely important for us today.

Some have assumed Walther taught that the "Missouri Synod" was the only true church on earth—the *Una Sancta*. In response, Walther warned in his evening lectures on *Law and Gospel*:

> May God keep you from becoming entangled with this false teaching concerning the Church, viz., that the Lutheran Church is the true visible church of Jesus Christ in the sense that one can be saved *only in this church!* [emphasis his]. The Lutheran Church is indeed the true visible church; however, only in this sense, that it has the pure, unadulterated truth. As soon as you add the qualification "alone saving" to the Lutheran Church, you detract from the doctrine of justification by grace through faith in Jesus Christ and confound Law and Gospel. May God keep you from this error for the sake of your own soul and those that will be entrusted to your care![26]

The consternation of the Saxon immigrants under the rule of Martin Stephan caused Walther and his fellow immigrants to dig deeply into the biblical teaching on the issue of church and ministry. The community realized that Stephan's claim to be the supreme ruler in all secular and spiritual matters was wrong.

In a similar vein, the controversy with J. A. A. Grabau (1804–1879) and the Buffalo Synod also created severe problems. Grabau, for example, taught that the power of the sacraments does not rest upon the Word alone, but that the true ministerial office must also be present. He maintained that the Office of the Keys does not belong to the congregation but to the ministry. This led to his insistence that "ordination has been permanently commanded by the apostles for the entire church, and in that sense is to be considered as a command of the Holy Ghost, as a divine command." But what was still worse is that Grabau taught that "the congregation owes obedience to its pastor, not only when he teaches God's Word, but also in things which are not contrary to God's Word according to Article 28 of the Augsburg Confession."[27] In this way, the office of the holy ministry was exalted by men, far beyond God's Word. In fact, Grabau described the polity of the Missouri Synod as "Anabaptistic, democratic stupidity."[28] After discussing the differences between the Buffalo and the Missouri Synods on church and ministry, twelve congregations and pastors of the Buffalo Synod joined the Missouri Synod. The remaining six divided into two groups, each claiming that they constituted the original Buffalo Synod. Christian Hochstetter, the author of the first major history of the Missouri Synod, left the Buffalo Synod in 1867 and joined the Missouri Synod.

In contrast to Grabau's errors, W. F. Hoefling believed that the ministry was a mere human arrangement. Walther taught that it had been established by God. Thus another dimension was added to the discussion.

Because of the doctrinal disagreements regarding church and ministry, in 1850 the Missouri Synod asked Walther to produce a treatise on the subject. Walther's book, entitled *Kirche und Amt* (Church and Ministry), was published in 1852, but the English translation by J. T. Mueller did not appear until 1987.[29]

Many discussions have been held in The Lutheran Church—Missouri Synod on the impact *Church and Ministry* has had on the church. The title page of the first edition, published in Erlangen, Germany in 1852, declares that it is "the voice of our church in the question of church and ministry." The Foreword goes on to state:

> Hence, the synodical convention held in St. Louis in the fall of 1850 asked this writer [Walther] to compose the present book. Its contents were presented to the synodical convention, held the next year at Milwaukee, either literally or substantially, and after they had been examined and respectively revised, it was resolved to publish the manuscript "in our name and as our unanimous confession" [that of the Missouri Synod].[30]

In considering the spokes of the church and its ministry on Walther's doctrinal wheel, we will refer to several other books he produced on this topic. The first was *The Form of a Christian Congregation*, which originally appeared in 1863. *The Form of a Christian Congregation* was the practical application of the role of the local congregation, providing a working agenda for all areas of its concern. Walther summarized the objectives of the book:

> In conclusion, the reader might be reminded that this work offers no untried new experiment in church polity, but that it represents a church organization which is in existence here for twenty-four years already and in which God's grace is not inconsiderable, annually increasing number of congregations, firmly united in one faith and confession and also outwardly joined in the works of [Christian] love, have been edified with richest blessings and are being edified today.[31]

The Form of a Christian Congregation, together with Walther's essay at the Iowa District convention in 1879, "Duties of an Evangelical Lutheran

Synod," go hand-in-hand. Here Walther emphasized that the Lutheran Confessions cement congregations together. To maintain that cohesion, faithful pastors and teachers subscribe to these historic Confessions as well.[32]

Walther enumerated a number of theses, spelling out the duties of the Synod. Those duties include, among others, the necessity to:

> Faithfully treat the congregations in an evangelical way … not assume a dictatorial role over them … assist them in acquiring upright pastors and teachers … protect them against pastors who err in doctrine, follow an offensive life-style, and are domineering in their office.[33]

In addition, he stated that a Synod must support its pastors and teachers, promote knowledge of congregational members in the truth in every possible way, strive for peace and unity in the truth and finally be intent on the growth of Christ's kingdom and the salvation of souls. The essay is extremely valuable and ought to be reviewed by congregations regularly.

Throughout Walther's writings, he repeatedly emphasized that the power of the keys belongs to the local congregation, as does the power to elect, call, and ordain pastors.

In other theses of *The Form of a Christian Congregation*, Walther emphasized the care for the poor, fellowship with orthodox congregations, congregational meetings, the scope of congregational decisions, calling a pastor, and the rites pertaining to the Sacraments of Baptism and Holy Communion. The congregation also has responsibilities when sickness and death occur and in providing Christian education. It is a vast agenda for the parish.

Elders are a necessity in the congregation, to serve as overseers. It is also the congregation's responsibility to introduce to its members only doctrinally pure books, such as hymnals, catechisms, and church and school books.

The Office of the Keys, to which Walther devoted 17 pages, speaks of impenitent and stubborn sinners, heretical errors of faith, excommunication in the congregation after a thorough examination, admonition, and review. "The congregation shall by a unanimous resolution put out of the congregation or publicly excommunicate through the minister of the Word."[34] If there are those "who do not agree to such an excommunication the congregation shall deal according to Christian discipline."[35] But a penitent person who has been excommunicated is to receive reinstatement as a member of the congregation.[36]

In thesis thirty-one, Walther emphasized the proper call of a pastor and also the seriousness of ending or terminating the call. There is no hint or provision for the "hire and fire" mentality.

> Congregations shall not be so presumptuous as arbitrarily to depose their pastors and others who administer an ecclesiastical office. But if they fall into pernicious errors and are found guilty by lawful procedure … and refuse to accept instruction from God's Word either by the congregation or by the pastors called for this purpose; or if they become manifest as contumacious impenitent sinners; or if they have committed an offense by which they have lost their good report among those who are without and by which they cause the enemies of the Lord to blaspheme, then Christian congregations in Christian order (to which under circumstances belongs a provisional suspension) must remove them from office as such as God Himself has put out.[37]

On religious unionism, Walther expressed his strong opposition in this way:

> Lastly, the congregation shall also see to it that neither the congregation nor individual church members enter into any church union with unbelievers or heterodox communions and so become guilty of religious unionism in matters of faith and church.[38]

It is difficult to determine what the "heterodox" communions are. Walther explained that the heterodox are those who "believe, teach, and confess" in opposition to God's Word and the Lutheran Confessions.[39]

Walther's *The True Visible Church* enlarges upon the "Altenburg Theses" of April 1841. This series of essays was begun at the Synodical Convention in St. Louis in 1866 and was continued at various district conventions up through 1871. A published volume appears under this title in 1867.[40]

Perhaps in no other work, except in the controversy on predestination, has Walther been more misunderstood than in his book *The True Visible Church*. For example, the *Lutheran Observer* incorrectly concluded that "the name Missouri has the meaning of being the only true Lutherans on earth!"[41] Nothing could be farther from the truth. When one reads the theses of this essay carefully, it is apparent that when Walther spoke about the "true visible church,"—that is, the church which the human eye can see—he specifically referred to the "Evangelical Lutheran Church." He never equated this with "Missouri." It is almost a generic use of the term. He defined it, as in the Altenburg debate, in Thesis 10:

> The Evangelical Lutheran Church is the sum total of all who without reservation profess the doctrine which was restored by Luther's

Reformation and was in summary submitted in writing to the emperor of the realm at Augsburg in 1530, and was treated and expounded in other so-called Lutheran symbols as the pure doctrine of the divine word.[42]

Immediately in the next thesis, Walther protested against equating the Evangelical Lutheran Church with the *Una Sancta*, the one holy Christian church outside of which there is no salvation. This needs to be emphasized because of the mistaken notions that have appeared over the years.

The Evangelical Lutheran Church bases all its teachings on the Word of God as the "sole and perfect source, rule, and norm, and the judge of all doctrine."[43] The marks of the church are "pure Gospel-preaching and unadulterated administration of the holy sacraments. Then it is the true visible church of God on earth."[44] Walther asserted that although churches may be polluted with errors, "one may still find true believers and hence members of the true visible church. ... Scripture calls even such visible communions 'churches' as are guilty of partial deviation from the pure Word of God as long as they retain God's Word essentially."[45]

Walther rarely used the term "denomination," as we are accustomed to when speaking of the various Christian churches. Nevertheless, he taught that it is possible that hypocrites and wicked people may be found in these "churches." He used the terms "sects" (*Sekte*) or "separatist bodies" (*Rotte*) of those churches where unity has been disrupted through doctrinal errors, personalities, or ceremonies, which have not destroyed the foundation of faith.[46]

ELECTION OF GRACE

The doctrine of election deeply disturbed Lutheranism in America and specifically The Lutheran Church—Missouri Synod in the late 1870s and early 1880s.[47] We have already noted this in chapter 3, but we will now look at it in more detail. The doctrine of election is another spoke in Walther's doctrinal wheel.

No internal controversy in the Synod was as violent, disturbing, and draining as the controversy on election of grace. The German term *Gnadenwahl* means "election of grace" and indicates that we are elected by God's grace alone. The opponents in this controversy believed that a minimal spark of activity, contributed by man, was essential for one's salvation. The controversy revolved mainly around this point, although countless books, pamphlets and other literature were written on the subject covering every facet imaginable.

Questions such as the following were asked: Does God save man arbitrarily? Does man contribute anything to his salvation? Does God do it all, while man does nothing? Does God expect man to "push" his salvation along? Walther, with his emphasis on justification by faith through Christ without the deeds of the Law, held that it is God who is exclusively responsible for our individual salvation.

In view of this, the term "predestination" is not a desirable term to use when discussing this issue. Predestination often has a Calvinistic connotation that God has decreed some to everlasting joy while others are decreed to eternal damnation. It is the question that has disturbed the church throughout the ages: "*Cur alii prae aliis?*" (Why are some saved in preference to others?). Walther consistently maintained that while God has elected some to grace, He absolutely did not determine that some are relegated to hell. Holy Scripture declares in no uncertain terms that man is saved solely by the grace of God through faith in our Lord Jesus Christ. On the other hand, Scripture also tells us that it is solely by the action of rejecting Christ and His salvific work that unbelievers are doomed to hell.

All of Walther's literature on the doctrine of predestination was written in German. One man who made a big difference in making Walther's works available in English was John Humberger[48] (1840–1907) who translated Walther's pamphlet "Doctrine concerning Election."[49] In this pamphlet Walther pointed out how extremely difficult it was for Lutherans in America when they had to deal with the doctrine of predestination. He wrote:

> God has imposed upon our American Lutheran church the difficult task, by the controversy which has broken out on predestination, to contend for one of the most mysterious doctrines of His Word, to judge which no human reasoners, no idle, curious, vainglorious spirits, no indifferent false Christians, but only true, enlightened, humble Christians being concerned about their salvation, who tremble before God's Word, are sufficient and capable.[50]

Walther's position on election was based on Scripture. He believed firmly that man cannot, even under the most marvelous circumstances, contribute anything to his salvation. His sinful nature has condemned him in God's eyes, but the sacrifice of God's Son, our Lord Jesus Christ, has brought eternal forgiveness. We are saved by grace alone, without the deeds of the Law. Consequently, for Walther, when a person is saved, it is a matter of giving all glory to God alone without granting even the smallest credit to man's ability to help God along with his salvation.[51]

In spite of the fact that Walther viewed the continuum of faith from Pentecost to the present, and often quoted the church fathers on their support of scriptural or biblical doctrines, he did not quote the Post-Reformation fathers in this controversy. This was because the term *intuitu fidei* (in view of faith) had at times been thoughtlessly or improperly used. Thus Walther searched the Scriptures for an answer and bounded right over the early church fathers and dogmaticians.[52] The term *intuitu fidei* allowed the idea that if an individual tried a little harder, perhaps God would see him or her as having faith, thus being worthy of election. Walther denied that man was capable of doing anything to attract God's attention through Christ or that he could contribute even a farthing on his way to Christ. The term "in view of faith" was rejected by the Missouri Synod in its "Thirteen Theses," which were adopted by the Synod in 1881.[53]

The Synodical Conference of North America had just been founded in July 1872 when suddenly there was a theological explosion that abruptly ended the halcyon period following its organization. Walther had presented another of his "*Soli Deo Gloria*" essays at the Western District convention in 1877. Three essays in this series, presented between 1877 and 1880, dealt exclusively with the doctrine of predestination.[54] Walther's 1877 essay was severely criticized for the content of thesis two:

> God's eternal election (*Wahl*) not only sees and knows beforehand the salvation of the elect (*Auserwählten*), but by the gracious will and pleasure of God in Christ Jesus is a cause which creates, works, helps, and furthers our salvation and all that pertains to it. Our salvation is so founded on this that the gates of hell cannot prevail against it.[55]

In the same essay Walther affirmed that the cause of God's election (thesis three) is not produced or launched by any action of man, such as:

1. The work of man or his sanctification;
2. Man's proper use of the means of grace;
3. Man's personal decision;
4. Man's longing and prayer;
5. Man's non-resistance;
6. Man's faith.[56]

No protests were made immediately following this presentation. In fact, what did occur was encouraging and exciting. Capital University and Seminary of the Ohio Synod (in fellowship with the Missouri Synod and a fellow member of the Synodical Conference) conferred the degree of

Doctor of Divinity on Walther on January 23, 1878. But a year later, on January 2, 1879, Professor F. A. Schmidt, a former student and colleague of Walther, raised objections to Walther's 1877 essay. Walther did not respond to Schmidt's criticism immediately.[57]

In a letter to J. A. Ottesen[58] dated February 8, 1879, Walther explains why he did not respond to Schmidt's critique earlier. He wrote that Schmidt had not asked for an answer, but had admonished him to come to the right position on the doctrine of election. Walther also mentioned that Schmidt had not referred to any specifics of the essay which he questioned, but only in general condemned the absolute predestination and enlarged on his own position. Walther further said that a full and complete response to the issue could not be handled properly in the scope of a letter. Moreover, Walther feared that Schmidt's threats of attack on the presentation were intended to bring him to his knees to beg for forgiveness.[59]

After a few weeks, Walther admitted that he should have responded to Schmidt's criticism even if only briefly. But by this time Walther thought that his response would be interpreted as an action due to Schmidt's threats. Furthermore, Walther stated that he did not consider Schmidt a false teacher. Yet he opined that if two people in doctrinal disagreement with each other are working together in the same congregation, they cannot do so with blessing because the disagreement will precipitate a schism.

Further complications set in as time went on, and a war of pamphlets soon broke out. Apparently the question of the position of the seventeenth-century dogmaticians was also raised by Schmidt. In the letter referred to above, Walther assured Ottesen that he did not consider the dogmaticians heterodox in the doctrine of election. He hoped that the expression *intuitu fidei* could be understood biblically, but stressed that it should immediately be followed by an explanation. Walther observed that anyone who desires to use that expression may do so, but he should make it very clear that God did not predestine us because of our good will which He had foreseen. Rather, we are saved entirely by grace. That issue became the crux of future discussions.

Walther observed that a wrong understanding of *intuitu fidei* could lead to the highest point of Pelagianism (the heresy that man is not totally depraved), "which we hate in the depth of our heart." Actually, according to Walther, he would rather die than be condemned by the entire world for having tolerated even the most subtle Pelagianism. Such subtle Pelagianism, Walther emphasized, would rob Christ of His crown.

In referring to the criticism of his essay, Walther stated that his words had not simply slipped out, but were the result of serious research in Scripture, the Lutheran Symbols, and the writings of Luther. Walther further noted that he had much earlier treated the doctrine of predestination in this way in his sermon on Septuagesima Sunday, 1852. Unabashedly, he had preached in the identical vein as he had done in his essay on predestination at the Western District in the late 1870s.[60] The text was Matthew 20:1–16.

The situation was bad. Walther had been privately attacked by Schmidt in a letter and regretted that he had not responded to it. So he suggested that the two meet after the Illinois District convention. Also in his letter to Ottesen he wrote:

> I wish nothing more than that a victory can be gained in peace, without hostility and fighting. ...

> Pray for our poor Zion because the devil only has evil in mind against us. May we pray that in the doctrine of election, we will not be wedged apart. Be sure that you study this doctrine properly in Article XI of the Formula ... Greeting you in an unaltered brotherly love, I am your partner in sorrow and member of the kingdom.[61]

Walther did not attend the Illinois District convention as proposed. Instead, he delivered an essay on the certainty of salvation at the Synodical Conference in July. In this essay he again confidently stressed that our sins are forgiven completely through the work of our Lord Jesus Christ. Schmidt and Walther met after the conclusion of this conference to discuss their differences, but nothing was settled.

Anyone who reads the 1879 Western District convention essay which elaborates on predestination will quickly note that Walther did not refer to Schmidt by name.[62] After this unsuccessful meeting between the two, Schmidt, together with some of his supporters, introduced a new publication in January 1880 entitled *Altes und Neues* (of Old and New). The entire controversy was now a public matter.

To consolidate its forces, the Missouri Synod under the newly elected general president, H. C. Schwan, convened a pastoral conference of all clergy in Chicago from September 29 to October 5, 1880. A total of 467 pastors attended. Members of other synods were also present. Only a few weeks later, Walther presented his third essay on predestination at the Western District convention (October 13–19) at St. Paul, Concordia, Missouri.

Another major attempt to resolve the controversy was held in Milwaukee, December 25, 1880 to January 5, 1881 during the Christmas recess. This time all the faculties of the Synodical Conference educational institutions were present. The meeting was convened by Professor P. L. Larsen, newly elected president of the Synodical Conference.

In this Milwaukee conference it was agreed that all discussions should be based completely on Scripture and not on the Confessions or the Reformation theologians. A pivotal passage was Romans 8:29, but very little progress was made because the verb "to foreknow" (*proegnoo*) caused inconclusive discussion. At these sessions, Schmidt declared that he had been commanded by God to wage war. To this Walther replied: "You wish war, you shall have it."[63]

No dialogue, no discussion, no debate assuaged the differences. The Missouri Synod finally disposed of the problem by adopting the "Thirteen Theses" on predestination at its convention in Fort Wayne, Indiana in May 1881.[64] To this day these "Thirteen Theses" are the basis of the Missouri Synod's position on predestination.

Three particular issues were under debate:

1. Is election the cause of faith or vice versa? Walther upheld the position that election is the cause of faith, while those who differed said that God elected those whom He foresaw would come to faith (*intuitu fidei*).

2. What is the relationship between universal grace and particular election? Walther taught that universal grace and particular election (God's choosing certain people for salvation) are two distinct doctrines which dare not be mixed together or confused. Those who differed with him argued that election is subsumed under universal grace.

3. What is the role of man's resistance in all this? Walther asserted that in their unconverted state all human beings resist equally and that the mystery of election cannot be explained by saying that some resist more and others less. If it were a lesser resistance on the part of man to God's salvation, it would be considered synergism. Walther's opponents did not agree.

The Formula of Concord, Solid Declaration, Article 11 is the only Lutheran symbol that treats predestination. A close comparison with Walther's Western District essays of 1879 and 1880 substantiates that Walther followed this article intimately in his presentations. The article itself acknowledges:

> There has been no public, scandalous, and widespread dissension among theologians of the Augsburg Confession concerning the eter-

nal election of the children of God. Nevertheless, this article has become the occasion of very serious controversies at other places and has involved our people also.[65]

The doctrine of predestination is in total opposition to human reason. Walther asserted:

> Admittedly, we can not resolve the apparent contradiction of temporary believers, because we are just poor, miserable creatures. But that shall not move us to reject the clear Word of God and thereby rob us and all Christendom of such an exceedingly comforting doctrine.[66]

It continues to be a mystery. Walther wrestled with this doctrine and said in his 1877 Western District essay:

> We have never had more reason to approach our doctrinal discussion with fear and trembling, and to despair altogether of our reason and all our wisdom as at this time. It is surely one of the most profound mysteries God has revealed to us through His Word, which we are to approach during these next days. The doctrine of predestination touches the very heart of the vast inscrutable mysteries of our salvation, into which the angels desire to look, without being able to fathom it. Oh, what horrible sin we could commit were we to inject our own thinking into the thoughts of God, yea, even pass off our own thoughts as the thoughts of God.[67]

Regrettably, the controversy was not resolved within the Lutheran family in America. Walther continued to proclaim that we must give all glory to God alone in all we believe, teach, and confess. We are justified by faith in Christ without the deeds of the Law.

Scripture and the Confessions

Walther had a high view of the Holy Scriptures, and he confessed the words of the Epitome of the Formula of Concord:

> We believe, teach, and confess that the prophetic and apostolic writings of the Old and New Testaments are the only rule and norm according to which all doctrines and teachers alike must be appraised and judged ... other writings of ancient and modern teachers, whatever their names, should not be put on a par with Holy Scripture. Every single one of them should be subordinated to the Scriptures and should be received in no other way and no further than as witnesses to the fashion in which the doctrine of the prophets and apostles was preserved in post-apostolic times.[68]

This is enunciated also in Article II of the original constitution of The Lutheran Church—Missouri Synod in 1847. There it appeared as a condition of membership: "Acceptance of Holy Scripture, both the Old and the New Testament, as the written word of God and as the only rule and norm of faith and life."[69]

The literature of Walther is firm and consistent. Like orthodox Lutherans of all ages, Walther had the utmost confidence in the inspiration, authority, and reliability of the Bible.

H. H. Walker gives an excellent description of Walther's position:

> Whatever the Bible declares to be the truth, that is truth, though the whole world may declare it to be false; on the other hand, whatever the Bible declares to be false and erroneous, that is false and erroneous though the whole world, yea an angel from heaven, declare it to be correct and true. He [Walther] did not allow human reason and intellect to sit in judgement over or correct truths revealed in the Scriptures. He did not follow church traditions nor listen to alleged new revelations. The Bible alone, the whole Bible, and nothing but the Bible in theology—that was Walther's position in regard to the Bible. Therefore also as to interpreting these Scriptures his principle was: Scripture is to be explained by Scripture, or in other words, the Holy Spirit speaking to us in the Scripture must explain Himself, must be His own interpreter, just as every man must be and is the best interpreter of his own words.[70]

All his life, Walther was a scriptural theologian, a student of the Bible. Present-day Christians might assume that Walther lived in the pre-critical era of Scripture studies. Yet already in his time, liberal scholars were attacking the inspiration and veracity of Scripture. This is one reason Walther remains so interesting and contemporary.

To Walther, Scripture was an eternal foundation built by God through which the Creator was speaking to people from generation to generation in an unchanging, unaltered fashion. Throughout the centuries, Satan and his cohorts have been determined to destroy this foundation. In our present era it may be of interest to note that for Walther the terms "Bible," the "Word of God," and "Scripture" were synonymous. All are names for the one source by which God proclaims His love for all mankind throughout the centuries, centering on Jesus Christ as Savior. This makes it God's great "love letter" for all time.

As early as 1867, Walther wrote a lead article in *Lehre und Wehre*[71] and in it presented four principles of Scripture. These, together with the literature he produced on "canonicity" and biblical interpretation, are the best anchors we have to understand his position on Scripture, which he conveyed to his students and to the entire Synod. With logic and firmness Walther wrote:

1. When we Lutherans speak of the "Scripture principle," or call Scripture the "formal principle" of our church and theology (in contrast to the so-called "material principle," the doctrine of justification by grace alone through faith in Christ) we thereby want to say: 1) That we recognize the canonical Scriptures of the Old and the New Testaments as the only source of our religious or theological knowledge; 2) That we therefore recognize the said writings as the only rule and plum line according to which all doctrines and teachers are to be judged and evaluated, as well as the only judge of all doctrinal controversies.[72]

2. In that we declare the canonical Scriptures of the Old and the New Testaments as our scriptural principle, we reject every other, whether: 1) Reason ... or 2) Tradition ... or 3) New revelations.[73]

3. When we recognize the Scriptures of the Old and New Testaments as our only principle of knowledge, we recognize at the same time: 1) That Holy Scripture, according to content and form, has been inspired by God. ... 2) That Scripture is complete, or that it contains everything for all the people to know and to believe that is sufficient for their salvation. ... 3) That Scripture is clear, or that everything that is necessary to know for salvation and for our godly life is revealed in it, that every alert reader who is of sound mind and knows the language can easily understand it according to its grammatical sense. ...[74]

4. When we declare that the canonical Scriptures of the Old and New Testaments are our only scriptural principle, we recognize that Scripture is not subject to individual or human interpretation ... but is to be interpreted out of itself (*aus sich selbst*).[75]

Strangely, this article is not signed, and therefore we cannot say with absolute certainty that it came from Walther's pen. His usual signature for articles of this type was a "W." But the four principles in thesis form are so identical to all the other Waltherian literature that we do not doubt its authorship.

Theses thirteen to twenty-one of Walther's *The True Visible Church* address the issues of scriptural authority and proper interpretation. This material includes the clearest hermeneutical teaching of Walther available.[76]

Walther stated in thesis thirteen that the Evangelical Lutheran Church recognizes the written word of the apostles and prophets as the sole and perfect source, rule, and norm, and the judge of all doctrine—not reason, not tradition, not new revelations.[77] In his usual fashion, this thesis is expounded in detail.

In thesis fourteen Walther commented that "the Evangelical Lutheran Church professes the perspicuity of Holy Scripture."[78] This leads into a discussion of the dangers of private views injected into scriptural interpretation as well as the issue of "open questions."[79]

Thesis fifteen states that "the Evangelical Lutheran Church recognizes no human interpreter of Holy Scripture whose *ex officio* interpretation must be regarded as infallible and binding; a) not any individual person, b) not any special estate, c) not any special or universal church council, d) not the whole church."[80]

After citations from the Confessions, Walther spoke about the value of the church fathers and how grateful we can be to have their insights. But, he said, these must be disregarded when they interpret Scripture in any way which sets it at variance with itself.

> Thesis sixteen: The Evangelical Lutheran Church accepts God's Word as it interprets itself; A) it leaves the decisions solely to the original text; B) in its interpretation of words and sentences, it adheres to the linguistic usage; C) it recognizes only the literal sense as the true meaning; D) it maintains that there is but one literal sense; E) it is guided in its interpretation by the context and purpose; F) it recognizes that the literal sense may be either the improper or the proper one; however, it does not deviate from the proper meaning of a word or sentence unless Scripture itself forces it to do so, namely, by either the textual circumstances, a parallel passage, or the analogy of faith; G) it interprets the obscure passages in the light of the clear; H) it takes the articles of faith from those passages in which they are expressly taught, and judges according to these all incidental expressions regarding them; I) it rejects from the very outset every interpretation which does not agree with the analogy of faith.[81]

> Thesis seventeen: "The Evangelical Lutheran Church receives the entire Holy Scripture [as God's Word], regarding nothing set forth in it as superfluous or unimportant, but everything as necessary and weighty; it accepts also all doctrines which necessarily follow from the Scripture words.[82]

Simply stated, Walther emphasized that Scripture is the only source of doctrine, that the Bible interprets itself, that the literal sense is the true sense of any passage, that the Word of God is infallible, that it is perspicuous, and that the context determines the meaning. But the dominating principle of understanding Scripture and its central message is justification of the sinner by faith alone through Christ. All other doctrines are merely the spokes around this hub.

One of the *Lutherstunden* (Luther Hours) lectures which Walther presented in the Baier Lecture Hall on Friday evenings from 1878 to 1879 deals with the divine origin (*Göttlichkeit*) of the Christian religion. Some of the theses presented at that time dealt with Holy Scripture. Toward the close of the presentation, Walther mentioned a series of lacunae or gaps that have crept into the biblical text and asked how this is possible if the Bible is God's Word. There are, he contended, many good practical answers. Walther's point was that students at the time were facing unbelief, doubt, and rationalism. But it was their job to continue to preach justification by faith and let the seeming scriptural inconsistencies take care of themselves.

In his 1873 Western District essay on the *Soli Deo Gloria* theme, Walther expounds on the statement in the Apology, Article IV, "Do they suppose that these words fell from the Holy Spirit unaware?[83]

> One needs to remember while reading Scripture that the Holy Spirit has inspired Scripture and has set down everything deliberately. Here our church confesses that every word, every sentence structure, every repetition of any word, every abbreviation, the entire manner and method of speaking has its origin in the Holy Spirit, who has inspired everything, not only the truths, not only the meanings, not only the "what" but also the "how," who has selected the words necessary so that the mind of God would be correctly revealed to us. That it is the teaching of Holy Scripture itself is clear to every Christian …

> It is not Isaiah, not Moses, not Paul who is speaking; but it is the Holy Spirit who is speaking. To a human being it will happen on occasion that he will unwittingly make a somewhat incorrect statement. But this never happens to the Holy Spirit. In short, this passage shows that the doctrine of the inspiration of Scripture as set forth in the seventeenth century by our venerable dogmaticians is already inherent in the symbolical books.[84]

Biblical criticisms, challenges to the doctrine of inspiration which occurred during Walther's lifetime and have escalated since that time, did not alter Walther's views. In a most interesting article in *Lehre und Wehre*, Walther took on these challenges.[85] He said that all the intellectual discoveries and elements of the day—whether in astronomy, physics, geography, or ethnography—had not in any way diminished his faith in Christ. The challenges of such men as Albrecht Benjamin Ritschl (1822–1889), the Goettingen University professor who denied the veracity of Scripture and original sin, or Christoph Ernst Luthardt (1823–1902), of Leipzig University, with whom Walther ran an ongoing doctrinal battle in their respective periodicals, should not disturb us.

In *Lehre und Wehre*, Walther reported on the debates held in Europe on the authority of Scripture.[86] The debates covered not only "higher criticism" but also the canon insofar as it impinged on inspiration. Walther observed that the modern theologians dealt with Scripture as though it had been a great secret, only for the elite. Common folks knew very little about it. Walther commented:

> Without a doubt these gentlemen (*Herren*) thought that even the non-theologians had advanced enough so that they could endure the rather glaring light that the Scriptures were full of errors. It appears, however, that these gentlemen miscalculated that also. Believing Christians in the East Sea provinces [where the discussions had been held] are the least likely ready for such wisdom. They became deeply disappointed, totally disturbed because they thought that up to now they still had a sincerely believing theological faculty [at Dorpat], but this dream has also been exploded.[87]

How did Walther express himself on the Antilegomena? This term historically has been applied to some books of the New Testament which had been questioned as being Scripture, while the Homologoumena had been universally accepted. In the 1850s this issue became a knotty problem because Georg Albert Schieferdecker had based some of his millenialist views on the book of Revelation. In response, K. A. W. Roebbelen wrote in *Der Lutheraner* criticizing Schieferdecker for basing any doctrine on Antilegomena.[88] Walther followed up in *Lehre und Wehre* by discussing whether it was heretical to question the canonicity of parts of the New Testament.[89] Walther basically followed Martin Chemnitz (1522–1586), affirming that the church does not have the authority to decide what is canonical and what is not. Scripture authenticates itself.

For Walther, Scripture was always the inspired Word of God. Although it was not popular in the early part of his life in America, Walther continued to uphold the position that the Lutheran Confessions were the *norma normata* (normed norm) as normed by Scripture, which is the *norma normans* (norming norm). Scripture is the absolute norm of faith while the Confessions are a secondary norm.

Walther lived during the period of Lutheran history in America when the authority of the Lutheran Confessions had reached the absolute rock bottom. This was due to several factors. One of the most significant was the language transition. The majority of Lutheran immigrants in colonial America had read and spoke German. Gradually, as they became acclimated to their communities, they became Americanized and increasingly used the English language. This happened at a time when very little of the confessional writings of the Lutheran church in the *Book of Concord* had been translated into English. This was also true of other German theological literature, much of which originally had been written in Latin. Tragically, Lutheran clergymen who had become anglicized could use neither the German nor Latin languages. This was just as true of the people in the pews. Realistically, this served Lutheranism in America from its European roots. Lutherans were soon homogenized with other American churches.

By 1851, the Henkels of the Tennessee Synod had produced an English translation of the entire Book of Concord.[90] But it was too late. The Lutheran Confessions had fallen into evil days.

It was Samuel S. Schmucker (1799–1873), professor of the theological seminary at Gettysburg, Pennsylvania, who searched for a theological document to which all Lutherans could subscribe. Thus, at a time when the Augsburg Confession had become largely unknown and in the course of a changing Lutheran theological basis, Schmucker and his friends produced the Definite Synodical Platform in 1855. Significant shifts included modifying the sacrament of Baptism and the Sacrament of the Altar. Schmucker anticipated that Americanized Lutherans would subscribe to it even with its altered theology. Only a few Lutherans accepted the Platform, however, while some ignored it and still others completely rejected it.[91]

To these changes Walther expended efforts to return Lutheranism to a confessional basis and renewed biblical studies. He had written two articles in which he forcefully urged that subscription to the Lutheran Confessions was essential for a Lutheran. The first appeared in *Der Lutheraner*, and was entitled "Why Should We, Even in This Day, Hold Unflinchingly to the Confessional Writings of Our Evangelical Lutheran Church?"[92] A second article was presented as an essay to the Western District, meeting in St. Louis in April 1858. The essay was entitled "Why Should Our Pastors, Teachers, and Professors Subscribe Unconditionally to the Symbolical Writings of Our Church?"[93] Here Walther argued:

Accordingly, as far as the primary purpose of a symbol is concerned, this is the intention: 1) that in it the church clearly and distinctly confesses its faith and teaching before the whole world, 2) that the church may thereby be distinguished from all heterodox communions and sects, and 3) that the church may have a unanimous, definite, and common norm and form of teaching for its ministers out of which and according to which all other writings and teachings that are offered for test and adoption can and should be judged and regulated. If the church requires of its ministers only a conditional acceptance of its symbols, 1) it thereby publicly retracts that it really has the faith and doctrine which it has there set forth, its alleged confession is not really its confession, and it can therefore justly be charged with duplicity and merely deceiving the world with its symbols. Moreover, by demanding only a conditional subscription to its symbols from its ministers 2) the church does not distinguish itself through its symbols from heterodox sects but places itself (with its symbols which admittedly contain errors) on the same level as the sects. In this case 3) it lacks a unanimous, definite, and common norm and form of teaching according to which everybody can both criticize his own teaching and judge all other writings and teachings.

There is a second thing that pertains to the purpose on whose account the church requires of its ministers that they subscribe to its symbols. This is 1) that the church may assure itself that those who wish to exercise a ministry in it really have the same orthodox understanding of the Scriptures and the same pure and unadulterated faith as the church itself possesses, and 2) that the church may obligate them by a solemn promise to proclaim this faith purely and plainly or to renounce the ministry in its midst, that is, either not to undertake it or, if one is already in it, to give it up rather than by false teaching to disturb the church and mislead its members. This purpose of confessional subscription on the part of ministers of the church is completely nullified, however, if the ministers are required to confess adherence to the symbols of the church only on a conditional basis. For when the church openly admits to its ministers that its symbols may contain doctrines which are contrary to the Scriptures, 1) it gives up the means of assuring itself concerning the faith of the subscriber through his subscription and 2) it thereby cancels the obligation of its ministers to proclaim the Word of God purely and without adulteration according to the symbols of the church as its doctrinal norm.[94]

With deep insight, Walther offered a summary of the effects Pietism and Rationalism had on confessional subscription:

Only with the appearance of Pietism in the Lutheran church was there an attempt here and there to express the subscription formula in a conditional way. The seed for it lay already in Spener's explanation, yet Spener still expressed himself rather cautiously. ...

Then when the rationalists finally came, they impudently tore down the already undermined bulwarks of the church and planted the banner of their reason and so-called "common sense" on the ruins. If our church, which is now lying in the dust, is to rise again, and if a church is not gradually to come into existence which has the semblance of a church but possesses nothing of the church of the Reformation except the name "Lutheran," there is no use in all the loud shouting about churchliness, in even the most precise restoration of ancient ceremonies and external customs, in the investment of the ministry with special glory and power. Nothing will help except an ever-renewed and more vital appropriation of the old, orthodox symbols of the church and an unconditional renewal of our confession of the same.[95]

Walther argued with those who said the Confessions were a coercion of faith, "A chain upon the spirit and the children's shoes of the past," and consequently must be abandoned in an enlightened age. He also met the criticism that the Confessions were "colored glasses through which a person sees the Bible," "polluted channels through which divine truth is not brought" in its purity, "but muddied through the mixing of human error." To all this Walther responded:

These are the objections which might well cause one who doesn't know to fall. But if they're carefully examined, we see that they are not valid. The fact that the church expects all its members to accept the symbols is called the coercion of faith. But who in all the world is forced to become a member of our church? Isn't that left to the individual? Isn't it his own right to join or not to join? And to separate himself from us or to remain with us? Where is the coercion? ...

Actually, for three hundred years the Lutheran church has been accused of insisting too rigidly, too firmly, on the symbols, on the very letters of Holy Scripture, but seldom has anyone dared to say—and never has anyone been able to prove—that they have departed from the Scriptures. If therefore we fell away from the teachings of the Symbols, we should not be falling away from the word of men, but from the Word of God. We should not be denying Luther, but Christ. We should not only cease to be true Lutherans but also yield the right to be called Christians. ...

Should we dissolutely throw away the fruit of the Reformation, the booty of the thousand-year-old battle of the whole Christian church, the spiritual inheritance of our spiritual fathers? Would we actually faithlessly surrender to our enemies, and sacrifice to the indifference of our times, what countless martyrs shed their blood for and what the church, after enduring the most terrible persecutions, has as its trophy of victory?[96]

With firm conviction Walther went on to encourage confessionalism:

Oh, let us, then ... be on our guard against those who refuse to build on the building of the church's past but would build something new. Consider what the apostle wrote in Ephesians 4—that there is one body, one faith, one Baptism, hence also one true church and one correct doctrine, which does not have need to be found for the first time, but which always was and will continue unchanged until the end of days, so that all new doctrines and new churches are false doctrines and false churches ... thus we participate in the victory of all true contenders for the unadulterated Word of God and become fellow heirs to the full blessings of the Reformation.[97]

In a work entitled *Der Innere Gang des Deutschen Protestantismus*, written by K. F. A. Kahnis (1814–1888), professor at the University of Leipzig, the author proposed various innovations on the inspiration of Scripture. In reviewing this book, Walther voiced his strong reactions as follows:

We must confess that we were dismayed when we read [the attacks made upon the inspiration of Scripture]. Who will want to join hands with a new theology which claims to be a legitimate development of the old Lutheran theology that abandons the doctrine of the principle of theology, that of Holy Scripture, of the *ratio formalis scripturae* [the formal principle of Scripture], that which constitutes the very essence of Scripture?[98]

There is a significant quotation from Walther's 1873 essay at the Western District convention on the topic of *Soli Deo Gloria*:

The Savior Himself tells the apostles that the Holy Spirit will reveal the "how" and "what" they are to preach (Matthew 10:19–20). The apostle also speaks "in words ... taught by the Spirit" (1 Corinthians 2:13), and the prophets without exception state when they begin to write: "The Lord is speaking!" And when the New Testament quotes the Old Testament, it also states: "The Holy Spirit spoke" (Mark 12:36; Acts 1:16, 28:25, etc.). The apostle Paul testifies that all Scripture is inspired by God. He does not say, "the Word of God" but "all Scripture." Exactly as the holy men have written it, so the Holy Spirit inspired it. That our Lutheran church believed and confessed this already in the sixteenth century is proved by the reference, among others, quoted from the Apology [Apol IV, 107]. Anyone who pledges himself to the symbolical books and permits himself to be installed into the ministry and does not believe this teaching is a miserable scoundrel.[99]

From its first edition to the current one, the LCMS Constitution has emphasized that both the Old and the New Testaments of Scripture are "the written Word of God" and "the only rule and norm of faith and of practice."[100]

In the article previously quoted in which Walther wrote on confessional subscription, he observes the relationship between Scripture and the Lutheran Confessions. He termed the Bible God's confession to us while the Symbols are our confessions to God.

> The Bible is the question of God to men: Do you believe My Word? The symbolical writings are the answer of men: Yes, Lord, we believe what You say! The Bible is the chest in which all treasures of wisdom and the knowledge of God lie hidden. The symbolical writings are the jewel room in which the church has deposited as in a spiritual store room all the treasures which in the course of hundreds of years she has with great effort drawn and dug out of the treasury of the Bible. The Bible with its teachings is the handwriting of God concerning our salvation, which Satan always wishes to falsify and declare as unauthentic. The symbolical writings contain the records which have been laid down, from which one can see how the church has believed these teachings from time to time and has ever held fast to them.[101]

This is the best description of Walther's position on the relationship between Scripture and the Lutheran Confessions.

NOTES

[1] C. F. W. Walther, *Essays for the Church* (St. Louis: Concordia Publishing House, 1992), Vol. 2, 66.

[2] Walther, *Essays for the Church*, Vol. 1, 264.

[3] Walther, *Essays for the Church*, Vol. 1, 54.

[4] Walther, *Essays for the Church*, Vol. 1, 63.

[5] W. H. Cooper, "Walther's Pen," *The Lutheran* 20:1 (October 6, 1937), 13.

[6] Erwin L. Lueker, "The 'Bright Torch' in Walther's Thought and Action," *Lutheran Witness*, 80:3 (February 7, 1961), 15.

[7] *Proceedings of the Western District*, 1859, 11–52. The eight theses of the lecture given at the Nebraska District in 1883 re-emphasize the same theme. See also Erwin L. Lueker, "Justification in the Theology of Walther," *Concordia Theological Monthly*, 32:10 (October 1961), 598–605 for further elaboration.

[8] C. F. W. Walther, *Kurzer Lebenslauf des weiland ehrwürdigen Pastor Joh. Friedr. Bünger* (St. Louis: Verlag von F. Dette, 1882), 29.

[9] *Proceedings*, Synodical Conference, 1872, 21.

[10] *Proceedings*, Synodical Conference, 1872, 20–21.

[11] Walther, *Essays for the Church*, Vol. 1, 170.

[12] Walther, *Essays for the Church*, Vol. 1, 59.

[13] Walther, *Essays for the Church*, Vol. 1, 62.

[14] C. F. W. Walther, *Convention Essays*, trans. and ed. by August R. Suelflow (St. Louis: Concordia Publishing House, 1981), 75.

[15] Walther, *Convention Essays*, 97.

[16] Walther, *Convention Essays*, 105.

[17] Walther, *Convention Essays*, 108.

[18] Walther, *Convention Essays*, 179.

[19] C. F. W. Walther, *The Proper Distinction between Law and Gospel*, W. H. T. Dau, tr. (St. Louis: Concordia Publishing House, 1986), 50.

[20] Walther, *The Proper Distinction between Law and Gospel*, 60.

[21] Walther, *The Proper Distinction between Law and Gospel*, 63.

[22] Walther, *The Proper Distinction between Law and Gospel*, 404.

[23] Walther, *The Proper Distinction between Law and Gospel*, 240.

[24] Walther, *The Proper Distinction between Law and Gospel*, 406.

[25] Walther, *The Proper Distinction between Law and Gospel*, 387–88.

[26] Walther, *The Proper Distinction between Law and Gospel*, 343.

[27] *Proceedings*, Buffalo Synod, 1848, 9–10, 14–16.

[28] J. A. A. Grabau, *Second Pastoral Letter*, 16; cited in *Ebenezer*, W. H. T. Dau, ed. (St. Louis: Concordia Publishing House, 1922), 130.

[29] C. F. W. Walther, *Church and Ministry*, trans. by J. T. Mueller (St. Louis: Concordia Publishing House, 1987).

[30] C. F. W. Walther, *Church and Ministry*, 9.

[31] C. F. W. Walther, *The Form of a Christian Congregation*, translated by J. T. Mueller (St. Louis: Concordia Publishing House, 1963), VIII. This work was reprinted in 1987 as part of the Concordia Heritage Series.

[32] Walther, *Essays for the Church*, Vol. 2, 6–63.

[33] Walther, *Essays for the Church*, Vol. 2, 7.

[34] Walther, *The Form of a Christian Congregation*, 112.

[35] Walther, *The Form of a Christian Congregation*, 113.

[36] Walther, *The Form of a Christian Congregation*, 122.

[37] Walther, *The Form of a Christian Congregation*, 128.

[38] Walther, *The Form of a Christian Congregation*, 137.

[39] Chapter 6 of this volume will elaborate on this.

[40] *The True Visible Church* was translated by J. T. Mueller in 1961 and published by Concordia Publishing House. In 1987, it was reprinted in the Concordia Heritage Series. Walther, *Essays for the Church*, Vol 1, 88–201.

[41] *Lehre und Wehre*, 18:11 (November 1872), 350.

[42] Walther, *The True Visible Church*, 42.

[43] Walther, *The True Visible Church*, 50.

[44] Walther, *The True Visible Church*, 50. An error crept into the printing of Thesis 12 in the English translation, with the omission of the word "Lutheran" on page 50. With the use of today's ecclesiastical terminology, this is an interesting lapse.

[45] Walther, *The True Visible Church*, 15.

[46] Walther, *The True Visible Church*, 29.

[47] For a comprehensive review of the entire controversy, See Hans R. Haug, *The Predestinarian Controversy in the Lutheran Church in North America*, 2 vols., Ph.D. Thesis, University of Michigan, 1967.

[48] Humberger was born in Thornville, Ohio on July 28, 1840. He graduated from the Columbus Lutheran seminary of the Ohio Synod and was ordained at Germantown, Ohio on August 27, 1865. He served in the active ministry of the Ohio Synod for more than forty years. He died on January 26, 1907. See *The Error of Modern Missouri* (Columbus, OH: Lutheran Book Concern, 1897), 788.

[49] C. F. W. Walther, "Doctrine Concerning Election" translated by J. Humberger (St. Louis: Concordia Publishing House, 1881).

[50] Walther, "Doctrine Concerning Election," 10–11.

[51] Walther, *Essays for the Church*, Vol. 2, 219.

[52] See "Church Fathers and Doctrine," 1884 Synodical Conference Essay in Walther, *Essays for the Church*, Vol. 2, 67–101.

[53] Walther quotes the Theses almost verbatim from the Formula of Concord.

[54] Walther's three essays on predestination are printed in *Essays for the Church*, Vol. 2, 102–220.

[55] *Essays for the Church*, Vol. 2, 106, as quoted from FC, SD, 11, in Theodore G. Tappert, trans. and ed., *The Book of Concord* (Philadelphia: Fortress Press, 1959), 617.

[56] Walther, *Essays for the Church*, Vol. 2, 106.

[57] See chapter 3.

[58] J. A. Ottesen (1825–1904) was an influential member of the Norwegian Synod and a pastor in Decorah, Iowa.

[59] Letter from Walther to J. A. Ottesen, February 8, 1879; transcription by W. K. Wadewitz at Concordia Historical Institute.

[60] See C. F. W. Walther, *Amerikanisch-Lutherische Evangelien Postille* (St. Louis: Concordia Publishing House, 1870), 88–89.

[61] Letter from Walther to J. A. Ottesen, February 8, 1879; transcription by W. K. Wadewitz at Concordia Historical Institute.

[62] See Walther, *Essays for the Church*, Vol. 2, 149ff.

[63] D. H. Steffens, *Dr. Carl Ferdinand Wilhelm Walther* (Philadelphia: Lutheran Publication Society, 1917), 346.

[64] See Erwin L. Lueker, ed. *Lutheran Cyclopedia* (St. Louis: Concordia Publishing

House, 1975), 766–67. The theses appear in the Appendix. The adoption of these theses is discussed in Chapter 3.

[65] Tappert, *Book of Concord*, 616.

[66] Walther, *Essays for the Church*, Vol. 2, 170.

[67] Walther, *Essays for the Church*, Vol. 2, 107.

[68] Tappert, *Book of Concord*, 464–65.

[69] Roy A. Suelflow, "Our First Synodical Constitution," *Concordia Historical Institute Quarterly*, 16:1 (April 1943), 3.

[70] H. H. Walker, "Carl Ferdinand Wilhelm Walther, D.D., the Luther of America," *Concordia Historical Institute Quarterly*, 29:4 (Winter 1957), 174.

[71] C. F. W. Walther, "Vier Thesen über das Schriftprincip," *Lehre und Wehre* 13:4 (April 1867), 97–111.

[72] Walther, "Vier Thesen über das Schriftprincip," *Lehre und Wehre* 13:4, 97.

[73] Walther, "Vier Thesen über das Schriftprincip," *Lehre und Wehre* 13:4, 98–99.

[74] Walther, "Vier Thesen über das Schriftprincip," *Lehre und Wehre* 13:4, 100.

[75] Walther, "Vier Thesen über das Schriftprincip," *Lehre und Wehre* 13:4, 103.

[76] Walther, *The True Visible Church*, 50–131; cf. *Essays for the Church*, Vol. 1, 156–201, for Walther's further elaboration on Theses 13, 17, and 18.

[77] Walther, *The True Visible Church*, 50.

[78] Walther, *The True Visible Church*, 56.

[79] The subject of open questions will be treated in chapter 6.

[80] Walther, *The True Visible Church*, 61.

[81] Walther, *The True Visible Church*, 66–90.

[82] Walther, *The True Visible Church*, 90.

[83] Apol IV, 107; Tappert, 122.

[84] Walther, *Convention Essays*, 27–28.

[85] C. F. W. Walther, "Was lehren die neueren orthodox sein Wollenden Theologen von der Inspiration?" *Lehre und Wehre*, 17:2 (February 1872), 33ff.

[86] C. F. W. Walther, "Zur Frage von der heiligen Schrift," *Lehre und Wehre*, 31:9 (September 1885), 275–79.

[87] Walther, "Zur Frage von der heiligen Schrift," *Lehre und Wehre*, 31:9, 278.

[88] K. A. W. Roebbelen, "Die Offenbarung St. Johannis," *Der Lutheraner*, 11:9 (December 19, 1854), 65–67.

[89] *Lehre und Wehre*, 2:7 (July 1856), 204–16; see also C. F. W. Walther, *Editorials from Lehre und Wehre*, Herbert J. A. Bouman, ed. (St. Louis: Concordia Publishing House, 1981), 24.

[90] *The Christian Book of Concord*, Ambrose and Socrates Henkel, trs. (New Market, VA: Solomon Henkel & Brothers, 1851).

[91] For a comparison of some of the significant articles of the Platform with the *Augsburg Confession*, see August R. Suelflow "Following the Frontier, 1840–1875" in E. Clifford Nelson, ed, *The Lutherans in North America*, (Philadelphia: Fortress Press, 1975), 222–23.

[92] Walther, "Warum sollen wir an den Bekenntnisschriften unserer evangelisch-

lutherischen Kirche auch noch jetzt unerschütterlich festhalten?" *Der Lutheraner*, 5:11 (January 23, 1849), 81–84.

[93] Walther, *Essays for the Church*, Vol. 1, 20–63.

[94] Walther, *Essays for the Church*, Vol. 1, 24.

[95] Walther, *Essays for the Church*, Vol. 1, 29.

[96] *Der Lutheraner*, 5:11 (January 23, 1849), 81–83.

[97] *Der Lutheraner*, 5:11, 83.

[98] "Neue Litteratur," *Lehre und Wehre*, 1:8 (August 1855), 248.

[99] Walther, *Convention Essays*, 27.

[100] Article II, Paragraph 1, of the Missouri Synod Constitution in *Handbook of The Lutheran Church—Missouri Synod*, 1998 Edition (St. Louis: LCMS, 1998), 9.

[101] *Der Lutheraner*, 5:11 (January 23, 1849), 83.

6

OTHER CHURCH COUSINS

Walther had a great zeal to unite all the Lutherans in North America who agreed on Scripture and the Lutheran Confessions. This was an enormous goal in mid-nineteenth century American Christianity when many Christian organizations and Lutheran groups had already formed into synods or independent Lutheran church bodies. It was a period when neither deep traditions nor doctrinal matters had crystallized into the denominationalism we know today.

Several events deeply affected American Lutheranism in Walther's day. The Definite Synodical Platform of 1855 was issued, the Civil War took place, and among Lutherans, the strident predestinarian controversy occurred in the late 1870s. During the decades of the 1850s, 1860s and 1870s, there was a re-evaluation of both Lutheranism and of the nation. It was a time for restoration, bold thinking, and deep searching about the Lutheran heritage.

As stated earlier, Walther had come to a steadfast position on Scripture as the revealed Word of God and the Lutheran Confessions as a correct interpretation of Scripture. He arrived at this through God's Spirit and especially through *oratio, meditatio, tentatio* (prayer, meditation, testing and anguish). He had lived with a troubled conscience just as Luther did. Hence Scripture and the Confessions remained strong bulwarks in his personal life, his family, and the church. He wanted his message to be shared and with others to proclaim the scriptural, Lutheran, Reformation theology that "God was reconciling the world to himself in Christ" (2 Corinthians 5:19).

The story of Walther's relationship with other Lutherans began with the very formation of the Missouri Synod. But this was not enough for him. He was eager to unite with other Lutherans who were in doctrinal agreement. He tried to achieve this by conducting "Free Conferences" and "colloquies" with other synods, and eventually with the formation of the Synodical Conference. These positive efforts—and disappointments—will be reviewed in this chapter, as well as some of Walther's principles in dealing with non-Lutheran denominations.

THE THEOLOGICAL CLIMATE

Precisely what was the theological climate in which Walther found himself? One problem was the effect of rationalism on Lutheran provincial churches in Germany and its introduction to America. The universities of Jena, Tübingen, and others had faculty members who taught pure rationalism to their students. For example, Johann Gottfried Eichhorn (1752–1827), known as the "father of modern higher biblical criticism," taught that Holy Scripture should be subjected to critical investigation just as any other ancient record. He no longer believed that the Bible was the inspired Word of God.

At Tübingen, Ferdinand Christian Baur (1792–1860) taught that Christianity had little more influence than demonstrating the ethics of Christ. He accepted as inspired only the reasonable accounts of the Scripture. He was soon followed by his student, Gottfried Friedrich David Strauss (1808–1874). While at Tübingen, Strauss produced his *Leben Jesu* in 1835 in which he denied the resurrection of Christ. He, too, believed that the Christian religion had undergone a gradual historical development somewhat comparable to heathen mythology, and strongly pointed out what he considered the mythological aspects of Scripture. Before long, the theological air was heavily polluted with rationalism.

Some Lutherans in America were also influenced by this anti-Christian theology of rationalism. It had been a creeping menace to Lutheranism in the North Carolina Synod, which expressed its interest in the catechism produced in Germany by Johann Kaspar Velthusen (1740–1814), the so-called *Helmstädt Catechism*. In the New York Ministerium, F. H. Quitman (1760–1832) had published a new English catechism in 1814 and a new hymnal in 1816 in which he introduced a strong rationalism and anti-trinitarianism to the church. The Unitarians lauded him. This readily opened the doors to unionism and revivalism.

Walther and his co-workers kept a wary eye on the struggles and problems of their fellow Lutherans in the East and in Europe. But when the Lutheran leadership attempted to adapt Lutheranism to Protestantism and to erase the denominational barriers, the Missouri Synod planned to defuse it.

Philip Schaff (1819–1893), one of the great church historians in America, presented a series of lectures when he visited Berlin in 1854. This presentation is noteworthy for American Lutherans and especially for those who are interested in the life of Walther and the Missouri Synod.

Though not a Lutheran, Schaff portrayed Lutheranism in America through his eyes and with his perception. In his presentation in Berlin, Schaff described three types of Lutherans—"neo-Lutherans," "moderate or Melanchthonian Lutherans," and "old Lutherans."

> In general one may speak of three tendencies in the American Lutheran Church.... For brevity's sake, we shall call them the Neo-Lutheran, the Old Lutheran, and Moderate Lutheran, or Melanchthonian.
>
> The Neo-Lutheran party originated out of a conflict and an amalgamation of Lutheranism with American Puritanism and Methodistic elements. It consists mostly of American-born Germans and proudly calls itself, in an emphatic sense, the American Lutheran Church. This group is probably the largest, undoubtedly the most active, the most practical and progressive, and is best acquainted with the English spirit. It is to a large extent English and un-German, not only in language, but also in all its sympathies and antipathies.
>
> Theological training and thorough education is not found among them, but instead mostly superficial American routine sophistication, gift of eloquence, knowledge of parliamentary order, and businessmanship.... Up till now it has carried the most weight in the so-called General Synod. One can best learn to know them through their organ, *The Lutheran Observer*, edited by Dr. Kurtz, and out of the numerous writings of Dr. Schmucker in Gettysburg, especially out of his *Popular Theology*.
>
> The Old Lutheran division has just recently immigrated to America from Germany, chiefly from Saxony (the Stephanites), out of Prussia (Grabau and Ehrenstroem ... and his adherents), and out of Bavaria (Loehe's missioners). They are still totally German and have not mixed in the least with the English and the American spirit. Even though outwardly they are progressing quite well, they are still strangers and foreigners, in a new world. With the second generation things will probably look quite different....
>
> The pastors of the Old Lutheran group are for the most [part] well indoctrinated, faithful, conscientious, and self-sacrificing, but at the same time, if a fortunate consequence does not hinder them, they are extremely exclusive and narrow-minded people (so much so) that they could hardly consider the most pious Reformed as a Christian and would not at any price partake of the Lord's Holy Supper with him. Luther is for them the highest human authority, and especially that Luther who in the discussion at Marburg, with tears in his eyes,

denied the brotherly handshake of Zwingli. "God's Word and Luther's doctrine pure" (as if these two were unconditionally identical!) "Shall in eternity endure" is the characteristic motto of the Lutherans from St. Louis. With honorable zeal and great sacrifice they have founded two theological seminaries in St. Louis and Fort Wayne. They maintain church order and discipline in their congregations and are concerned about their schools. Compared with the latitudinarian and uncertain experimentation of the Neo-Lutherans they have the advantage of a firm principle, a well-formed dogmatic basis, and a logical consistency....

Concerning the doctrine of the ministry, which has also become a firebrand of controversy among the strict symbolical Lutherans in Germany in spite of all honorable agreements of doctrinal unity, they are spread into two enemy camps and are vying with each other in their church papers from week to week with an antipathy and bitterness which in truth is not an honor to Lutheranism and Christianity and does not in the least command respect from the Anglo-American concerning this section of the German Christianity....

The Synod of Missouri, which was organized in 1847 and since then has grown rapidly, represents in this controversy, especially through [Der] Lutheraner, edited by Professor Walther, the usual Protestant point of view, which considers the ministerial office as the mouthpiece of the universal priesthood and bases its belief on the published documents of the Lutheran Church and the private writings of their outstanding theologians. The Synod of Lutherans Immigrated from Prussia presents the catholicizing doctrine. This is set forth in The Informatorium, edited by Pastor Grabau in Buffalo, New York.... Mr. Grabau, it is said, each year on Maundy Thursday is cursing and damning everyone from his pulpit, from the Baptists and Calvinists down to the Missouri "would-be-Lutherans and factious spirits" (Maullutheranern und Rottengeistern), who does not belong to the church, that is, his little synod, which is composed of about a half dozen Lutheran preachers. His anathematizations, however, are quite harmless....

The moderate Lutheran tendency standing as in the center of these two extremes ... really has the oldest American Lutheran tradition on its side, because the first missioners came for the most [part] out of the Halle Orphanage and from the Spener and Francke schools of Pietism, which were known to be not very strict symbolically and really half-Reformed. This group is represented by the oldest and largest synod, the so-called Pennsylvanian, and in some degrees also by the Joint Synod of Ohio, which a few years ago has announced that the Symbolical Books, including the Formula of Concord, are obligatory. It does not sympathize with the exclusive spirit of the Old Lutherans, since its leaders are too Americanized already and know the English Reformed Church better than to accuse them of heresy unhesitatingly. *The Lutheran Standard*, which appears in Columbus, may in a manner be considered its organ. A goodly number of the preachers, especially among the older men, have few firm convictions, are poorly educated, stagnant, and are much more concerned about building programs and politics than theology and church affairs. They follow almost blindly a few leading intellectuals. However, we must excuse them when we consider that twenty or thirty years ago there were no regular opportunities to gain a theological education in the German Church of America.

A deeper spiritual life and a church consciousness developed within recent years in the Pennsylvania Synod. The most influential man in this movement in the last two decades was without a doubt Dr. R. Demme of Philadelphia, who was born in Altenburg. He is an outstanding pulpit orator and a man with a noteworthy solid, strong, and a true German personality, the author of the liturgy and new hymnbook in use in this synod.... To this group are also added many promising young theologians, some of whom were trained in America and some of whom have emigrated from Europe, who follow the same tendencies for the most part. The true task of the old Pennsylvania Synod lies herein, not only to be a conciliatory force between the ecclesiastical Old-Lutheranism and the Puritanic Neo-Lutheranism, but also at the same time to mediate between the European-German and the American interests and thereby effect a drawing together and consolidation of the different elements in the Lutheran Church of America.[1]

Schaff's presentation was much longer in the original, but the reduced text is directly pertinent to an understanding of Lutheranism in America in 1854, seven years after the LCMS was organized and one year before Schmucker issued his Definite Synodical Platform in which he denied the power and benefits of the sacraments of Baptism and the Lord's Supper.

The Platform was written by three leaders of eastern Lutheranism. The first was Samuel S. Schmucker, who graduated from Princeton Theological Seminary at a time when Lutherans did not have an institution for the training of their own pastors. He was considered the best educated young man in the church, and later as the most influential man in the General Synod. Others who collaborated with him were Samuel Sprecher

(1810–1906), a student of Schmucker and also his brother-in-law. At the time he was president of Wittenberg College in Springfield, Ohio. The third leader was Benjamin Kurtz, who had just finished a debate with J. W. Nevin (1803–1886), a Reformed professor at the Theological Seminary in Mercersburg, Pennsylvania.

In addition to rationalism, the second major problem was revivalism, to which some Lutherans in America were deeply attracted. During its heyday in the early nineteenth century, Benjamin Kurtz tried to defend the revivalistic system while Nevin opposed it. In his *Lutheran Observer* Kurtz carried on a running battle with Nevin and argued:

> If the great object of the anxious bench can be accomplished in some other way, less obnoxious but equally efficient—be it so. But we greatly doubt this. We consider it necessary in many cases, and we believe there are circumstances when no measure equally good can be substituted. Hence we are free to confess that we go for this measure *with all our heart* [emphasis in original].[2]

Schaff and Kurtz's positions well illustrate the environment in which Walther found himself. While Walther emphasized subscription to the Lutheran Confessions, which included Luther's Small Catechism, Kurtz argued:

> Has the Dr. [Nevin] forgotten that we [the Lutherans] have no "creed" or "catechism" which requires uniformity of belief in non-essentials? That we allow our members to believe what they think the Bible teaches provided they agree in fundamental points; in a word, that we have adopted the Melanchthonian maxim: *In certis unitas, in dubiis libertas, in omnibus charitas.* [In certain things unity, in things uncertain liberty, in all things charity.] Hence we bear and forebear; agree in some points and differ in others; but are we therefore "split into different divisions"?[3]

Schmucker stated his position clearly when he wrote an article entitled "Vocation of the American Lutheran Church":

> For them [Gettysburg Seminary] to inculcate on their students the obsolete views of the Old Lutherans, contained in the former symbols of the church in some parts of Germany, such as exorcism, the real presence of the body and blood of Christ in the Eucharist, private confession, baptismal regeneration, immersion in Baptism, as taught in Luther's Large Catechism, etc., would be to betray the confidence of those who elected them to office, and defeat the design of the

Institution, not one dollar of whose funds was contributed by synods or by individuals professing these views."[4]

A contemporary of Schmucker and Kurtz, Joseph A. Seiss (1823–1904), at one time president of the Pennsylvania Ministerium and a co-founder of the General Council which he headed as president, reflected a few years later:

> A happy thing would it have been for our church, its usefulness and success in this country, if their successors and descendants [of the early Lutheran leaders in colonial America] had all and always remained steadfast to the true confessional basis on which the Lutheran Church in this new world was started. But a long period of defection came 1) a period of rationalistic and then Methodistic innovations, 2) a period of neglect of the Confessions and of the doctrines of the Church as Luther and Muhlenberg taught them, 3) a period of self-destructive assimilation to the unsound and unchurchly spirit of surrounding sects, by which the life and vigor of our churches were largely frittered away, 4) a period from which the Lutheran Church in America is only now beginning effectually to emerge.[5]

With such divisions among Lutherans and given Schaff's description of Lutheranism, it is small wonder that Walther and the Missouri Synod who took no part in such excesses and theology were called separatists and isolationists. Their theological convictions forced them to preserve tenaciously in the American environment what they had learned to be the greatest treasures—God's Word and a solid confessional platform.

FREE CONFERENCES

All of this deeply concerned Walther who worked arduously on uniting his fellow Lutherans. But then came the Definite Synodical Platform in 1855 in which Schmucker identified five errors in the Augsburg Confession which had always been accepted universally by all Lutherans. The alleged errors Schmucker identified were:

1. The approval of the ceremonies of the mass;
2. The approval of private confession and absolution;
3. The denial of the divine obligation of the Christian Sabbath;
4. The affirmation of baptismal regeneration;
5. The affirmation of the real presence of the body and blood of the Savior in Holy Communion.[6]

Even though the Platform was only mildly attacked by the Missouri Synod, Walther nevertheless extended a general invitation to all Lutherans to participate in "free conferences," that is, inter-Lutheran conferences designed to discuss matters of doctrine. He set forth both a procedure and goal in *Lehre und Wehre*:

> So we venture openly to inquire: would not meetings, held at intervals, by such members of churches as call themselves Lutheran and acknowledge and confess without reservation that the Unaltered Augsburg Confession of 1530 is the pure and true statement of the doctrine of sacred Scripture, and is also their own belief, promote and advance the efforts towards the final establishment of one single Evangelical Lutheran Church of America? We for our part would be ready with all our heart to take part in such a conference of truly believing Lutherans whenever and wherever such a conference would be held, pursuant to the wishes of the majority of the participants; at the same time we can promise in advance the support of numerous theologians and laymen to whom the welfare of our precious Evangelical Lutheran Church in this new fatherland is equally a matter of deepest heartfelt yearning and with whom we have discussed the thoughts here expressed.
>
> Since it is true that many differences of opinion still exist among those Lutherans who hold with all their heart to the fundamental confession of our church the treatment of which in our periodicals can more easily hinder than advance unity among us, the personal and verbal statements and expressions of opinions would above all else surely bring about this unparalleled blessing, namely, that the contest within our church (which will always be necessary) will receive and keep the nature of a mutual competition among brethren of the faithful preservation of the precious gem of doctrinal purity and unity.[7]

The appeal was successful. A total of seventy-three individuals came from vast geographical areas for the first conference in 1856. In a day when few Lutherans knew each other and travel was difficult at best, this was a significant number. It took thirty hours just to go from St. Louis to Chicago. Two conditions were important in arranging the conference: 1) The participants pledged themselves to the Unaltered Augsburg Confession and 2) they did not officially represent the synods in which they held membership. This was an auspicious beginning within Lutheranism which appeared to be divided into hostile camps. Walther had high hopes that a large segment of Lutherans in America could be united.

When it was time to set the agenda, all voted that the Augsburg Confession itself, article by article, should serve as the basis of the discussions. No agenda, not even a set of theses, was prepared for this meeting.

Altogether four conferences were held: the first in Columbus, Ohio, October 1–7, 1856; the next in Pittsburgh, Pennsylvania, October 29–November 4, 1857; the third in Cleveland, Ohio, August 5–11, 1858; and the last in Fort Wayne, Indiana, July 14–20, 1859. A fifth conference had been scheduled for Cleveland in June 1860 but because the two leaders, Walther and Lehmann, were unable to attend, it was never held.

In some instances it is difficult to determine how many were present at the conferences. The participants did not represent synods, and so the secretaries listed those present in various ways. The first conference, we know, was attended by seventy-three persons (fifty-four pastors and nineteen laymen). Of these, sixteen were members of the Missouri Synod. In all, members of the following synods were represented at one time or another: Missouri, Ohio, New York, Tennessee, Pittsburgh, and the Norwegian Synod. The average attendance at these conferences appears to have been around forty people.

All the conferences were opened with devotional exercises, usually including hymns, prayers, and sometimes the Apostles' Creed, and concluded with the Benediction.

F. W. Lehmann (1820–1880), a professor at the seminary in Columbus, Ohio and later president of the Ohio Synod and of the Synodical Conference, served as chairman of the first three conferences. The German and English secretaries of the conference were H. C. Schwan (1819–1905), who in 1878 succeeded Walther as president of the Missouri Synod, and Matthias Loy (1828–1915), who later became president of Capital University, Columbus, Ohio and president of the Ohio Synod.[8]

The sole topic under discussion at the conferences was the Augsburg Confession: at the first, Articles I-VII; at the second, Articles VIII-X; at the third, Articles XI-XIII and XXV; and at the fourth, Articles XIV and XXVI-II. As one looks at these articles, it is truly amazing that such unanimity was attained on the doctrines of Holy Baptism and the Lord's Supper, the two sacraments that Schmucker had altered. In fact, during the four conferences, most of the articles of the Augsburg Confession were accepted without any dissent, when earlier they had been bitterly disputed.

What caused the demise or termination of these conferences? Two reasons surface. The first was that Walther, one of the leaders, was very ill with a "racking cough," probably some throat and lung ailment, and therefore was not able to attend the fourth conference in 1859. Strangely enough, Lehmann, who had chaired the first three conferences, also was absent at the fourth, as was Loy. There were only one or two Ohio Synod pastors present at the fourth conference.

Fred W. Meuser has speculated on the second reason for the demise of the conferences:

> Missouri received into its ministerium a pastor who had accused President Lehmann of Ohio of a lax attitude in regard to secret societies; Ohio accepted a pastor who had difficulties in the Missouri Synod. Shortly after the fourth and the last of the free conferences was held, antagonism had reached the point where the *Lutheran Standard* editor could write: "There are some good Lutherans who would covet no greater honor than to be abused by [*Der*] *Lutheraner* … perhaps it would be as well anyhow for the Missourians to resign the assumed supervisory generalship of all other Lutheran Synods and attend better to their own affairs."[9]

A fifth conference had been scheduled for Cleveland, Ohio in June 1860. Notices appeared in *Der Lutheraner* (May 15, 1860) and elsewhere. The Ohio Synod withdrew its support in its official German organ, *Kirchenzeitung*, because of the strained relationships between the two synods.

What began as a great challenge and joy for Walther now ended in disappointment. After the first free conference, Walther had expressed his great pleasure:

> The spirit which permeated the conference was the spirit of truth, of love, and of peace. Naturally, it was too much to expect that among the members of the conference, who in most instances saw each other face to face for the first time, differences in doctrine should not at first become evident. At the same time, however, it became apparent in the clearest possible way that no one present would not have been ready to conform to recognized truth. Every voice heard testified that in all hearts there lived an upright and yearning desire for unity in spirit through the bonds of love and peace."[10]

Was Walther inclusivistic or exclusivistic in his relationships with other Lutherans? This can best be answered in his own words—words which bear significantly on his attitude towards fellowship:

> The Lutheran Church is not limited to those people who from their youth have borne the name "Lutheran" or have taken that name later on. To every person who honestly submits to the whole written Word of God, bears the true faith in our dear Lord Jesus Christ in his heart

and confesses it before the world, we extend our hand, regard him also as a fellow believer, as a brother in Christ, as a member of our church, no matter in which sect he may lie concealed and captive.[11]

GENERAL COUNCIL

In the 1850s and 1860s, American Lutheranism was restive, ambivalent, and uncomfortable. It appears that the three modes or positions Schaff had outlined earlier were well in place. The prospects for uniting Lutherans in America seemed close and yet so far. The Pennsylvania Ministerium, which had been organized under the leadership of H. M. Muhlenberg in 1748, was represented at the first of the free conferences, but not the subsequent ones. On the heels of the disintegration of the free conferences and the General Synod's theological decline, Dr. Charles Porterfield Krauth (1823–1883), professor of the Lutheran theological seminary in Philadelphia, who had opposed the Definite Platform, issued his "Fraternal Address" in 1866.[12] This communication proposed the organization of a new federation of Lutheran synods based distinctively on the Unaltered Augsburg Confession and Lutheran principles. This was to result in the organization of the General Council later that year. Did the impetus for such a body come as one of the results of the free conferences?

The Missouri Synod delegated Walther, Wilhelm Sihler (1801–1885), and J. A. F. W. Mueller (1825–1900), the first graduate of the Altenburg, Missouri seminary and then pastor in Pittsburgh, Pennsylvania to attend the preliminary meeting of the General Council.[13] Only Mueller was able to be there. Walther described his inability to get to Reading, Pennsylvania in December 1866 for this meeting. On December 14, 1866 he wrote to his daughter Magdalene (Lenchen) and son-in-law Stephanus Keyl:

> If the Pennsylvania convention, as originally planned, had been held in Pittsburgh, I would have undoubtedly personally attended. Since, however, it was held in Reading, eight days later than originally scheduled, we submitted our vote in writing and requested Pastor Mueller, our third synodical commissioner, to attend. This he did, as we have been informed in writing. I am living in the deepest anticipation of the results."[14]

Only a few days later, on December 27, 1866 his anticipation was modified by a report issued by Mueller. In a letter to his son-in-law, Walther confided:

I do not regret that I didn't go to Reading. It would have been extremely painful for me to meet with such false spirits [*falschen Geistern*] as the Iowans, Canadians, among others. My witness would have been lost even as that of our dear Mueller. It is true, the resolutions are for the most part fairly acceptable [*meist sehr schön*], but it is alarming if one considers all those who have subscribed to them, people who are in part open hypocrites, or who do not fully realize what they have done. I feel profoundly sorry for such people as Krauth, Krotel, Schaeffer, and others, because they were so weak and sought strength in the union of such elements. God give me the wisdom that when I need to write about this publicly, I may do it so that this good matter [*Sache*] which is in the works may not be hindered, but may be furthered.[15]

What actually did happen? Walther had been in Buffalo, New York to conduct a colloquy with the Buffalo Synod from November 20 to December 5, 1866 at the request of the Buffalo Synod. He had hoped to go from Buffalo to Pittsburgh, Pennsylvania on his way home. But, since the dates and place had been changed, he was unable to follow his original plan. In addition, both Walther and Sihler, who also was at the Buffalo colloquy, had been gone from their homes and their work for more than two weeks when the Reading convention began.

As indicated, Mueller attended the meeting in Reading in December 1866. The minutes of the first convention reveal that Mueller opened the fourth session with prayer[16] and presented a paper during the course of the convention.[17] At the end of the sixth session held on the afternoon of December 14, both delegate Mueller and F. A. Schmidt (Walther's great opponent during the predestination controversy) took leave of the convention "expressing their joy in meeting so many brethren in the Lord and hoping soon to have a united Lutheran Church in this country."[18]

The Missouri Synod opted for "free conferences" instead of organizing a new federation (General Council) which it considered premature. At the Western District convention of 1867, the invitation and response to the General Council was discussed. At this convention Walther presented a part of *The True Visible Church*. He covered theses three–six. The theses dealt primarily with church fellowship, sectarianism, heresy, and unionism synonymous with the seventeenth century "syncretism." Walther did not refer at all to the formation of the General Council. The Western District, however, adopted a response which the other districts (Northern, Central, and Eastern) ratified in the course of their subsequent conventions. The General Council had specifically invited the Missouri Synod to its next convention. However, the four districts responded that while they considered it a special privilege to be accorded this invitation:

> [W]e have arrived at the conviction that we dare not avail ourselves of so honorable a proposal. In view of the relation we sustain toward different members of the Church [General] Council, in reference to doctrine and churchly practice, we must be apprehensive that the consideration and discussion of differences still existing in the convention of the Church Council, might give rise to the reflection that we intended to interrupt the bringing about of the unity, and are therefore fearful lest our participation, instead of leading to an agreement, might be productive of greater alienation.... We beg leave to declare it again, as our conviction, that "free conferences," such as are separated from officially organized conventions of ecclesiastical bodies, on the basis of the Symbols of our church as contained in the Formula of Concord of 1580, are the only proper means for an exchange of such convictions, as are still divergent, and which by the grace of God, may lead to a unity on the basis of our beloved Confession.[19]

At the same time the General Council was faced with several important questions known as the "Four Points." These included issues which disturbed Lutheranism at that time, namely: the 1000-year reign of Christ on earth (millenialism); permitting non-Lutherans to commune at Lutheran altars; permitting non-Lutheran pastors to preach in Lutheran pulpits; and membership in secret societies. Both the Ohio and Iowa Synods had asked for clarification on these issues. By 1872 the famous "Akron Rule" emerged, but too late to provide the necessary clarification for several synods. Missouri was dissatisfied. The Wisconsin, Minnesota, and Ohio Synods, and others withdrew.

In retrospect, the "Akron Rule" stands as a significant contrast to today's practices. It declared that:

> I. The rule is: Lutheran pulpits are for Lutheran ministers only. Lutheran altars are for Lutheran communicants only.

> II. The exceptions to the rule belong to the sphere of privilege, not of right.

> III. The determination of the exceptions is to be made in consonance with these principles, by the conscientious judgment of pastors, as the cases arise.[20]

The Iowa Synod decided it could not enter into full membership in the General Council. Together the Minnesota and Illinois Synods withdrew in 1870. This in turn opened up a much broader prospect for the Missouri Synod in seeking fellowship with other synods. It ushered in the period of "colloquies" which Walther and the Missouri Synod conducted in a fast-paced series from 1866 to 1872 to seek unanimity. Walther continued in his sincere desire to develop a united Lutheranism in America, even if it was not by means of the General Council.

With respect to the formation of the General Council, the Missouri Synod, via its four districts, rendered the opinion that the Council was being organized too hastily and prematurely. It recommended instead a series of "free conferences" by which the participants would be strengthened and convinced that "unity of spirit must first be sought and attained before external union can follow.…"[21] A formal reply by the officers of the four Missouri Synod districts, with the concurrence of their respective districts, underscored the necessity of free conferences and insisted that the free conferences must be separated—distinct from—officially organized conventions of ecclesiastical bodies. Such conferences, however, did not materialize. This virtually terminated Missouri's dialogue with the General Council.[22]

COLLOQUIES

During the period following the Civil War, Lutherans aiming to achieve unity among the various Synods in America moved in one of two orbits. One was to consolidate the General Council, and the other to hold "colloquies" conducted by the Missouri Synod with seven different synods. These differed from the "free conferences" in that each synod which was engaged in seeking unanimity in doctrine either elected or appointed specific representatives to attend. These were official meetings called "colloquies" (in German they were referred to as *colloquia* from a Latin term meaning "coming together to speak"). Each of these colloquies had a heavy doctrinal agenda which generally covered the issues of church and ministry, confessional subscription, "open questions," chiliasm, pulpit and altar fellowship, the Word of God, and secret societies.

Seven different colloquies were conducted in a short span of six years, while at the same time district and synodical conventions were held. Walther led each of these colloquies, in addition to his ongoing regular responsibilities. He was indeed deeply involved.

BUFFALO SYNOD

After years of controversy, it was a decided breakthrough when a major portion of the Buffalo Synod invited Missouri to send colloquants to a meeting held from November 20 to December 5, 1866 in Buffalo. The doctrines of church and ministry had been the primary cause of differences. J. A. A. Grabau interpreted the office of the ministry in a hierarchical fashion, giving the office too much authority, claiming that ordination was mandated by God, and insisting that a congregation owed obedience to its pastor even in areas that were not mandated in the Word. He had a restricted view of the church, believing that his own synod was the only true church. This is demonstrated by the fact that in 1858 Grabau and the Buffalo Synod excommunicated the entire Missouri Synod. The barrage of printed literature identifying the theological differences is almost unbelievable.[23]

Discussions at the 1866 colloquy convinced almost two-thirds of pastors and congregations of the Buffalo Synod that they should join the Missouri Synod. The remaining Buffalo pastors experienced a split among themselves. One group joined the Wisconsin Synod on an individual basis while the other continued until the formation of the first American Lutheran Church in 1930.

IOWA SYNOD

Major differences existed between the Iowa and Missouri Synods going back to the early 1850s when Wilhelm Loehe disagreed with Walther and the Missouri Synod on the office of the holy ministry, "open questions," subscription to the Lutheran Confessions, millenialism, the Antichrist, and the like.

The doctrine of millenialism was one of the chief issues on which the Missouri and Iowa Synods disagreed. Millenialism is the belief that there will be a literal 1000-year reign of Christ on earth. Some teach that Christ's return will take place at the beginning of the reign (pre-millenialism) while others say it will occur at the end (post-millenialism). It is primarily based on a misreading of Revelation 20:1–7.

Georg Albert Schieferdecker, who had been expelled from the Missouri Synod in 1857 because of his views about the millennium, contributed to the position of Loehe and the Iowa Synod on this false doctrine. Already in the eighteenth century Johann Albrecht Bengel (1687–1752) had become involved in setting the date for Christ's return to earth in 1836. He had been a part of the German Lutheran pietistic movement. Among American Protestants, William Miller (1782–1849) predicted Christ's second coming for 1843. When that did not occur, he admitted a mathematical error and reset the date for October 22, 1844. Nothing happened on that date either. The Adventist movement in America developed as a result of Miller's efforts.

The colloquy between Missouri and Iowa was conducted November 13–19, 1867.[24] Because the Iowa colloquants were planning to attend the meeting of the General Council in Fort Wayne one day later, the meeting was cut short and yielded little progress toward unity. It is of note that Schieferdecker, who had supported the Iowa Synod's chiliasm, later joined the Missouri Synod with his friends in 1875.[25]

The penetrating issue of "open questions" also caused strong debate between the two synods, with Iowa advocating a broader tolerance in this area. This position basically held that doctrines taught in Scripture, but which had not been confirmed in the Confessions or in the development of new ecclesiastical confessions, could be considered "open questions." Some felt that anything not explicitly taught or defined in the Confessions was still "open." Besides, only the articles in the Confessions that were introduced with "we believe, teach, and confess" required subscription. Open questions, then, could include every scriptural doctrine which was not adequately covered in the Lutheran Symbols. Thus, questions concerning the authority of Scripture and its relationship to the Lutheran Confessions became a much discussed issue, and continue to be today.[26]

OHIO SYNOD

Although there had been any number of contacts between the Ohio and Missouri Synods, it must be remembered that those who disagreed with the Ohio Synod's position on anglicization and confessionalism in 1845 became the nucleus of those who formed the Missouri Synod two years later. Nevertheless, Ohio participated in the free conferences and provided considerable leadership. Missouri and Ohio had an "on again, off again" relationship over the years. When Ohio requested a colloquy with Missouri, this was readily accepted and was held on March 4–6, 1868 at Columbus, Ohio. Only district presidents (Central, Eastern, Northern, Western) participated in these doctrinal discussions. The fact that the colloquy was limited to district presidents (all ordained men) was an innovation, especially since Walther always insisted that lay people be involved in doctrinal discussions. The primary doctrine considered during the three-day sessions dealt with church and ministry. Agreement was reached in all of the doctrinal areas discussed, and this later led the way to the formation of the Synodical Conference in 1872. In fact, the Ohio Synod took the initiative in organizing that federation.

WISCONSIN SYNOD

The meeting with the Wisconsin Synod was held in Milwaukee, Wisconsin, October 21–22, 1868. Although Wisconsin had been organized as early as 1850, there had been considerable animosity between the Missouri Synod and the Wisconsin Synod up until 1868. The differences consisted in the influence exercised over Wisconsin by its earlier leaders who sometimes were more Reformed than Lutheran. Consequently, Wisconsin had been less committed to Scripture and the Lutheran Confessions than Missouri. But a strong Reformation theology emerged in the 1860s, and this was the genesis of the colloquy. Wisconsin's theological students began to be trained at Concordia, St. Louis beginning in 1869.

The colloquy was highly successful. Within two days the two synods reached a concord on "open questions," church and ministry, inspiration of Scripture, subscription to the Confessions, millennium, and the Antichrist. Wisconsin, too, participated in the formation of the Synodical Conference. The following points were adopted by the colloquants between Wisconsin and Missouri:

1. Acknowledging each other as believing and confessing correctly....

2. Acknowledging the right to send representatives to each other's synodical conventions.

3. Calling pastors from another of these two synods was acceptable and when pastors accept their call into the other synod they are urged to join the new Synod.

4. If opposition congregations arise—both synods [Wisconsin and Missouri] should pledge to do everything possible in order to solve this.

5. When a new congregation is organized in a disputed location, then the synods should render a decision.

6. If it is discovered that some readers of the other synod disagree with something that has appeared in the publication of the other, this matter should be reviewed privately first, in a brotherly way.

7. When individual members present false doctrine, then the synod responsible for this should try to determine what is right according to the Word of God.

8. Both Synods pledged to attend each other's conventions, etc.[27]

Almost a century later, the relationship between the two synods was deeply disturbed, resulting in the withdrawal of the Wisconsin Synod from the Synodical Conference in 1961. The problem was basically over the question of "church fellowship," and the requirements necessary for pulpit and altar fellowship.

The 1869 convention of the Missouri Synod was the high watermark of Missouri's efforts towards Lutheran union.[28]

ILLINOIS SYNOD

In rapid succession Missouri conducted another colloquy, this time with the Illinois Synod, August 4–5, 1869 in St. Louis. Illinois had briefly been a member of the General Council but had withdrawn its membership in 1870 because of the "four points." As a result of these sessions with Missouri, a new concept of "state synods" was introduced, and Illinois merged with Missouri that same year when the agreement was ratified at the 1869 convention. Doctrines under discussion at this colloquy were fellowship, chiliasm, open questions, pulpit and altar fellowship, and secret societies. In 1909 the Missouri Synod divided the state of Illinois into three separate districts.

MINNESOTA SYNOD

Just prior to the organization of the Synodical Conference in July 1872, a colloquy was held between the Minnesota and Missouri Synods. This, too, resulted in complete agreement in doctrine. In fact, in this case it was announced that agreement in doctrine had already existed prior to the meeting as evidenced from the convention reports. Minnesota entered into a union with the Wisconsin Synod in 1893.

ENGLISH CONFERENCE

The last in the series of colloquies was held with the "English Conference of Missouri" in Gravelton, Missouri in August 1872. This group was an extension of Eastern English Lutheranism, especially those Lutherans from Tennessee. At the colloquy, F. A. Schmidt preached in English at the divine service. Points of discussion included the Word of God, total depravity, the work of Christ, faith and good works, the sacraments, Christian liberty, church and ministry, and the Antichrist. At the colloquy, Walther presented his "Sixteen Theses" covering these issues. The conference adopted each of the theses one by one, after they had been delivered. These theses constituted the epitome of Walther's theology.[29] Unanimity was reached also with the English Conference which continued to be closely affiliated with the Missouri Synod until it became the English District in 1911.

THE SYNODICAL CONFERENCE
AND EXPANDING HORIZONS

These were exciting days in the history of the Missouri Synod. Under Walther's leadership there was a constant and continued effort to unite the Lutherans in America. The Norwegian and Missouri Synods already had a good working relationship, as described in chapter 3. Arrangements were reached with the Norwegians that its seminarians be trained for the ministry at Concordia, St. Louis. According to this agreement, the Norwegian Synod established a professorship at St. Louis but with the reservation that ultimately it wanted to establish its own educational institution. As noted earlier, Lauritz Larsen was the first to be appointed to this position in 1859. The arrangement was temporarily disrupted by the Civil War. Thereafter he was succeeded in 1872 by F. A. Schmidt who served until 1876 when the Norwegians established their own seminary in Madison, Wisconsin.

The Ohio Synod, with immediate support from the Missouri, Wisconsin, and Norwegian Synods, was instrumental in arranging a preliminary meeting working towards the organization of a new federation which would become the Synodical Conference. The meeting was held January 11–13, 1871 in Chicago. A second such meeting was held the following November. This enabled the participants to organize the Synodical Conference in Milwaukee, Wisconsin on July 10, 1872. The "Plan of Union" had been adopted earlier by the representatives of these synods and was referred to the constituent synods for ratification. The constitution was adopted in 1872.[30]

Two articles of this constitution are of special historical interest to this biography. First of all, the Synodical Conference in Article II adopted one of the briefest confessional and scriptural subscriptions of almost all Lutherans in America. It simply read:

> The Synodical Conference accepts the canonical books of the Old and New Testaments as God's Word and the Confession of the Evangelical Lutheran Church of 1580, called the *Concordia*, as its own.

The second constitutional article of interest was Article III, which dealt with objectives and was Walther's strong hope for the ultimate goal of uniting all Lutherans in America. The fifth paragraph of this article stated as its objective: "To unite all Lutheran synods in America in one orthodox American Lutheran Church." This was Walther's dream!

Another noteworthy clause in the constitution was the emphasis that the new organization was a "conference" or federation, rather than a church. It also declared that all member synods were committed not to enter into "official church relations with other church bodies" without the prior agreement of all other synods which were members of the conference.[31] This would later prove to have grave reflections on the Wisconsin-Missouri relationships in the 1940s.

Members of the new conference were the Missouri, Ohio, Wisconsin, Norwegian, Illinois, and Minnesota Synods. It was a wonderful achievement to reach doctrinal unity among six synods. Not until 1944 did the Synodical Conference significantly modify its fifth objective to read: "To strive for true unity in doctrine and practice among Lutheran church bodies."[32]

In the mid-1870s, the Conference spent considerable time discussing the dissolution of all member synods and creating new synods based largely on state boundaries. A feeble response took place when the Concordia Synod of Virginia became a district synod of the Ohio Synod, the Illinois Synod was absorbed by the Illinois District of the Missouri Synod in 1879, and the Missouri Synod organized districts in Illinois, Iowa, Nebraska, and Kansas in anticipation that they would become state synods and members of the Conference. At the 1878 convention of the Missouri Synod, these issues of polity and unity were discussed pertaining to the Synodical Conference.

A second major plan, one which was later abandoned, was the attempt to create a single theological seminary with German, English, and Norwegian faculties. The 1879 convention of the Synodical Conference heard reports on both of these projects. But right at this time the predestinarian controversy was brewing, thus making it impossible to move the work ahead, and Walther moved quickly thereafter to erect a new seminary in St. Louis, dedicated in 1883.

During this period, the Missouri Synod was hindered in its English work primarily because it operated with the principle that English work in the Synodical Conference was especially the responsibility of the Ohio Synod, which quickly was becoming anglicized. As early as 1877, the Synodical Conference was urged to establish its own mission program. Its members recommended that the Conference consider work among African-Americans and Native Americans.

Work was soon begun among African-Americans when J. F. Doescher was commissioned on October 16, 1877. The work was highly successful. After the demise of the Synodical Conference in the 1960s, the pastors and congregations of the black mission were transferred to the Missouri Synod with the exception of one pastor. Two periodicals were produced to encourage support for these missions: the German *Die Missions-Taube*, and the English *The Lutheran Pioneer*. Both were established by resolution of the same 1878 convention of the Conference. Prior to that time, J. F. Buenger, pastor of Immanuel, St. Louis, Missouri had already proclaimed the Gospel beyond his congregation wherever he found listeners among African-Americans, Chinese, and Jews. In each he saw redeemed people in the Lord Jesus.[33]

As a result of the predestinarian controversy in 1879 and the years following, the unity existing in the Synodical Conference was soon shattered. It is fair to say that Walther and the Missouri Synod underwent a radical change in their attitude toward other Lutherans as a direct result of the predestinarian controversy. The bitterness and antipathy that were provoked caused the Missouri Synod to change its position on prayer fellowship. Because Missouri had been accused of crypto-Calvinism, a delegate at the January 1881 Milwaukee colloquy urged that if this were true then Missourians ought not to pray with these other Lutherans who had lodged this accusation.

Because the Missouri Synod had been accused of heresy, this pastor refused to pray with his Lutheran accusers. Consequently, the January 1881 meeting, which had been opened and closed with prayer daily, finished only with silent prayer.[34] This was probably the first time in its history that a Missourian had refused to pray with other Lutherans when discussing theological issues.

It was an extremely severe, painful, and isolating experience. Whereas prior to this time Walther was ready, under all circumstances, to discuss theology on the basis of Scripture and the Lutheran Confessions, his thinking now changed. This is a period of time in which Missouri felt so deeply hurt that it began to withdraw from opportunities for establishing fellowship. The Synodical Conference received its first major setback when the Ohio Synod left the Conference at a special meeting it convened in 1881 under the presidency of Matthias Loy. A number of clergymen and congregations withdrew from the Ohio Synod and organized the Concordia Synod of Pennsylvania and Other States. It joined the Synodical Conference in 1882 and merged with the Missouri Synod in 1886.

All the great plans of establishing a joint seminary and state synods had fizzled. The Norwegian Synod, working very closely with the Missouri

Synod in pastoral formation and in the Synodical Conference, withdrew from the Conference in 1883 in order to provide greater understanding and strength internally. This action precipitated a severe schism within that synod. Shortly afterward, in 1887, the Norwegian Synod lost almost one-third of its membership under F. A. Schmidt.[35]

What might have become the climax of all of Walther's efforts in relationship to other synods was virtually lost. The drive toward Lutheran unity had started so well in the formation of the Missouri Synod itself, in the "free conferences," and the "colloquies." It had culminated in the formation of the Synodical Conference. But much came to naught. Indeed, the Synodical Conference continued, but by the mid-1960s it came to a complete dissolution.

GLOBAL INTERESTS

In 1851 the Missouri Synod convention delegated F. C. D. Wyneken and Walther to travel to Neuendettelstau Germany to meet with Wilhelm Loehe. The primary purpose was to re-cement fellowship with Loehe. Even though initially the relationships with him were friendly, they had deteriorated and needed fixing.

The two traveled by train from St. Louis to New York on August 15, 1851 and took the ship *Africa* to Liverpool, England. The trip was not only a homecoming for them, but they also made it a point to meet with a large number of theologians at various universities. Among them were H. E. F. Guericke (1803–1878) who initially had been an influential opponent of the "Prussian Union."

In a letter to his wife shortly after his arrival in Erlangen, Walther noted that this was his first visit back to his old fatherland after the immigration. After having visited his birthplace at Langenchursdorf, he wrote:

> You can well imagine how joy and nostalgia contended within my heart. My dear mother was no longer there [she was living with her daughter and son-in-law in Hartmannsdorf, Germany], and of my father I [only] found his grave mound. But I thank God that I again saw my sister with her large family. It had just barely become known that I was there and the rooms were full of former acquaintances to see me and to speak to me.[36]

Later in the same letter he expressed his great love for his new fatherland.

I do not have to reassure you how much I yearn for America and to be with you again, with my precious family and those fellow believers and fellow soldiers of the Lord closest to me. As much good as we see and enjoy here, it is still my wish to live in America and to die there and nowhere else, and this resolve has grown not weaker but ever stronger. As much as God has done here toward improvement, yet I have to say after observing many things in Germany that induce me to praise God, the greatest thing God has done for us [is] in America. Please greet all relatives and brothers and sisters in Christ over there with a greeting of my fervent love.[37]

For Walther, the old university town of Leipzig, his alma mater, constituted a special joy. Here he met several of the faculty, including K. F. A. Kahnis (1814–1888), who had earlier been a friend of the immigration. When his views concerning Scripture changed, Kahnis had distanced himself from that movement.

Of very special interest was a visit to Dresden, where Walther's old friend from the immigration in 1838, Franz Adolph Marbach (1798–1860) was now living. Several years later, when Walther made a return trip to seek improved health in 1860, he was privileged to attend the funeral of Marbach who had died on June 6, 1860. He was most grateful that he had the opportunity to meet with Marbach both in 1851 and in 1860 and that any differences between the two had been resolved.

In Erlangen Walther met a large number of faculty when he arrived on October 5. He spent an entire month in the city and at the university. Here he met with J. W. F. Hoefling (1802–1853). At first the two felt comfortable with each other's theology, but as noted earlier, they disagreed on the role of the congregation and the pastor (church and ministry). In opposition to Walther, Hoefling "nearly combined the professional ministry with the universal priesthood."[38]

Another faculty member with whom Walther met was Johann Christian Conrad von Hofmann (1810–1877), who taught a limited atonement, namely, that "Christ suffered on our behalf, not in our stead." Gottfried Thomasius (1802–1875), professor of dogmatics at Erlangen, was in agreement with Kahnis' teaching that Christ had given up his deity when he lived on earth. Walther taught that he had not given up his divine nature, but had used it only infrequently. Another professor he saw was Heinrich Schmid (1811–1885), who became influential in America through the H. E. Jacobs and C. A. Hay translation of his *Doctrinal Theology of the Evangelical Lutheran Church* in 1875.

Finally there was Adolf von Harless (1806–1879), who had been a professor at both Erlangen and Leipzig and later the court preacher in Dresden. This was quite an array of great and active theologians in Europe during Walther's time. The itinerary and description of the visits appeared in *"Reisebericht des Redakteurs"* (*Editor's Travel Report*), a series of articles in *Der Lutheraner*.[39] These visits, including Langenchursdorf (where his sister was living), Brauensdorf, and Leipzig, took place between August 27 and September 6, 1851.

As for the work of the church, the three meetings in Nürnberg with Wilhelm Loehe (1808–1872) were the most important. The first was held on August 6, and the second when Walther attended a pastoral conference with Loehe on October 9. A final meeting with Loehe was held on November 14 and lasted almost a week. In spite of the friendly meetings they experienced and the apparent overcoming of their differences with respect to the doctrine of the church and ministry, a complete break in relations was to develop after Walther returned home. Wyneken and Walther started their way back to America and took a ship from Calais on December 30. They arrived in New York on January 16, 1852 and in St. Louis on February 2.

The break between Loehe and Walther was inevitable. Walther published his *Kirche und Amt* (*Church and Ministry*) which dealt with a major question discussed in theological circles in Europe at this time. Walther had undertaken his visit to Loehe with much anticipation, but shortly after his return to America, he learned that J. A. A. Grabau also subsequently had visited Loehe, and the fragile unanimity that had been achieved was destroyed.

Although there were no immediate results of Walther's trip to Europe, in 1871 a group of Lutherans separated from the Saxon State Church and organized an independent church. When they requested Walther's support, he suggested they call F. T. C. Ruhland (1836–1879) as pastor. He accepted and sailed for Saxony, arriving on April 5, 1872. Missouri had once more returned to Saxony! Ruhland served first in Dresden and later in Planitz.

Through the association with Friedrich Brunn (1819–1895) and other pastors and congregations, the synod of the Evangelical Lutheran Free Church of Saxony and Other States was organized on November 6, 1876. Walther rejoiced at this and supported Ruhland through frequent letters and financial aid. Georg Stoeckhardt, later Walther's pastor in St. Louis, was one of the founders. An excellent relationship between the "Free

Church" and Walther continued until his death. Today the church is known as the Selbständige Ev. Lutherische Kirche (SELK) and it has a seminary in Oberursel near Frankfurt, Germany. Theodor Harms of Hermannsburg also recruited students in Germany for the Missouri Synod after the Civil War.

Connections with Australian Lutherans were established in 1875. At that time, President E. Homann began correspondence with Walther after having become acquainted with him through *Lehre und Wehre*. The Australian church asked for a candidate and Caspar Dorsch, an 1881 St. Louis graduate, accepted the call to become pastor of a congregation in Adelaide. A close affinity developed between the Murray and the Mississippi.

Walther has been called a true peace theologian—*ein rechter Friedens Theologe*. Walther seized every possible opportunity he had to share his views of Scripture and the Confessions so that Christ might be exalted. Love for Christ and His redeemed motivated Walther. The Good News was for all people.

FELLOWSHIP ISSUES

Walther's efforts to unite Lutheranism in America were heroic. We take a look now at the principles he put forth concerning the church and its divisions, denominationalism, sectarianism, and heresy. There are two primary sources on which we will elaborate to trace his thinking and theology—the Constitution of the Missouri Synod and Walther's *The True Visible Church*.

Two articles in the LCMS constitution are especially significant. When the original, preliminary text of the proposed synodical constitution was prepared, it was disseminated in *Der Lutheraner* in September 1846, following the last preliminary convention to organize the Synod held in Fort Wayne in July 1846. The constitution was publicized because it was to be acted upon during the Synod's organizing convention in April 1847. While the articles we will discuss still appear in the present synodical constitution, they are in different locations than originally. Nevertheless, the terminology, which is still the same, is of great value in understanding Walther and his relation to other Lutheran and Christian organizations. The footnotes in *Der Lutheraner* explaining the meaning of these articles give us valuable insights.

The first article appeared in the original Chapter 1 (Article I) of the constitution in a paragraph entitled "Grounds for Establishing a Synodical Fellowship" (*Synodal-Verbandes*). The primary objective of the Synod was:

> The conservation and promotion of the unity of the pure confession (Ephesians 4:3–6; 1 Corinthians 1:10) and the common defense against schism [*Separatistischen*] and sectarian confusion [*Unwesen*].[40]

The footnotes explain "separatism," "schism," "sectarianism," and heresy. Since Walther was the primary drafter of the constitution, these footnotes are extremely valuable in understanding the synodical constitution today. Walther used the word *absondern* to define those who separate or sever themselves from the church. He made a distinction between "separatism" and "sectarianism." These may be considered fine points, but they are necessary to understand Walther's attitude toward the ecclesiastical environment in which the Missouri Synod found itself. The footnotes read:

> Separatists (schismatics) are those who at first separate themselves [*absondern*] not from the doctrine, but only from the fellowship of the church, because of the hypocrites who are intermixed. Such the church would gladly send off because they are only lip Christians [*Maulchristen*] who are also hypocritical in their faith but who have not become guilty of outward sins. Much more the [church] must judge according to Matthew 13:29–30 and according to the actions of the Lord as He dealt with Judas. Only revealed and stubborn sinners the church will finally expel, after all steps of admonition according to Matthew 18:15–17 have been taken, and have proven fruitless.
>
> Sectarians or heretics in contrast, are such who separate themselves from the pure doctrine and in this or that article deny Scripture, bring up false doctrine, spread it, or attach themselves stubbornly to it or defend it. Such the church after futile admonitions should avoid and expel according to Titus 3:10, Romans 16:17, and Galatians 1:8–9, to condemn them not absolutely according to their person (as they might come to repentance) but rather as carriers of a soul-destroying false teaching. It often happens, furthermore, that out of separatists sectarians will develop shortly.

These explanations aid us in understanding the current constitution in Article III, 1 and also Article VI, 2, a, b, and c. In addition, Chapter 2 (Article II) of the proposed 1847 constitution identified the "Conditions of Membership" as including, among others, the following stipulation:

Renunciation of unionism and syncretism of every description such as a), serving congregations of mixed confession, as such, by ministers of the church; b), taking part in the services and sacramental rites of heterodox congregations or of congregations of mixed confession [*gemischter Gemeinden*]; c), participating in heterodox tract and missionary activities.

This paragraph was followed immediately by an insistence on the "exclusive use of doctrinally pure church books and school books."[41] All of this is echoed in Article VI of the present constitution.

The original constitution called this *Glaubensmengerei*, that is, "ecclesiastical and confessional mixing together." It could also be translated as a homogenization of various faiths or blending them together. *Gemischter Gemeinden* refers to congregations where differing faiths or beliefs have been mixed together. The preliminary draft of the constitution in a footnote defines such mixed congregations as:

Those consisting of Lutheran and Reformed or the so-called Evangelical (united Protestants) mixed together, often served by so-called Lutheran pastors, who are therefore naturally duplicitous. Whatever is Lutheran should be Lutheran, and Reformed should be Reformed.[42]

The footnote consequently makes it very clear that this refers to pulpit and altar fellowship with non-Lutherans. In part, America had inherited such "co-mixtures" with Lutherans and Reformed. As Lutheranism had been transformed by pietism and developed into rationalism, it was in danger of losing the inspired Scriptures and subscription to the Lutheran Confessions. The rule of reason had made great changes in doctrine. In Saxony, Stephan, Walther, and their adherents left the state church because of the negative, anti-scriptural impact it had made upon them. In Prussia, on the other hand, King Friedrich Wilhelm III had forcibly tried to merge Lutherans and Reformed in his lands and, consequently, J. A. A. Grabau and thousands of others immigrated to America to avoid such coercion from the state.

But America had received immigrants from both the German Reformed and Lutheran faiths. In colonial America these two often worshiped together in a single church building because they could not afford two different structures and at times two different pastors. These congregations developed into the so-called "union churches," where people comfortably shared a worship facility and a clergyman. Frequently the people intermarried as well, and the community embraced an indistinctive faith and worship. Some of them practiced no liturgical worship and used a common German hymnal. Walther warned against such "unionism" in the two articles of the synodical constitution under discussion. In the early history of the Missouri Synod, there were several localities served by synodical pastors which had begun as mixed or union churches—Lochner in Toledo, Ohio, Buenger at Olivette, Missouri, Selle in Chicago and many others. In this context, "unionism" or the "co-mixture" usually related to the Reformed, unionistic, rationalistic, or Methodist Germans in America.

In his *Pastoral Theology*, Walther explicitly applied the theology of fellowship to the practice of the Sacrament of the Altar:

> Anyone who does not confess the faith that the true body of Jesus Christ is truly and really present in the holy Supper and so is received by all communicants, worthy and unworthy, cannot discern the body of the Lord (1 Corinthians 11:29) and so he is not to be admitted to the holy Supper under any circumstances ... but even one who confesses cannot ordinarily be admitted if he is and wants to remain, not a member of our orthodox church, but rather a separatist, Romanist, Reformed, so-called Evangelical or Unionist ... for the Sacrament, as it is a seal of faith, is also the banner of the fellowship when it is administered.[43]

Several statements from Walther in *The True Visible Church*, an essay he presented to the Western District convention at Immanuel, Chicago, Illinois in May 1867, will serve to shed further light on Walther's views regarding fellowship. Theses four, five, six, seven, and eight are especially apropos:

> Thesis four: Scripture calls even such visible communions "churches" as are guilty of a partial deviation from the pure doctrine of the Word of God as long as they still retain God's Word essentially.

> Thesis five: Fellowships which, though retaining God's Word essentially, nevertheless err obstinately in the fundamentals of the Word of God are, insofar as they do this, not churches in the sense of Scripture but factions or sects, that is, heretical fellowships.

> Thesis six: Fellowships that disrupt the unity of the church through errors not destroying the foundation of the faith, or because of persons, ceremonies, or matters of life, are, according to God's Word, sects (schisms) or separatistic fellowships.

> Thesis seven: Communions that call themselves Christian but do not recognize the Bible as the Word of God and so deny the Holy Trinity are, according to God's Word, not churches, but synagogues of Satan and temples of idols.

Thesis eight: While ecclesiastical writers at times call those communions true or real churches that retain God's Word essentially, in distinction from those that are not churches, nevertheless a true visible church in the full [*uneingeschränkten*] sense of the term, in opposition to heterodox churches or sects, is only that in which God's Word is proclaimed in its purity and the sacraments are administered according to the Gospel.[44]

In his essays Walther shared further definitions. In his explication, he defined what it meant to be "sectarian," "heretic," or "cult." In preparing these definitions he wrote:

It certainly was very wicked of Grabau to decry as a heretic and sectarian everyone who in any way opposed him, and to declare every congregation that wished to join our Synod to be a sect and a cult.... You see, any person, regardless of who he is, who has never been warned or has at least not been warned repeatedly and whose actions do not allow us confidently to conclude that against better knowledge and conscience he persists in holding and defending his error, *that person is not a heretic* [emphasis added], no matter what he believes and teaches.[45]

A heretic is one:

Who has been admonished once or more than once and has condemned himself, i.e., his conscience tells him that the person who is admonishing him is right, but he stubbornly refuses to admit this. This is a strong indication that such a person is a heretic and that he is not merely in error as we all err daily in both worldly and spiritual matters.[46]

A heretic usually has three characteristics: 1) Not only does he err, but he refuses to accept admonition; 2) He defends his error and tries to build up a group of adherents; 3) He disputes recognized truths and refuses to admit his error, because he is afraid of being disgraced.[47]

Walther held that the Christian church was one church, wherever it existed throughout the world. However within this one church (and Walther emphasized "within," in contrast to the Roman Catholic position) there were aberrations, which Walther referred to as "sects" [*Sekte*], or "cults" [*Rotten*]. These he defined as:

… adherents who gather around a heretic…. In a churchly sense only that communion is a cult which, despite repeated admonition, refuses to give up faith-destroying errors.[48]

Walther also lectured about a "pernicious sect" (schisms, sects, or separatistic fellowships) which he defined as follows:

1) It must go contrary to the foundation of the Christian faith; 2) defend its error with premeditation; 3) cause divisions and offenses in the church; 4) resolutely refuse correction, insist that it is right, and obstinately persist in its heresy.[49]

Later Walther submitted a quotation from Baier's *Compendium Theologiae Positivae*.[50] Walther observed:

This quotation teaches us the proper attitude toward unionism, which was known as "syncretism" during the seventeenth century. It is very important that we not have brotherly communion (*Gemeinschaft*) with individual weak members of the sects. For it is not a question of whether such a person has faith or not, which would be an "accident," but it is a question of having the pure Word and properly administered sacraments.[51]

In his *Pastoral Theology*, Walther applied his theology to the practical, everyday world of the pastor. His applications are as relevant today as they were when he wrote them. Regarding the "Requirements of Public Preaching" Walther stated:

In a congregation that does not yet know the correct doctrine, it can only have a harmful effect to preach much against false doctrines. Such a congregation will either be filled with antipathy toward the preacher as a loveless debater and controversialist because it cannot yet perceive the importance of doctrinal unity, and so it will be frightened away from pure doctrine and filled with sympathy for false doctrine; or it will thereby be made fanatical and brought to an unreasoning zeal against the sects, and it will place its Christianity and Lutheranism, not in true and living faith, but in zealotry for orthodoxy and the customs of the orthodox church.[52]

While Walther was adamant regarding the importance of the faithful practice of church fellowship, he also recognized the importance of witnessing to other churches when this could be done without compromise. J. A. Friedrich wrote in his memoirs that he had learned from Walther himself that he approved when a pastor of the Synod was invited to preach in a sectarian church. He could do so without being reprimanded if he was given complete freedom to conduct the entire service as his own.

Any portrayal of Walther as a strict, unfeeling militant in his defense of pure doctrine completely misrepresents the man. Walther was compassionate and empathetic not only to his own family and friends, but also to people with whom he disagreed theologically. He responded to them the way Joseph in Egypt did to his brothers. An unidentified writer stated:

> Professor Walther declared that he often, in the polemic, felt like Joseph, who spoke harshly to his brothers, but then went into his chambers and had a good cry, and after he had washed his face came out again among the people.[53]

And Walther was not unable to appreciate those with whom he did not fully agree. When Wisconsin Synod theologian John Philip Koehler (1859–1951) was a student at Concordia Seminary, the renowned Dwight L. Moody (1837–1893) came to St. Louis for a visit. Koehler reported:

> When Moody was in St. Louis at the end of the 1870s and proclaimed the Gospel of grace in a wonderfully fine manner, Walther, in the classroom, could not refrain from paying him recognition in the friendliest fashion, without then toning this down with reservations in respect to his errors. One could feel that Moody was very dear to Walther. That won my heart at that time for the gospel of Moody and Walther.[54]

Philip Schaff (1819–1893), the prolific American church historian and professor at Union Theological Seminary, visited Walther in 1883, just after the splendid new seminary on Jefferson Avenue had been dedicated. Even though Schaff was not a friend of confessional or "old" Lutherans, he nevertheless recorded in his diary that when he visited Walther personally and was shown the new seminary buildings, he was dumbfounded that these "strict Lutherans," as he called them, could accomplish so much. He also stated that his visit with Walther was one of his most pleasant and memorable experiences. Throughout his life Walther was a hospitable host, even when the facilities were limited and rustic.

Schaff, who lectured extensively all over Europe, referred to Walther as "the leader of the strict old Lutherans." During his visit he also met with all the seminary professors, by whom he "was most cordially received." According to Schaff's companion on the visit, all conversations were carried on entirely in German, "as but one of the professors was able to speak English.... He returned homeward in a joyous mood, telling me that it was one of the most pleasant days in his life."[55]

On the whole, however, Walther's relationship with "outsiders" was mostly with other Lutherans. Walther looked upon the developing Lutheran church in America, including the Missouri Synod, as struggling to understand and adhere to God's revelation. He firmly believed that when the truth of God's revealed Word was understood, and the Symbols of the church were held as true and unadulterated statements and expositions of the Word, fellowship in every respect could be practiced. His hope for Lutheranism in America was that all the organizations and synods could come to an agreement, as he so optimistically had anticipated through the "free conferences" and the "colloquies." It was God's honor and revelation that Walther hoped could be accepted by all who call themselves Lutheran.

NOTES

[1] "Nietzsche and Schaff on American Lutheranism," translated by August R. Suelflow, *Concordia Historical Institute Quarterly*, 23:4 (January 1951) 148–51; original text in Philip Schaff, *Amerika, die politischen, socialen, und kirchlich-religiesen Zustaende der Vereinigten Staaten von Nordamerika mit besonderer Ruecksicht auf die Deutschen, aus eigener Anschauung dargestellt* (Berlin: Wiegandt and Grieben, 1858); cf. Philip Schaff, *America: A Sketch of Its Political, Social and Religious Character*, Perry Miller, ed. (Cambridge: Harvard University Press, 1961), 150ff.

[2] Benjamin Kurtz, "Notes on the 'Anxious Bench,'" *The Lutheran Observer*, 11 (December 1, 1843), 3.

[3] Kurtz, "Notes on the 'Anxious Bench,'" *The Lutheran Observer*, 11, 3.

[4] Samuel Simon Schmucker, "Vocation of the American Lutheran Church," *Evangelical Review*, 2 (April 1851), 509.

[5] Joseph A. Seiss, *Ecclesia Lutherana: A Brief Survey of the Evangelical Lutheran Church*, 4th ed. (Philadelphia: Lutheran Bookstore, 1871), 223–24.

[6] Richard C. Wolf, *Documents of Lutheran Unity in America* (Philadelphia: Fortress Press, 1966), 103.

[7] "Vorwort zu Jahrgang 1856," *Lehre und Wehre*, 2:1 (January 1856), 3–6. See also Erwin L. Lueker, "Walther and the Free Lutheran Conferences," *Concordia Theological Monthly*, 15:8 (August 1944), 534ff.

[8] An original printed report of these conferences is entitled: *Auszug aus den Verhandlungen der freien, ev.-lutherischen Konferenz* (New York: H. Ludwig Verlag u. Buchdrucker, 1858).

[9] Fred W. Meuser, *The Formation of the American Lutheran Church* (Columbus, OH: Wartburg Press, 1958), 49–50.

[10] C. F. W. Walther, "Die allgemeine Konferenz," *Der Lutheraner*, 13 (October 21, 1856), 33; translated in Lueker, "Walther and the Free Lutheran Conferences," *Concordia Theological Monthly*, 550.

[11] "Von dem Namen 'Lutheraner,'" *Der Lutheraner*, 1:1 (September 7, 1844), 3; translated in Lueker, "Walther and the Free Lutheran Conferences," *Concordia Theological Monthly*, 537, footnote 18.

[12] For the text, see S. E. Ochsenford, *Documentary History of the General Council of the Evangelical Lutheran Church in North America* (Philadelphia: General Council Publication House, 1912), 128ff; cf. Wolf, *Documents of Lutheran Unity in America*, 141–48.

[13] *Proceedings*, Missouri Synod, 1864 and 1866, 85f.

[14] Ludwig Fuerbringer, ed., *Briefe von C. F. W. Walther … an seine Freunde, Synodalgenossen, und Familienglieder* (St. Louis: Concordia Publishing House, 1915), vol. 2, 62.

[15] Fuerbringer, *Walthers Briefe*, vol. 2, 71.

[16] *Proceedings* of the Convention Held by Representatives from Various Evangelical Lutheran Synods in the United States and Canada Accepting the Unaltered Augsburg Confession, 1866, (Pittsburgh: Bakewell and Marthens, Printers, 1867), 14.

[17] *Proceedings* of the Convention Held by Representatives from Various Evangelical Lutheran Synods in the United States and Canada Accepting the Unaltered Augsburg Confession, 1866, 8.

[18] *Proceedings* of the Convention Held by Representatives from Various Evangelical Lutheran Synods in the United States and Canada Accepting the Unaltered Augsburg Confession, 1866, 18.

[19] Carl S. Meyer, ed., *Moving Frontiers* (St. Louis: Concordia Publishing House, 1964), 256.

[20] Wolf, *Documents of Lutheran Unity in America*, 170.

[21] Meyer, *Moving Frontiers*, 255.

[22] Wolf, *Documents of Lutheran Unity in America*, 162–65.

[23] See Roy A. Suelflow, "Relations of the Missouri Synod with the Buffalo Synod Up to 1866," *Concordia Historical Institute Quarterly*, 27:1 (April 1854), 1–19; 27:2 (July 1854), 57–73; 27:3 (October 1854), 97–132.

[24] "Das Colloquium," *Der Lutheraner*, 24:7 (December 1, 1867), 56.

[25] August R. Suelflow, "Georg Albert Schieferdecker and his Relationship to Chiliasm in the Iowa Synod," B.D. Thesis, Concordia Seminary, St. Louis, 1946.

[26] See "The False Arguments for the Modern Theory of Open Questions," ["*Die falschen Stützen der modernen Theorie von den offenen Fragen*"] presented by Walther in *Lehre und Wehre*, 14:4–10 (April-October 1868). William Arndt and Alex Guebert translated the entire series of articles in the *Concordia Theological Monthly*, 10:4–11 (April-November 1939). President J. A. O. Preus considered this article so important that he had it reprinted in 1971 in the LCMS *Proceedings*, 1971, 227–44.

[27] "Wieder Eine Friedensbotschaft!" *Der Lutheraner*, 25:5 (November 1, 1868), 37–38.

[28] *Proceedings*, Missouri Synod, 1869, 26–30, 87–92.

[29] C. F. W. Walther, *Essays for the Church* (St. Louis: Concordia Publishing House, 1992), vol. 1, 229–43.

[30] The agreements of Missouri, Ohio and Wisconsin appear in Wolf, *Documents of Lutheran Unity in America*, Documents 82–87. The original constitution appeared in the *Denkschrift, enthaltend eine eingehende Darlegung der Gruende, weshalb die zur Synodal-Conferenz …* (Columbus, OH: Druck von Schulze und Gassmann, 1871), 5.

[31] See Wolf, *Documents of Lutheran Unity in America*, 197.

[32] Synodical Conference Constitution, 1944, Article A 42.

[33] C. F. W. Walther, *Kurzer Lebenslauf des weiland ehrwürdigen Pastor Joh. Friedr. Bünger* (St. Louis: Verlag von F. Dette, 1882), 99.b

[34] Roy A. Suelflow, "The History of the Missouri Synod During the Second Twenty-five Years of Its Existence," Th.D. Dissertation, Concordia Seminary, St. Louis, 1946, 158.

[35] See E. C. Nelson and E. L. Fevold, *The Lutheran Church Among Norwegian Americans*, 2 volumes (Minneapolis: Augsburg, 1960).

[36] Roy A. Suelflow, ed., *Selected Writings of C. F. W. Walther* (St. Louis: Concordia Publishing House, 1981), 18.

[37] Suelflow, *Selected Writings of C. F. W. Walther*, 24.

[38] Holsten Fagerberg, *A New Look at the Lutheran Confessions*, trans. Gene J. Lund (St. Louis: Concordia Publishing House, 1972), 226. It is this functional concept of the ministry which Walther rejected.

[39] *Der Lutheraner*, 8:13–21 (February 17, 1852–June 8, 1852), 97–102, 105–8, 113–15, 132–34, 137–38, 145–47, 153–57, 161–65.

[40] *Der Lutheraner*, 3:1 (September 5, 1846), 2.

[41] *Der Lutheraner*, 3:1 (Capital II, 3–4), 2.

[42] *Der Lutheraner*, 3:1 (Note on Capital II, 3), 2.

[43] *Der Lutheraner*, 3:1, 148.

[44] Walther, *Essays for the Church*, vol. 1, 107, 114, 124, 129, 132. See also John M. Drickamer, ed., *Walther on the Church* (St. Louis: Concordia Publishing House, 1981), 156–68.

[45] Walther, *Essays for the Church*, vol. 1, 115.

[46] Walther, *Essays for the Church*, vol. 1, 115.

[47] Walther, *Essays for the Church*, vol. 1, 117.

[48] Walther, *Essays for the Church*, vol. 1, 116.

[49] Walther, *Essays for the Church*, vol. 1, 119.

[50] Baier, *Compendium Theologiae Positivae*, vol. 3, 665, 671.

[51] Walther, *Essays for the Church*, vol. 1, 123.

[52] C. F. W. Walther, *Pastoral Theology*, trans. and abridged by John Drickamer (New Haven: Lutheran News, 1995), 79.

[53] *Lehre und Wehre*, 25:2 (February 1879), 49–50.

[54] *Faith-Life* 25:9 (September 1952), 11.

[55] Reported by Samuel J. Niccolls of St. Louis, who accompanied Schaff. David S Schaff, *The Life of Philip Schaff* (New York: Charles Scribner's Sons, 1897), 184.

7

LOVE, HONOR, AND RESPECT

THE WALTHER HOME

What was it like to be in the Walther home? Did the family occupy a mansion, as one might expect? Was it a place of quiet and solitude? By no means! It was first and foremost a model of Christian love, honor, and respect for and by spouses, children, in-laws, and grandchildren. For almost thirty years the family lived in small, congested quarters, but the beauty and happiness of a blessed marriage, family, and house guests were always evident. One would expect that with all the books and articles he wrote and all the essays he presented, Walther would have the means to live comfortably. To the contrary, Walther's will at the time of his death reveals that his total worth was a mere $4,000. Two factors undoubtedly play a role in this respect: 1) the salaries of pastors and synodical faculty were low, at best, and 2) Walther consistently gave away whatever money was paid him for his literary works to charitable organizations and special projects in the church.

Hospitality reigned supreme in every apartment or home the Walthers occupied. Their home was always open to visitors and guests of all descriptions: to pastors and their families awaiting a call, to travelers who stopped for short or long visits, to the destitute or those in unfortunate circumstances who needed shelter and food. Seminary students were regularly invited to share Sunday dinner with the Walthers.

The roots of the family were established when Walther was pastor of Trinity Church, St. Louis, and Emilie Buenger, his future bride, lived with her brother Ernst in Perry County, Missouri. The two had known each other and their families in Germany. Emilie, at the age of 26, traveled with her six siblings on the *Copernicus* as part of the Saxon immigration in 1838–39. Because of family immigration problems, Emilie's widowed mother, Christiane Buenger, stayed behind in Bremen with a son and daughter. The three later sailed for America on December 11, 1838, and arrived with the "New York" group in Perry County, Missouri, on May 12, 1839.

It is unlikely that Walther and Emilie saw much of each other in the "new country," given the difficulties of travel on the Mississippi River between St. Louis and Perry County. But a spark of interest between them prevailed and grew ever stronger as time went on. Rather suddenly and perhaps even somewhat precipitously, Walther proposed marriage to Emilie in a letter addressed to her. Not only did he propose marriage, but in the same letter unabashedly suggested a date and place for the wedding—subject, of course, to Emilie's consent.

August 10, 1841

Dear heartily beloved Emily:

As little as I have till now had the right to write to you, and particularly with such a greeting, yet I cannot do otherwise if I am to be honest with you. Nearly two years have gone by, as you will perhaps recall since through your dear brother Fritz [John F. Buenger] I at least indicated from afar a precious, sublime wish of my heart which no one in the world but you can fulfill. But how wonderful have been the ways in which our heavenly Father has led me during the past two years! I do not need to tell you anything of this; my life has been an open book for you....

Therefore I cannot wait any longer to express this my wish frankly, also to you. It is this: Will you, dearest Emilie, become my life's companion? Can you return at least in some degree the love which, as I now confidently hope, God has enkindled in my heart for you? Do you believe that you can live with me happily, contentedly, and God-pleasingly in a union as intimate and inseparable until death as the holy estate of matrimony is?

You know me, my character, my faith, my failings and weaknesses, my outward position; you know that you will find no temporal fortune, no honor before the world, no assured future with me. I can therefore only add my pledge that you will have in me a spouse who will love you dearly and by God's grace faithfully. I have no one whom I could ask to speak for me to you; I have therefore prayed the dear Lord Himself to be my Eliezer and to direct your heart according to His holy will and to our mutual temporal and eternal welfare. Follow His guidance and then inform me by return messenger of your God-directed decision.

As communication between here and Perry County is often long interrupted, you will not, as I hope for your love, think ill of me for making the following suggestion. If you can, in God's name, say yes to my question, then we shall look upon your declaration as the completion of our betrothal, since your dear mother today and my good mother already in Germany in advance have given their parental consent there to. I would therefore in this event not come to Perry County before our marriage. If this is agreeable to you, I should like to have the publication of the banns of the marriage made in Frohna and here on the 13th, 14th, and 15th Sundays after Trinity (5th, 12th, and 19th of September) and the marriage ensue perhaps on the Monday after the last date, namely September 20th in the church at Frohna. The day of my arrival and that of your dear mother would be, if you accept my suggestion, God willing, on the 15th or 16th of September....

I am almost surprised at myself for daring, in this first letter, to speak so freely of betrothal, of publishing the banns of marriage, etc.; how much more will you perhaps be astonished! May you, however, recognize this as nothing else than my wholehearted confidence in you, that you will, even if you could not give me your hand, certainly grant me the privilege of having at least vividly imagined myself out of pure grace without my merit or worthiness, in the position of seeing you as my God-given dearly beloved bride!

May He give you a joyous decision and then make your heart firm, sure, and certain that you rest in His grace and under His holy benevolence; and if God brings us together, we will mutually serve Him day and night without ceasing, faithfully, until death, by the power of His omnipotent grace in Christ Jesus, your and my Savior. Amen.[1]

And what was Emilie's response? Just a week later, on August 17, 1841, she wrote most endearingly:

My Most Precious, Most Dearly Beloved, God-given Betrothed:

I received your precious, dear letter Sunday after church in Altenburg, over which I was very happy, to hear from my folks—my brother Ernst was not there, and I thought that the letter was from my dear brother Fritz [John F. Buenger of St. Louis], but I opened it and found it was addressed to me.

I was at first a little shocked by the contents of your precious letter—it came so unexpectedly—but I did not neglect to resign myself into the faithful hands of the heavenly Father, who will also lead and guide me in this serious affair, and may He show me His holy will, according to His holy will which has decided nothing except that which brings us blessings. The heavenly Father and the Lord Jesus Christ, who is my *Brautwerber* [intercessor], have convinced me that it is the will of the Lord. Therefore I give you my yes and say that I want to be your wife.

May also the Triune God lend His Yea and Amen to this, since your dear mother and my dear mother have no objections, for which I am all the more happy. Yes, I love you, my beloved, betrothed, with all my heart, and on all the earth there is now nothing more dear to me than you, out of pure grace without any merit on my part. Also here I well see how God's Word is being fulfilled, how He as a true Father adopts the forsaken orphans as His own children, and how He provides for them when His time and hour have come. If He gives sorrows, then again He gives joys. May the Lord thus lead both of us through sorrows and joys to heaven, where we can together praise and thank Him for everything He has done for us. Thus I believe that with the help of the Holy Spirit I can live with you happily, blessedly, and God-pleasingly in such an intimate union, indissoluble unto death. I was concerned about the fact that I am so old and that I would be but a very poor helpmeet for you, who would be unworthy of you, but since you had no concern about this and since God has guided things thus, this [concern] has left me.

My temperament, my faith, my shortcomings and weaknesses are well known to you, and therefore it is not necessary to go into detail. Every day I pray to God [that He would grant me] to desist from all impropriety. I believe and hope assuredly that God the Almighty will keep both of us in His grace till death and that He will not remove His hand from us, for which both of us will want to pray together day and night. I am satisfied with everything which you consider good and right, but the announcement [of the marriage] and the wedding seem a bit rushed to me, and I would have desired to postpone it a little, but since you, my heartily beloved betrothed, have already designated the days for the publishing of the banns and for the wedding, therefore I am satisfied, and it pleases me very much that I am to be announced and married in Frohna by the Rev. Keyl, who was always concerned about me in such a fatherly way. The pastor and your dear sister received the news as unexpectedly as I did, but they were happy about it, especially your dear sister. May God be with us both also in this engagement that the time [of engagement] may be a God-sanctified time for me, in which I will daily plead with God in prayer for you. I have submitted myself entirely to God, and He will also, through our Lord Jesus Christ, bless this step, both in body and in soul, which we have begun with Him.

May the Lord keep you healthy, and if it be His will, bring you and my dear mother safe to us on the 15th or 16th of September, about which I am especially happy, to have you with us soon.

Loving you most sincerely,

[Signed]

Your betrothed,

Emilie Buenger[2]

Walther did not wait long to respond to Emilie's letter. He wrote on August 25, 1841. A few glimpses tell us much more about the bride and groom.

St. Louis, Missouri

August 25, 1841

In Christ Jesus, my dearly beloved bride:

After a long yearning wait, your precious answer is finally in my hands. As I see with great joy from your answer, God has assured you of His gracious will, that we should together journey through this earthly life toward heaven. May His holy name be praised eternally! Let us now daily beseech our good and gracious God for His Holy Spirit that we may enter into the estate of marriage in His grace and fear. A chief purpose of matrimony is that thereby the Christian church is expanded and edified. Oh, join me in praying in the name of Jesus, that our Lord would grant grace that on the day of our wedding that we may lay the first cornerstone for a little house-church (Romans 16:5). How I long to see our home as a true model for a genuinely Christian family in which God dwells and all God's children are stirred up to praise our Father in heaven! (Matthew 5:16)

Your Ferdinand[3]

Twelve days later Emilie wrote to Walther again, but apparently the letter to which she is responding is no longer in existence.

August 29, 1841

In Christ Jesus, Dearly Beloved Betrothed:

I was very happy to receive a letter from you so soon. Every day I think of you in love, and I pray God that He may send us His Holy Spirit, so that we may in His grace and in fear of Him enter on our new estate. Sometimes I feel that I am incapable on account of the seriousness of the position, but then I stay close to the Word, for God has ordered it so and wants it thus. May in all things not my will, but the will of the Lord be done. I know that I am not fit for any good thing, but I have the confidence in God that He does not forsake anyone who puts his trust in Him, and I am also confident that God will, out of grace, guide and lead us with His fatherly hands till He will receive us into the heavenly dwelling—the great promise in Psalm 28. Oh! Our blessedness! With this blessing we will cast all our cares upon the Lord and hold fast to this precious Word in good and evil days.

I also thank you for having referred me to the Book of Tobit and to Dr. Luther's wedding sermons, and I have read in Luther the explanation of the Sixth Commandment, and have also begun to read the sermons, but I knew hardly anything of this holy estate which Luther calls the most important of all estates, and also the Book of Tobit has been enlightening and constructive for me. May God also help me that I may become a Sarah like that, that I may with the same God and only through grace establish with you such a God-pleasing marriage in and with God.

[Signed]

Your Emilie[4]

Both Emilie and Ferdinand excelled in expressing their love for each other and the marvelous joy they had in anticipation of their marriage. She was 29, he was 30. In preparation for the wedding ceremony, Walther traveled on the Mississippi River to Perry County. He brought with him a box of cigars. For the wedding dinner he had planned a special entrée: venison. Shortly after arriving in Perry County, he asked a young man from the community to shoot a deer to be served at the dinner. Walther paid the selected hunter in advance with cigars instead of money. The hunter, however, sat all day smoking Walther's cigars instead of looking for a deer. By late afternoon the box of cigars had been consumed, but a shot was never fired! So the wedding dinner did not include venison.

The wedding ceremony took place on September 21, 1841 in Dresden, Missouri. E. G. W. Keyl [Walther's brother-in-law] officiated.[5]

When they returned to St. Louis, the couple moved into the home owned by Emilie's mother, Christiane Friederika Buenger, located between 1st and 2nd on Poplar Street. Ferdinand and Emily occupied the first floor, while Christiane and another daughter, Clementine and her husband (Gottlob G. Neumueller) lived on the second floor. This was Ferdinand and Emilie's home for nine years, where five of their children were born. It was in these small quarters of the home on Poplar Street that the second preliminary meeting to organize the Missouri Synod was held in 1846, at which the Walthers hosted four pastors: Lochner, Sihler, Fuerbringer, and Ernst. Lochner, who later married Lydia Buenger (Emilie's sister) described the limited quarters:

> The first floor consisted of a living room, which doubled as a bed-room for Walther, his wife, and two children, a study and a small sum-mer kitchen, which extended from the house. The study served as the guest room. When it was time to go to sleep, the lounge was unfold-ed and the double bed served Sihler and Fuerbringer. A trundle bed underneath served as a bed for Pastor Ernst and me. After breakfast the improvised sleeping room once more became the study.[6]

It was also at this home on Poplar Street that several tragedies occurred in the Walther family. During the devastating cholera epidemic in 1849, "Grandma Buenger" (Emilie's mother) died of the dreaded dis-ease on July 11, at the age of 61. Her son, J. F. Buenger (Walther's broth-er-in-law) lost his first wife to the same disease at the age of 26, together with their baby, only a year old. In the same home a year earlier (July 24, 1848) Walther's oldest son, Hermann Christoph, fell down the basement stairway and died the same day. The home that once was so cozy in 1846 had become filled with many sorrows by 1849.

Slightly larger living quarters became available when the Walther fam-ily moved to the first floor of the new Seminary wing in 1850. The entire wing was only 42 x 36 feet. The Walthers occupied one-half of the first floor (about 750 square feet), and the Adolph Biewend family lived in the other half. The Walthers had five children living with them at the time. Even though the quarters in this new apartment were quite limited, Walther hosted many students who were unable to go home for Christmas. The students lived on the second floor of this wing. Joseph Schmidt (1846–1931), first president of the newly-organized Michigan District and subsequently also president of the Fort Wayne college, described an 1860 Christmas in the Walther apartment:

It was very likely around Christmas time, 1860, that a few of our students, among them myself, received an invitation to the *Christbaumpluendering* [plundering the Christmas tree] in the family circle of the Walthers. Professor Walther himself directed the distribution of the gifts. Whenever he got a gift down from the tree, he asked, *"Wer soll das haben?"'* (Who shall get this one?) Then the one to whom this question had been addressed, with 'his back turned toward the tree, designated the recipient. After the distribution Professor Walther conducted a mock trial. He himself took over the office of judge. The name of the plaintiff has escaped me. I myself was the defendant, accused of I know no more of what capital crime. After the accusation the trial proceeded with the regular taking of testimony. Then I was given the floor for argument in my own defense. In spite of my brilliant apology—his Honor himself commended me—I was condemned to, I no longer remember, what kind of punishment. This little sidelight in the life of my great teacher I have, despite the many intervening years, not forgotten.[7]

THE CHILDREN

Ferdinand and Emilie Walther were blessed with six children, only four of whom reached adulthood. They were:

1. Christiane Magdalena (Lenchen), born November 22, 1842. She was married October 29, 1862 to Stephanus Keyl (son of E. G. W. Keyl) who died on December 15, 1905. The couple had twelve children, at least five of whom died prematurely. Two were born and died in Philadelphia; the other children at Port Richmond, Staten Island, New York.

2. Hermann Christoph, born October 25, 1844, who died at the age of four on July 24, 1848 of cerebral epilepsy as a result of a fall on the basement steps of their home.

3. Ferdinand Gerhardt (twin) born February 23, 1847. Ferdinand became a pastor and on May 27, 1873 married Bertha Biltz. He died at the age of 86 on May 25, 1933. His wife Bertha died November 10, 1944. The couple had five children.

4. Constantin (twin) was a miller and worked at various locations; ultimately he owned and operated his own mill in Norborne, Missouri. He married a widow, Sophie Kuntz Lau, on October 29, 1875. Constantin died September 21, 1905 and Sophie, three months later, on December 21.

5. Emma Julie (Julchen), born July 27, 1849; died November 24, 1904. On October 8, 1872 she married Johann Heinrich Niemann (born

April 11, 1848; died March 15, 1910). They had a son who lived less than two years, and a daughter, Ottilie, born in 1874, who reached adulthood.

6. Christian Friedrich, born June 29, 1851, who died of dysentery as an infant on October 29, 1852.

The four children provided Emilie and Ferdinand with some twenty grandchildren, but only about fourteen reached adulthood. Walther and Emilie were deeply devoted to their children and grandchildren. With so many untimely deaths occurring among their grandchildren, Walther wrote some very stirring and emotional letters of sympathy to the parents, always directing them to Jesus Christ as their Savior and reminding them of their eternal home in heaven where they would all be reunited.

NEW HOME

It was not until 1870, when Walther was 59 years old, that the family had its own, free-standing home. From 1850 to 1870 they had lived on the first floor of the south wing of the Seminary. There were two apartments on this floor, one Walther's and the other occupied by Professor Biewend. Later Walther purchased a lot on Texas (Clara) Avenue for $800. The lot was unused until after the Civil War, when his friends started to build a house, planning to present it to Walther. But Walther had none of that! When he became aware of the plans, he inserted a special announcement in *Der Lutheraner*, entitled "Something Personal." It declared:

> After I thoroughly considered and thought it through [the gift of a home], I have concluded to express very sincere thanks to the dear friends who have had this plan in mind. But under no consideration whatsoever would I accept the gift now or in the future. Since this matter is a matter of my conscience, I am petitioning those friendly givers, if they do not consider their friendship valueless, not to proceed and press this any further on me. Absolutely nothing will alter my decision, but any further attempts will cause me deep heartache.

> It is not my prerogative to make recommendations as to what to do with the completion of the planned construction. Nevertheless, I believe that I may venture the suggestion that I release my ownership of the lot, so that the house being erected on it may be sold and the income given to those generous givers.[8]

In a gesture of magnanimity, the house on 3632 Texas Avenue was made available to Walther but owned by the Synod. This is the home in which Walther died in 1887. After his death, it was occupied first by Martin Guenther (1887–1893) and later by Georg Stoeckhardt, who lived in it until 1906, when it was razed to make room for an annex to the Seminary known today as Holy Cross Hall. A favorite Russell drawing shows the house lightly covered with snow when the coachman came to pick up Walther in the carriage in the early dawn to preach at a Christmas service. At Walther's funeral, the house was draped in black crepe cloth.

Few descriptions are available of the interior of the house on Texas Avenue. At the front entrance to the right was the family room or parlor, containing Walther's grand piano given to him by his congregation. A long hall intersected the entire house from front to back. Behind the parlor was a large dining room, so often filled with numerous guests. Behind the dining room was a kitchen with an extended summer kitchen. The stairs to the second floor were next to the hall. Above the kitchen on the second floor was Walther's enlarged study, arranged by removing a wall between two rooms in 1881. The rest of the second floor provided sleeping quarters for the Walthers, their children, frequent overnight guests, and the housekeeper Katharina Huesemann.[9]

Marguerita Lenk, who with her husband and children lived with the Walthers during the time her husband was waiting for a call, wrote a book entitled *Fifteen Years in America*. In it she shared some glimpses into the Walther household, some inaccurately told on the basis of "synodical" tradition. She recounted that Mrs. Walther had told her that food did not mean anything to her husband. It would not make any difference to him, she admitted, whether she had prepared a roasted turkey or served cornmeal mush. Walther's favorite food was egg custard. In the course of the conversation with Mrs. Lenk, Emilie revealed that Walther's mother fixed egg custard for his birthday or on occasion as a consolation whenever he had a childish worry. It was somewhat similar to scrambled eggs and sweet soufflé. Even when others served it, Walther insisted that only his mother knew how to make good custard. Incidentally, Walther also liked sauerkraut, and another favorite was "head cheese" which he got from Perry County, Missouri.[10]

In his letter to Emilie, written May 2, 1860 while on board the ship to Europe, Walther lovingly spoke of Emilie's cooking. After relating the miserable, bitter cold they had experienced on board ship and the storms that buffeted them day and night, Walther said: "A journey on a sailing ship is, for the most part, uncomfortable." He continued:

I had difficulty getting used to the relatively good, but very heavy ship's fare; it was also the cause of a rather painful swelling of the finger joints which I have not gotten rid of yet. In all that, we often wished we could eat your cooking at least once a week and be able to enjoy your tasty and wholesome dishes.[11]

Paul Lehmann was a grand-nephew of Walther and lived in the Walther home in 1886–1887. In the fall of 1886 the family arranged a waterbed for the aged patriarch. Beginning at Christmas time, 1886, Walther gave up almost all his previous responsibilities. Before he became ill, he normally had breakfast at seven in the morning and then conducted family devotions, which consisted of Scripture and prayer. Immediately after breakfast Walther went back upstairs to his study. In mid afternoon, the housekeeper, Katharina Huesemann, served Walther beer. Evening devotions were conducted at 9 p.m. and usually Walther stayed up until midnight working in his study.[12]

In addition, Theodore Walther, son of Ferdinand, also lived in the Walther home beginning in 1884 so that the two young boys could attend confirmation classes and parish school in St. Louis. Theodore wrote: "When we got to St. Louis, Grandmother was still with us. She died the summer of the next year."

The boys reminisced that they always preferred Walther to apply butter to their bread because he was much more generous than others. Soups were the favorite, probably because Walther could not wear his dentures. Lenk also reports that Mrs. Walther stood at the bottom of the steps to the second floor study and called her husband to a meal, "Please be so kind!" If there was no response, she would repeat this call several times. Sometimes she was irritated when he didn't respond at all and sadly said: "He doesn't want to eat again! I must send coffee up to him."

One of the famous visitors to the Walther home was Philip Schaff of Union Theological Seminary, New York. He reported:

I must not fail to mention a most interesting acquaintance which I made lately. I recently visited the general president of the Missouri Synod, who is the pastor of a congregation here and a professor at Concordia College, where the young pastors-to-be are theologically educated for their profession.

Professor Walther is a thoroughly lovable, gentle-minded man with sharply-chiseled features, and bright, shining eyes. His conversation is in every respect positive and constructive. In his mouth everything takes shape and form and is molded before the eyes of the listener. He enters into all questions.[13]

Walther could become so engrossed in his research and reading that he actually did skip meals, sitting and puffing his long-stemmed pipes. His filing system consisted of pigeon holes in his desk. He took his notes on little slips of paper and, according to his own filing system, inserted them into these holes. There he preserved the quotations, references, and other notes he had copied from his voracious reading of Scripture, the Confessions, Luther and the Reformation fathers, the latter almost entirely in Latin.

Among the seminary students who were frequent dinner guests at the Walther home were his nephews, Theodore Buenger and Ludwig Fuerbringer, also two other students, W. Mueller and Karl Craemer. When special guests were present for dinner, Walther served wine. According to the French custom, he also placed some sugar lumps into his coffee. There was always a lively dinner conversation where Walther "was naturally the speaker." Ludwig Fuerbringer apologetically wrote:

> I regret that I did not put into writing what he said on such occasions, and thus start a little volume of *"Tischreden"* [*Table Talk*] of Walther.... Occasionally he also sent me on errands, and I remember very well that I took the distinguished naturalist Alfred Brehm from the hotel to Walther's home for dinner and again back to the hotel, traveling, of course, in the rather primitive streetcars, drawn by mules.[14]

THE CIVIL WAR AND WALTHER'S HOUSEHOLD

Walther and the faculty closed the Seminary on April 26, 1861 because of Civil War skirmishes. Shortly thereafter Walther moved his family to the Kerckhoff Farm in Sandy Creek, Hillsboro (Jefferson County), Missouri, for their safety.

Emilie's brother, Theodore E. Buenger, a teacher in Chicago, had encouraged the entire family to come and stay with him. Walther graciously responded on May 7, 1861 that he had already sent the family out of the danger zone. Other faculty members with their families moved in several directions also. Only Saxer and Walther stayed behind to look after the Seminary. In a letter to J. M. Buehler (first Missouri Synod pastor in California), Walther described the conditions in St. Louis at the time, concluding with the words, "Saxer and I are living alone in solitary like two eccentrics in the attic."[15]

Two of Walther's letters addressed to Emilie during this period of separation were preserved. In the first, dated May 10, 1861 Walther wrote that the battle had begun in St. Louis and that the Union troops were pursuing the Missouri state troops.

> Don't be concerned about us because you know that even a sparrow does not fall from the sky without God's knowledge.... I am there where God has placed me ... since I don't know whether the city will be locked up temporarily, so that no one can leave or come into it, I want to visit you shortly after the holidays.... May God grant that the dear children are living in the fear of God and that they will learn to pray particularly in the time of need. May our dear Savior have you under His wings, like a hen, and the Holy Spirit pour comfort and peace into your hearts.[16]

Walther added in a postscript that the soldiers had returned to the arsenal and to the Marine Hospital with great shouts of victory, and that they had taken the weapons of the state troops and driven the Confederates out of their camp. Shortly thereafter Walther visited his family in Hillsboro.

In a second letter written on May 28, 1861, Walther wrote Emilie that he had returned home safely after having visited her at the Kerckhoff farm. Then he makes this comment:

> I arrived back in St. Louis at 9 p.m. [May 28]. Since the evening was so beautiful.... I got off the train at Carondelet [now Broadway] so that I could stay overnight in my dear college. I am so grateful that all of you are well....[17]

Walther then relates matters of a domestic nature in his letter:

> Mrs. Hefele has done well in taking care of our things. The garden is in good condition and she is preparing it for the future, as she says. The berries on the lot are doing quite well and the Biewend children are picking them as soon as they are ripe.... Mrs. Hefele has also brought the cow back, taking good care of her, and is making butter for us and for her household. Saxer's garden, she told me, was being taken care of by Madame Biewend. Consequently I can't send anything to you.

> I don't know whether I should encourage you to come back or not, which I don't know myself. But this much I should say that you do not have to remain in the country because of the political situation, since it is pretty quiet here and no new turmoil is expected. I will leave that entirely up to you if you want to return soon. If you think that it is

healthier for the children and that they have better activities in the country, especially if we have to go on half rations in a few months, then stay. The synodical treasury is exhausted. If you think, on the other hand, that the children are neither healthier nor benefitted to live in the country then by all means, come as soon as it is convenient for you. But don't rush. The difference, undoubtedly, is not great. I am living here in my loneliness and not very comfortably. If you decide to return shortly, I don't know whether you will need any money for the return trip. If you are short, then please write me. Undoubtedly, it will be best if you return by train. Be sure to ask the Kerckhoffs how much we owe them for the rent.[18]

In a letter to Friedrich Brunn, dated August 23, 1861, Walther indicates that the Seminary had been closed for three months (June, July, and August), and perhaps a few days in May and in September. Walther's family, however, returned to St. Louis on June 6.[19]

WALTHER'S FAMILY AND CHILDREN

Walther's letters, written over the years to friends and family, reveal that he was an individual with deep feelings and emotions. In his essays and literary works alone, he is a giant. But there is a genuine sparkle in his correspondence with friends and family. Walther is not only a many-faceted person, but a man who dearly loved his wife, his children, and his grandchildren. Each family member had special meaning for him and constituted the beauty of their home together. Neither the size of the living quarters nor its furnishings were essential; only the family living there made it important.

Throughout his letters—and not all have been preserved—he uses nicknames for his children: Magdalena becomes Lenchen, Julie becomes Julchen, while the two boys Ferdinand and Constantine retained their full names. His parental love followed them throughout their lives. Even the grandchildren had names of endearment. His grandson Theodore was "Thodo," and grandson Ferdinand was "Nand." The two granddaughters were Emilie, nicknamed "Milie," and Emma, whom he called "Emmchen."

The oldest daughter, Christiane Magdalene (Lenchen) married Stephanus Keyl on October 29, 1862. Stephanus accompanied Walther on his journey to Europe in 1860 to regain his health. He remained in Germany afterward and studied at the University of Leipzig for about a year.

Most interesting is the letter written by Stephanus Keyl, dated June 24, 1862, in which he asked Walther for the hand of his daughter Lenchen. In response, Walther admitted that he was surprised by the request, and that he had petitioned God to give him an answer. Since Keyl was the son of Walther's deceased sister, he wrote Stephanus that he had consulted with various faculty and clergy members to get their opinion and had also discussed it with his dear wife. Walther spoke most lovingly of his 20-year-old daughter:

> I have also discussed this with Lenchen, who is unspeakably dear to us, who immediately responded positively, as did Rebekah. She has never saddened us and has been the joy of my life. For some time it has been my prayer that God would provide her with a good husband.... Three times others have proposed marriage. The first one was much older than she and the other two she rejected, because she neither had love nor respect for them. Happily you finally came knocking.... I know you intimately and you are aware of her weaknesses and consequently will deal patiently with her as a gift from God's hand.... She is completely overjoyed ... so take her! May the Lord, merciful and compassionate, tenderly intertwine you through His fear and tender grace sanctified in love. May His blessing rest upon you now and forever.[20]

The marriage of Lenchen and Stephanus Keyl was fraught with enormous tragedies. While Stephanus was pastor in Philadelphia, both of their first two children died. In 1867, Stephanus became extremely ill so that he had to resign his pastorate. Then, for a while he operated a cigar store. Later, and throughout the rest of his life, he was the immigrant missionary in New York City.

Next in line of the Walther children were the twins, Ferdinand and Constantin. Walther tells the story in an interesting fashion in a birthday letter to Ferdinand (a student at Ft. Wayne) February 19, 1865:

> You know that you had two brothers, both of whom were strong and healthy. I had looked to them with tremendous hope and received them from God's hand. The first, when he blossomed forth as a majestic rose, at the age of four, God permitted a most unfortunate and violent tumble down the steps. He died 24 hours later. The other did not even live to his first birthday. [The little boy was born on June 29, 1852, and died on October 29, 1852.] He had become as sweet as a lily.

When you and Constantin were born, I immediately thought that I would not have you for too long a time; you were both so small and needy that I thought that the next summer complaint would tear you away from us. But look, both of you remained alive, even if Constantin, who showed that he was the weaker of you two, demonstrated greater understanding than you. Even as a little boy, he spoke of wanting to study for the ministry, when you seemed to have much more interest in a secular occupation. With the result I thought that even if you were not studying for the ministry, then at least he could do so. But everything turned out totally different than what I had thought. Though you alone were left I had high hopes that you would carry on my name on the roster of the servants of the church and my name would not die out. I pray that this, my last hope, will not be taken from me. May God Himself equip your heart and awaken in you the desire and love to undertake the hardest, the most blessed, and the most wonderful call in which a man can be.

I don't want to force you because God does not want anyone pressured to become His servant; besides, I do not know whether God may have selected you for some other task. I pray that it may be His blessed will that you will proclaim God's Word someday, save people from the devil's fangs, and build the ark of the church, then I will be extremely happy. The teachers will shine in the heavens who bring many to salvation as the stars forever and ever. It is especially in these latter terrible times, where the devil has sent out his masses, that the Lord needs fighters on Christ's side, and to battle with the banner of the cross, that not everything will fall prey to hell. May God therefore give you confidence and joy that God may "draft you" for the spiritual battle so that the poor world will not be murdered, but become lively, not plundered and destroyed, but be made rich and blessed. Trust alone in the Lord, He will give you what your heart desires. Even if others have more gifts than you do, God can provide what is needed. Even the most gifted frequently go down in the ground, where they become arrogant; but to the humble God often gives the grace and provides the lowliest that we will see that it is not we ourselves, but God's work, my dear Ferdinand.[21]

The *Abendschule* also published a second letter which Walther wrote to Ferdinand on April 2, 1865. He wrote that Constantin was now in Altenburg, Missouri, working with Mr. J. H. Weinhold.

He will be working toward supplying the earthly bread to people as a miller, and you will be distributing the heavenly bread; ... if both of you will be performing the tasks set for you in God's and your neighbor's love, I will be very satisfied. I am looking forward to seeing you both together, Constantin in a white coat, and you in a black one; that should be an odd couple! If God permits, you should visit Constantin during your summer holidays and see if he can already start the mill by himself.[22]

From the Jubilee edition of the *Abendschule*, we also learn of Constantin's wedding on October 29, 1875, at the age of 28. The parents invited only relatives and colleagues to the small wedding. He married a widow, Sophie Kuntz Lau, who had three children from a previous marriage. They later had two children together, a boy and a girl. Four years after the marriage, Constantin became involved in a milling venture in Eufaula, Alabama.

Things did not go well with Constantin. In a letter dated June 4, 1886, Walther wrote to his nephew Johannes that since "Constantin has considerably plundered my treasury," he was unable to send as much of the cash birthday gift as he would have liked. He also wrote that Constantin had bought a mill in Norborne, Missouri, for which Walther had given a bond. At the time of Walther's death in 1887, Constantin owed his father $720 to cover the real estate of a house and lot, according to Walther's will. Towards the end of his life Constantin worked at Concordia Publishing House. He died on December 31, 1905.

The other twin, Ferdinand, lived until the age of 86; he died on May 25, 1933. As a young man, Ferdinand was called as pastor to Brunswick, Missouri. The story was written by John J. Trinklein, an 1882 graduate of Concordia Seminary, St. Louis, as told to him by Ferdinand Walther himself. John F. Buenger, Walther's brother-in-law and President of the Western District (1863–1875), ordained and installed Ferdinand. On a Friday, Buenger and candidate Walther traveled to Brunswick without having made any particular missionary calls. No Lutheran service had ever been conducted there. All that Buenger knew was that "hard-headed Germans, both Protestant and Catholic," were living there. However, Buenger had received a letter from a nominal Lutheran inviting the Lutherans to come.

> Buenger, the very soul of a true missionary, took counsel with Walther, and they proceeded to the small town that was from now on to be on the map of the young Missouri Synod.

> On Saturday morning he told [young Ferdinand] Walther: "Now we have to go around and drum up a congregation for you so that I can ordain and install you tomorrow as their pastor." They both went

down Main Street. Buenger buttonholed every passerby that looked like a German and remarked: "You are surely a German and a Lutheran, are you not?" Upon an affirmative answer he introduced Walther with a summary information: "Here is your young pastor, who will be ordained and installed tomorrow. Come by all means with your whole family!" Time and place of services were duly indicated, also the request made to bring along as many as they could of their acquaintances.

One he met who told him that he was a Catholic. Buenger laid both his hands on his shoulders commiserating by remarking: "Oh, you poor fellow! Nevertheless come to the services tomorrow and the ordination of Pastor Walther." After having so canvassed all points within reach, they retired for the night to await the results of Buenger's improvised missionary preliminaries. At the appointed time a fair-sized multitude had found their way to church. Buenger conducted the services by singing the altar service and reading the Sunday's epistle and Gospel before entering the pulpit to preach.

After the sermon he presented Walther as their new pastor. Two questions he put to the assembly: First, whether they wanted to form a Lutheran congregation, and secondly, whether they wanted Walther as their pastor. Both these questions were answered in the affirmative. So Buenger proceeded to the rite of ordination and installation with a good conscience. He was correct to a dot even if a little less formal. The good people made good their first and second resolution. Buenger left Walther to attend to all further details of organization....

Pastor F. Walther never left New Brunswick, but spent his whole lifetime there, a rare occurrence. There are very few that can point to a life-tenure in their first and only charge.[23]

When Ferdinand was ordained into the ministry in Brunswick, Missouri, Walther wrote him a most significant letter dated September 9, 1871. The letter deals plainly with the holy ministry. Following are some valuable excerpts.

I have lived to see the oft-coveted time when you are in the holy ministry. You are now ordained to the service of Christ, in His church by the old apostolic rite of laying on of hands. That means that the demand is made of you as one vowed to the Lord to have no other goal in this world until your death than to lead souls to the Savior (which He has bought so dearly with His blood), on your part to spread truth and holiness on the earth and to help to edify the kingdom of God or the church. You are already now beginning this duty and are engaged with the congregation assigned to you.

Oh, what a happy man you will be if you now administer your office faithfully! Your work is the most honorable, the holiest, the most blessed, and the happiest that a man can perform. It also has the most glorious reward, for the teachers are to shine as the splendor of heaven and, in leading many to justification, as the stars forever and ever (Daniel 12:3).

I have an evil, idle flesh and blood.... But my dear son, the less you trust in your corrupted heart, so much the better. Indeed, you cannot be faithful by your own strength. But each morning bend your knees and ask Him to cleanse your heart, to sanctify it, to fill it with His Spirit and to urge you on; then God will help you also to overcome yourself and to live only for your holy office.

The dear Lord has called you Himself and say to God daily and confidently: "You have sent me; oh, make me able now. I would readily have stayed away from this difficult office, but You have directed me through my parents from my childhood so that I had to become Your servant. Oh, help me now to carry out everything well!" Then God will not forsake you nor let you get stuck, but will give you the necessary wisdom in all things. Only let God's Word be your counselor and prayer your refuge. Never do anything hastily! First consider everything carefully! Remain humble and modest over against God and men! To the humble God gives grace and to the sincere He allows success....[24]

Ferdinand Walther experienced spiritual difficulties in his ministry, especially during his early years. At times he had bouts of depression and self-doubt. Perhaps he felt he was not able to carry out his responsibilities as he should and compared himself with his illustrious father. He shared his feelings with his father, who always responded with words of encouragement and comfort. In a letter written on December 3, 1871, Walther wrote:

Your last letter still contains the complaint that despair often overcomes you, so that your heart would nearly break. But I hope that our faithful God will not permit you to go under completely in this your need. For He has created you, redeemed you through the blood of His Son and in Baptism has received you as His child and heir. And He has called to all sinners through the prophet Isaiah: "Though your sins are like scarlet, they shall be white as snow; though they are red like crimson, they shall become like wool." God has worked in you the will not to serve sin, and thus He will not permit the spark of your faith to be extinguished, but will blow it up into a bright flame by the breath of His mouth through the Word....

You wrote that when you preach you show others the way to salvation, but feel that you yourself are going lost and that your preaching is only lip service. But this is only the voice of the flesh and the wicked foe, who wants to throw you into despair. In all confidence continue to preach Christ and praise His grace, for that is the doctrine which the Lord has commanded His disciples to preach. This preaching is therefore the best work you can possibly do in your present calling. And believe what you are preaching, and thus your preaching will not only benefit your listeners but also yourself. That's the way your preaching should be....[25]

Ferdinand was married to Bertha Biltz, whose father was F. J. Biltz, a member of the Saxon immigration. He later served as President of the Western District (1875–1891). Ferdinand and Bertha were married on May 27, 1873. They shared the same birthday (February 23), one born in 1847 and the other in 1853. Their first child, a boy, died as an infant. Later they had four more sons and one daughter. In order of their births, they were: Theodore Ferdinand, also known as "Thodo," born February 4, 1876; Ferdinand Arthur known as "Nand," born December 5, 1878; Paula, born July 16, 1881; Rudolf, born July 23, 1885; and Julius A., born May 4, 1888. The oldest, Theodore Ferdinand, graduated from Concordia Seminary, St. Louis, in 1898 and served as a pastor.

As was his custom, Walther annually wrote a birthday letter to his children. One such letter, addressed to Bertha and Ferdinand, shows his genuine concern for them.

February 20, 1874

May the new year of your life which you are about to step into be especially blessed and joyful. God has given you the ability without any groaning to look into the future where you know that beside the joyful, there have also been sad days in the past as you have experienced. However, God never tempts us more than we can endure and does not give us a greater load than we are able to carry. His anger lasts only a moment. Even if the weeping lasted long into the evening, the morning, nevertheless, brings joy. May the heavens envelop you in the new year even if the thunder is rolling over your heads. The clouds will soon disappear; the thunder will be silent, and the sun, in divine friendliness, will provide laughter in your life. May God's

Word continue to be the light on your path, even as you walk through its dark valley. You will soon come to the places where the shadow will give you relief from the hot glaze of the sun and the fresh source for your spiritual thirst.

Addressing his son Ferdinand particularly, Walther continues the letter:

Above all my heartily beloved son, I wish for you ever greater joy in the holy ministry in which you are and richly bless you in the faithful service you are rendering to blood-bought souls. May God give you, my well-beloved Bertha, such a heart that you will be satisfied with the circumstances and the lot God gives you. May God, through His hand of grace, protect you from all misfortune in your home and permit the sweet bond of love, which has embraced you, never to be unraveled, but always grow tighter in an inner fashion.[26]

Two years later in his annual birthday letter Walther prays:

May the heavenly Father continue to strengthen your dear wife and keep her, as well as your little sprout [*Sprössling*] with its sweet-smelling savor. May God also give you the power, wisdom, and the joy to take care of your ministry and richly bless your work.[27]

Ferdinand and Bertha had their first living son, Theodore Ferdinand, on February 4, 1876. Walther was overjoyed! After receiving a telegram announcing the birth, he responded immediately the next day to express his great happiness, particularly also because it was a son. He reminisces:

February 5, 1876

I can still recall clearly the time when my first child Lenchen [Magdalene Keyl] was born. It was nothing less than if I had won the grand prize. I would not have given up this treasure for anything in the world. Now when I went out of the house, it seemed to me as if I had a magnet at home that continually drew me homeward. It will be the same with you. Even if marriage has worked out ever so well, it first becomes a perfectly happy one when it is blessed with children. They preeminently are the heart-bands between man and wife.

Even if it had been a girl, I would have rejoiced royally; but because it is a boy, my joy and certainly also yours, is increased still more. After all, one wishes that one's own name should not die out; the boys are the only ones who perpetuate the father's name. Now both of us have a little male descendant [*Stammhalter*] to carry on the line. What joy!

Oh you dear children, let us also therefore wholeheartedly say thanks to our faithful God because He has done great things for us. We are indeed not worthy of such great mercy and goodness; but rather, we deserve nothing but punishment. For this reason, immediately make a covenant with God, that you resolve to dedicate your little son, whom the Lord gave you, to the Lord and to rear him to His glory, to the child's own salvation and for the benefit of the world. Promise this to our God! Then such a vow is a constant reminder when the flesh wants to become weary and lazy. A child dedicated to God is the greatest jewel in the home. After all, a child is of more worth than all the stars in the heavens and the whole globe, for all of these will perish, but a child is born for eternity.

Would to God that I could hurry to you now! How fortunate I would prize myself if I could take your little son [*Büblein*] into my arms, press him to my heart, and kiss him! However, I must forego that. If God will only keep the sweet little boy healthy for you! I hope (if I myself will not die before that) to see him with both of you here on the occasion of this year's synodical convention. [The Western District in St. Louis, May 3–9, 1876.][28]

Theodore Walther (Ferdinand and Bertha's son) later studied for the holy ministry, and lived with Walther in St. Louis at the time of the latter's death in 1887. He graduated from Concordia Seminary, St. Louis, in 1898. He served pastorates at St. John's, Meta (near Jefferson City), Missouri, 1898–1902; Concordia, Kirkwood, Missouri, 1902–1914; and Grace, Wellston, Missouri, 1914–1949 when he retired. Later Walther's son Ferdinand also retired in Wellston, Missouri and lived with his son until his death on May 25, 1933.

In a later letter to Ferdinand, Walther suggested several names for their newborn son: Rudolph, which means counsel and help, as Luther states; Christopherus, someone who carries Christ in his heart; or Renatus, which means born again. Later in the letter he refers to the baby as his little crown prince, and quickly adds that the prerogative of giving a name to this son belongs to the parents alone. He adds:

You have no idea how anxious I am to see the golden youngster. Hopefully I will have this opportunity at the forthcoming convention.... Mother also greets you for your birthday a thousand times.[29]

The fifth of the Walther children was Emma Julie (Julchen), born in 1849 while the Walthers were living in the Buenger home where Seminary classes were being conducted. Julchen was born in the midst of the severe cholera epidemic in St. Louis. In a period of eighteen days, several of Walther's close relatives died: his mother-in-law, his sister-in-law, and a nephew.

While growing up, the Walther children were surrounded by Seminary students as well as children of faculty members. At that time the Seminary still consisted both of the preparatory school and the Seminary until 1861, when the preparatory institution was moved to Fort Wayne.

It appears that Julie was physically weak. In a letter addressed to his daughter Lenchen in New York in 1870, Walther described in some detail Julie's illness with smallpox [*Blattern*]. He writes that she had a high fever, was in severe pain, and was covered with pox blisters from head to foot. He continued in the letter dated January 9, 1870:

> Thank God the illness was not evil, but helpful. Consequently we hope the dear patient will not have any after effects of the pox. We praise God that she had a remarkable patience and submission to God's holy will…. We are certain that this most difficult suffering will serve our Julchen for the welfare of her soul, will strengthen her faith and direct her on a heavenly course. Because of that, we do not sorrow, and much less murmur against God's marvelous counsel…. Life on this earth has value only when we are prepared for our eternal salvation. Why should we complain that God led our dear Julchen through the cross in order to provide her with magnificent glory and protect her against eternal pain. How long will it be that this poor life will come to an end? Then one will not be asked, "How magnificent one has been, but how faithful and God-like one has lived. Then we will see that the fortunate days are only an empty kernel [*taubes Korn*], and the days of tears are filled with golden, nourishing wheat, yes, which produced a huge crop of sheaves."
>
> Our dear mother who has not left the bedside of our patient day and night, and Julchen herself greet you heartily—I myself have suffered for almost two weeks with a stubborn catarrh and therefore was unable to preach; but now I am much better.

In his letter, Walther regrets that they did not have any money and consequently were unable to send the Keyls a Christmas gift. He expressed the hope that soon they would be able to make up for that loss. He ends by asking that Lenchen will kiss her dear, sweet children.[30]

Julie was married on October 8, 1872, at the age of 23, to Johann Heinrich Niemann. After their engagement had been announced, J. A. Ottesen of the Norwegian Synod wrote the Walthers a letter of congratulations. Walther responded in a letter written more than a year before they were married as follows:

Hearty thanks for your congratulations! I thank God that my Julie has just become engaged to the dear Pastor Niemann. I think that he is suited to her admirably. He is a 'man' in the good sense of the word … but with a great tenderness while at the same time a proper Christian with tremendous understanding and outstanding gifts. Julie loves him so very dearly that I almost say that she is *schwärmerisch* [enthusiastic], as she highly honors him, holds him in great esteem, and will render him obedience. As it appears, the personalities are not the same. He graduated two years ago and had served as our librarian at the Seminary. For two years he has been a pastor in Little Rock, Arkansas, and is well beloved there even though he has had some difficult battles in the congregation.… The wedding will be held next year, perhaps even after the next convention of the Synod, which hopefully you may be able to attend and if you attend, hopefully you will be able to be present at the wedding. Even though Julie will be at some distance from us, she has responded that when one is in love, nothing is too difficult.…[31]

Walther's letters to Niemann indicate his joy about the future marriage, as do his descriptions of Julie's response. Niemann was a graduate of Concordia Seminary, St. Louis, in 1869. Born in Melle, Hanover, Germany, he was called and ordained as pastor of First Lutheran, Little Rock, Arkansas in 1869 as successor to Martin L. Wyneken. Niemann remained at this church until 1875. In 1876 he became pastor of Trinity, Cleveland, Ohio, where he remained until his death on March 15, 1910. He served as president of the Central District for a period of almost thirty years (1880–1909).

The couple had one daughter, Ottilie, who survived to adulthood. A son born in 1876 died shortly after birth.[32]

At the time her mother, Emilie Walther, died in August 1885, Julie had undergone surgery and was unable to attend her mother's funeral. She was also ill when her father died in May 1887 and was unable to come to St. Louis for the funeral. Her husband, however, was present.

Walther and His Grandchildren

Walther loved his grandchildren profoundly. He demonstrated this in his correspondence again and again. He seemed to be completely taken in by them when they came to visit. The letters following show his deep emotional love for these little ones, a facet of Walther's life which has often been overlooked. During the summer of 1866, daughter Lenchen (Keyl) and her two children visited the Walthers in St. Louis. Walther describes in depth little Emilie Keyl's 3rd birthday in a letter to her father.

August 4, 1866

Little Emilie parades around the entire day up to the lunch hour. After lunch she prefers to take her pillow and go into the guest room for a nap, sleeping because severe demands had been placed upon her in governing everything. In the shadow of the seminary building and its elegant, ornamental trees, she walks through with an expression as though the management of all the precincts of Concordia were entrusted to her. Her energy has already become famous among the children of the entire neighborhood. Above all, with her great amiableness, a large measure of a strength of character, without having the power of speech, nevertheless [she] expresses her own will. She has recognized that in her own district there is a higher authority who can take the beautiful little branches of the Acacia trees for a purpose other than to give shade. Up to now this has not been necessary because all I did was show her the rod. I had to raise the window of my study, and with my deep bass voice use it when the little romper was determined to exercise her own will as the highest law of the house. In spite of all of this, she has the greatest confidence in her grandpa [Grosspapa], who allows her many innocent endeavors which her mother would be inclined to deny. I need only to sit down when she comes running with her beaming face in order to sit on my lap.

The dear Theodorchen is equally most precious. He is such a sweet child that he cannot defend himself from all the kisses received. He is complaining only when he is teething. There is never a lack of arms and hands to carry him. Grandma [Grossmama] would dearly love to teach him how to eat in order to spare his mother, but it seems to be the hardest lesson for him. He adheres to the apostolic: "I have given you milk to drink and not solid food because you are not ready to receive it." I believe rightly, besides the spiritual understanding of this passage, there lies a natural truth and the basis that little children need their mother's milk. We have trouble with his mother [Walther's daughter]; because she dislikes beer. It is in the air, even if simple, that the valuable food prepared by the Grossmama excels. We have nothing else to do than to pray to our loving God that He will continue with His blessing to lead the dear little ones with His eyes, permit them to grow. You see these little rosebuds smelling even better as they were when you allowed them to come here. The heavenly gardener provides the rest.... May the Lord be with you in your loneliness![33]

After Lenchen and her children returned to Philadelphia, Walther, in his concern for their safety, wrote, The Lord has carried you on eagle wings to your home." But he missed his daughter and her children! He wrote on:

December 14, 1866

The whole house is empty and forlorn. During the past almost a quarter year, the joyful meals now seem as the meals of death. Missing was the garnishment which your dear little ones brought to the table with their lark-like chatter. The variety of tasks that we had with these little ones were so pleasant that one continues to be deprived of such a great benefit. The entire college, after your departure, appeared like an aviary, but without the song of a single bird.... I am grateful for having experienced the real fatherly joys.[34]

The great joy that Walther expressed at the visit of his daughter Lenchen and her children is contrasted with the previous Christmas of 1865. Their younger daughter Julie traveled to visit the Keyls in Philadelphia, which left the parents all alone for Christmas for the first time in their lives. Walther wrote about the quiet and somber Christmas he and Emilie experienced. In early January, he wrote to his daughter Julie:

January 8, 1866

We had very joyous holidays in the spiritual sense, but in the physical sense the days had been really quiet. It was the first time in my life that at Christmas time I was at home alone with Mother. You can imagine how much we have missed you. So much more vividly we have thought of you. In spirit we saw you laughing, and saw the little Emilie jumping around for joy and clapping her hands and we saw the little Theodorchen with his popping eyes in front of the sparkling, illuminated Christmas tree.

Since the very hard winter has set in, our beautiful choir has suddenly wilted. There were many who were going to participate in it, but there were not enough men who wanted to help in getting together the young ladies living so scattered about and then to take them home again. Therefore, it was decided that the choir take its summer vacation in winter—then in Spring when the flowers bloom again, to emerge in its full beauty once more.[35]

Other letters written by Walther to his family also reflect his deep love and concern for his children and grandchildren. When his daughter Lenchen was expecting a child, Walther wrote a remarkable letter on the marvels of being a mother.

April 18, 1867

I noted with joy in your last letter that the Lord has again blessed you with maternal hopes. That, of course, again poses a heavy burden for you and brings with it many a care and also some danger.... Ever since I have known of it, therefore, I have daily implored our dear God to continue to be with you, to protect and keep you in all your ways, to lighten your burden and in His time safely deliver you and make you a happy blessed mother of children.

But at the same time I must also remind you not to forget in your cares and burdens what a great gift of God it is to be blessed with off-spring that way. Think of it, is it not something great that God deems you worthy to bestow life and existence on an immortal human called to eternal life and dearly redeemed through Christ? If that little babe is successfully born into the world, this is a greater achievement than one thinks. For the little child is then there in order to know God, in all eternity and to praise Him and receive salvation. If God would give you a million dollars, this would be a lesser gift than a little child. Gold and silver will not only pass out of existence on the day of judg-ment, as will also the whole world, but in dying you must leave every-thing behind here; but not so with a little child, whether it dies before you or after you, it still remains your little child; and when through God's grace that little one learns to know the Savior and to believe in Him, you will rejoice with it in all eternity.

Therefore do not be sad about the present inconvenience which the blessing of children brings with it, but thank God for it and spare your life and your strength, because the second life is now dependent upon yours—a precious, costly treasure, more splendid than precious stones and pearls. This you certainly are experiencing daily in your little ones, namely in your Emilie and your Theodor. Isn't it true, you would not be willing to trade them for a whole kingdom? See from this how God has enriched you.[36]

Late in 1868, Walther received a telegram that another one of the Keyl children, little Theodor, had died at the age of less than two years. Walther's heart was torn apart. With a deep sense of grief, he wrote a very moving letter to the bereaved parents.

December 12, 1868

Now a new grief is spread over you and tears from your parental hearts flow when your only son, so very sweet, has been taken home.

We thought that the blows of taking your first two children would be enough ... we thought that when the dark and foggy night would be over and the light of joy arise again, that the face of God would smile on you so that the wounds would heal—but no, even when the old wounds are still bleeding, the unsearchable God takes His sword and cuts even deeper into your soul!

What should we say to that? Oh, you dear ones—what else than "Your will be done. God, you cannot mean evil?!" If that were the case, God would not be the Father, the wonderful Father over all children in heaven and earth, who acknowledge Him as such. Is it possible God can cut wounds without intending them for your welfare? Wasn't it inexpressively painful when you witnessed your sweet little Theodorchen suffer so? Could God be disposed with evil toward us when He now sees our lamentations? God could have preserved your sainted baby, when we so often cannot help our own children. What could God have done other than to take your dear child to Himself in heaven, so that He could preserve him and you in all eternity—dare we who are now grieving that God, in this dangerous world, took the sweet smelling flower and placed it into His heavenly garden, even before sin, like a worm destroys it and causes it to wilt? Dare we grieve that God has taken that trusting child quickly but relieved him of all grief and trouble? He has redeemed him and placed him into the fellowship of all joyful angels and fellow redeemed.

You undoubtedly will say that—no, never. But isn't this the real cause why our hearts are bleeding? We gladly grant our little Theodorchen his early glorification. But not to be able to see this amiable angel child, no more to hear him babble, no more being able to kiss him and press him to our hearts, and never dare we forget his blessed fellowship and his earthly needs. No longer can we teach him to pray and to lead him to his Savior, and more importantly, fulfill the parental duties and to watch him with joy as God's little plant unfolds and grows in age and grace before God and men—that, it is, over which our poor heart cannot be comforted. Oh, my dear children, I can readily enough see that now we pray the third petition in the midst of your great tragedy ... my fatherly heart has been torn and my hand writes as my eyes are filled with hot tears. But, because of that, does the Word become untrue: "The Lord has made all things well?" Whom God loves, he chasteneth. We must enter the kingdom of God through great difficulties and troubles. For those who love God, all things will turn out well. No, it is and will remain certain that even this, our hard blow, is a blow of love.... This comfort not even the devil can take from us....

I cannot express my unspeakable sorrow that I will not be able to look at the little cherub face and no longer be able to plant a kiss on his cold lips. How very realistically we can still see in my soul, the beloved child, at the time when we last saw him. I also realize that I was with you then when my soul prayed: "Oh, if only God will continue to grant this great earthly treasure to my dear Lenchen...." The child with his lovely personality made a profound impression on me that I could not get rid of the thought that you would retain such a child.[37]

God gave the Keyls another son, Theodor Stephanus, in 1874 and three additional children.[38]

ANOTHER TRAGEDY

During the summer of 1872 the Keyl family again visited the Walthers. Keyl had attended the synodical convention in St. Louis in April. He returned to New York, while his wife Lenchen and their two children stayed behind for an additional visit. But a great tragedy occurred. Little Emma Mathilda died while at the Walther home. It fell on Walther to inform his son-in-law of the girl's death. One can only imagine the depth of grief and sadness that surrounded the family. Walther wrote his son-in-law, Stephanus Keyl, a most touching letter.

May 22, 1872

Two children were left to us, but one, our dear, sweet Emmie, He took from our lips, from our lap, and from our arms. Besides the measles, Emmie had pneumonia and just at the time when she was teething. For God these three enemies of that young life would not have been overwhelming, but for the tender little child it was too much and since the Lord of life had resolved from eternity that this innocent child should never know the evil of the world, there was no delay; God hurried it out of this miserable life and refreshes it now even with joy before His own countenance.

She never cried, never expressed the least impatience. As a lamb she lay there, and only the quick, short breathing sounded like a constant sighing and moaning. The doctor did everything he could. He was very tireless, and his visits were never hurried. It seemed as if the course of the illness would turn for the better, but we soon saw that this was only outward appearance. As human beings are always encouraged at every flicker of small hope, so also we were here. Yet, the Lord's will had to be done.

We know that the blessed child only preceded us to receive us there above with joy whenever our own hour has come and then to be with us there eternally. We also know that when God lays a cross on us, this is not His anger, but rather a sign of His love.... We are thereby to become like the father of all believers, who was required to prove his faithfulness, thereby, that when God required him, he had to lay his own son, whom he loved, as a sacrifice on God's altar. But above all, we are thereby to become like the picture of the Son of God Himself, who never laughed but wept much in this vale of tears....

We are exceedingly sorrowful that you now, in your loneliness, receive this tragic letter, and would God we could fly to you and weep with you and comfort you; but even this also is God's gracious leading. He will certainly strengthen you, also to bear this cross. God already has led both of you through the school of affliction and has exercised you herein, so that with His help you will also this time not murmur against the Lord but bring Him also this offering, even though with tears....[39]

Walther had baptized Emma on August 20, 1871, when he had traveled by train to New York to visit the Keyls. Regarding that visit he wrote to his wife Emilie on August 21, 1871 as follows:

Stephanus, to my great joy, met me at the train station; otherwise I would have been completely lost in this large city, like Peter in a strange land.... At 4 p.m., we went to Port Richmond, where I met Lenchen hale and hearty with all her children. Yesterday, a Sunday, we had the baptism. I baptized the little Emma Mathilda. We had a high time. The whole circle of friends was there. We were overjoyed and we thought of you with a heartfelt wish that you could be in our midst too.[40]

Walther never hesitated to express his deep feelings and love for his children and grandchildren, as well as his profound grief in times of bereavement. His letters clearly demonstrate that in spite of all his responsibilities in teaching, preaching, writing, and speaking, the needs of his family were his first and foremost priority.

EMILIE BUENGER WALTHER

A poem which Walther wrote to his beloved Emilie for her 32nd birthday (July 21, 1844) demonstrates the deep love which prevailed between the young couple. At that time they had one little girl,

Magdalena. The poem was attached to a new red dress which Walther gave
his wife as a birthday present.

> Here is a dress, my precious sweet,
>   It is my gift to you,
> In joy and sorrow always meet
>   For one so sweet and true;
> It's small enough, and modest, too,
>   The gift your eye does see,
> But with it goes my heart anew,
>   Which loves you ardently.
> So take it and believe me, dear,
>   Though dresses will grow old,
> My love for you from year to year
>   Will gleam like purest gold.
>
> But look not on the gift alone
>   I offer you this day;
> For with it goes, my dearest one,
>   A wish for life's far way.
> For as I tender you this dress,
>   I ask the Lord on high
> To grant me in His graciousness
>   The boon for which I cry:
>
> As in Baptism's holy stream
>   You put the Savior on,
> May He abide, for peace supreme,
>   With you your whole life long;
> And may He deck you with the dress—
>   The best gift of the soul—
> Of His own perfect righteousness,
>   Your fairest aureole!
>
> The dress is of a scarlet hue
>   Which on this day you wear;
> Oh, let it tell me, dear, that you
>   Will truly love me e'er,
> That as on our glad wedding day
>   Your heart still beats for me
> And I with happy joy may say:
>   My dear you'll always be![41]

Walther exerted a great deal of effort to reunite the members of his
family at their home, especially after some had left the parental roof.
Lenchen returned home with her two children in 1866. In a letter Walther
admits that he would have responded earlier to Stephanus Keyl if he had

the necessary travel money for both Lenchen and Julchen. This letter indicates that he now has the money available and is therefore planning for them to come. He expresses great joy in anticipation of this visit.

July 10, 1866

To: Stephanus Keyl

How profoundly I am rejoicing to have children about me for a longer period of time. Ferdinand also will be here in July and August. I can hardly describe my great joy. Your concerns about the disturbances are unfounded. Actually I can't think of anything more sweet and wonderful than the pleasant unrest brought on by our own children and grandchildren. My only concern is this, that you will not have your helpmeet and your children during this time. I am hoping confidently, however, that staying at our healthful college will be most beneficial to Lenchen and your children, especially in this present summertime; which will make your loss a little more acceptable.... It would be great if you could be here with all of us. Perhaps you may be able to stay with us a short time before the convention and our family reunion would be a great joy. Until then, we will remember you in our heart and kiss your dear little children....[42]

Two years later the Walthers visited the Keyls in Philadelphia. Walther had given a lecture at the Central District convention held at Trinity, Zanesville, Ohio.

On another occasion in 1879, Walther missed Emilie's 67th birthday on July 21. He was meeting at the time with the Synodical Conference in Columbus, Ohio, just when the Predestinarian Controversy had begun. Walther wrote to Emilie as follows:

Columbus, Ohio

July 18,1879

To My Dear Wife:

Because your 67th birthday is next Monday, I will hurriedly use a free quarter of an hour this evening to congratulate you on your birthday.

Above all, I join you in thanking our benevolent and gracious God because He not only has had you in his keeping so long, but also has provided so richly for all the needs of your body and life. He has shielded you from so many threatening misfortunes and has led and guided you so kindly, and preserved you by his Word and his grace.

Indeed, I have ample cause to thank the Lord right heartily for that, because you have been the faithful help and companion of my life in joy and sorrow until this hour. At the same time my fervent wish is not only that the Lord will grant you many more years of life, and will permit me to enjoy your wifely faithfulness, but also that He may permit the evening of your life to be a very joyous one and blessed in body and soul. May God grant that I do not carry you to your rest, but you, me. An old widower is clearly more helpless than an aged widow.[43]

By 1879, both Emilie and Ferdinand anticipated that the end of their lives was near. The "dear guests" referred to in the letter above included the Walthers' daughter, Julchen Niemann, who came to visit Emilie at this time. The entire family took every opportunity to visit whenever possible.

When the controversy on election to grace had flared up to an incendiary peak, Walther attended the Missouri Synod Convention in Fort Wayne, Indiana, a convention sometimes referred to as *"Die Gnadenwahl Synode"* (The Election to Grace Convention). A letter he wrote to Emilie on May 13, 1881 gives us some unique insight into Walther. The debate was acrimonious; the Missouri Synod was on the verge of schism. In spite of that, however, Walther wrote Emilie that he had arrived safely, and that he was pleased and personally satisfied with the way the convention was going.

Everything is going well at the convention. The opponents are sitting with their red faces and note that they are not able to tear the Synod apart, which they had hoped they could achieve. Although final decisions have not yet been made, the outcome looks very good.

Walther stayed at the home of Pastor H. Sauer in Fort Wayne. President Schwan and Joseph Schmidt also stayed in the Sauer home. However, Walther had a room by himself. In this same letter to Emilie, Walther assured her:

In spite of all the disputation, I am sleeping well at night. My bedroom is broad and deep and filled with fresh air. I am the only one and have this all to myself.[44]

This was a period of testing in Walther's life. Additional meetings were held to resolve the controversy, tensions were high, and about the same time a seminary student committed suicide. The hectic schedule of preaching, delivering essays, and writing articles continued to demand serious portions of Walther's time. In the meantime Emilie did everything

possible to keep her husband happy and well. Visits with the family continued especially in 1883, when the parents traveled to Cleveland and Port
Richmond, Staten Island to see their children. A marvelous climax to all of
this was the dedication of the grand new seminary in September 1883.

FAITHFUL HELPMEET

Emilie's greatest ambition was to serve her husband, her family, her
church, and the community in which they lived. She never permitted her
needs to be first; the needs of others were her priority. She was a loving
person, whose care-giving made a deep impression on many people. What
she may have lacked in concern for society generally, she more than made
up for in her concern for Seminary students and their welfare, for wholesome food for her family and house guests, and cleanliness (*Reinlichkeit*).
The sewing circle which she organized soon after they were married
(known as "Mrs. Walther's Sewing Circle") is another concrete demonstration of her life of service to others.

Although Emilie had slight bouts of illness at various times, she never
suffered serious illnesses during her lifetime. She was a plucky person
whom illness could not get down. It is amazing that she could travel by
train alone as she did to Chicago, Philadelphia, and elsewhere. However,
in late spring of 1884 she became ill and was confined to her bed. Walther
describes her condition in a letter to his son Ferdinand dated April 19,
1884. With deep concern he wrote:

> Unfortunately I have to inform you that Mother has been ill with a
> most painful rheumatic fever [*Rheumatischen Fieber*]. Right now she
> seems just a bit better, but even at best, recovery will be very slow
> since our precious patient suffers from great weakness. Please pray
> God that He will grant her recovery and sustain her for us once again.
> It would be shocking to me if I were in my old age to lose my very
> indispensable helpmeet. I am not giving up hope that when you come
> to us for the synodical convention, she will be our busy Martha once
> more.[45]

Ludwig Fuerbringer states that Emilie "revered" her husband, and
that Walther often expressed his gratitude that his "good wife took care of
all externals and, above all, took the very best care of him.[46]

In late summer of 1885 Emilie again became ill and her end was in
sight. Walther wrote to his son-in-law Stephanus that Emilie was very ill
in bed. At that time he called it "Malaria Fever." Breathing was extremely

difficult for her day and night. She was also growing weaker and weaker with the result that Walther was extremely concerned for her life. He elaborated that if she was not improving quickly, then with the consent of his homeopathic doctor, he would call in Dr. Schade "so that nothing would be neglected." He continued,

> Please support us in our prayers. There would be no harder blow for me than if in my last days my wonderful helpmeet who has always been standing at my side, would be lost.[47]

At about this time Walther wrote to his good friend, U. Koren, among other matters, that

> My wife is gravely ill in bed with heart disease which so often denies her the ability to breathe. I am in great need. It would be an immense sorrow if I would lose my faithful helpmeet.[48]

On Sunday, August 23, 1885 Emilie's soul was taken to heaven. Her funeral was conducted on Wednesday, August 26th.

Walther sent a telegram to each of his children informing them of their mother's death, but because of various circumstances, none of the children was able to come for the funeral. Magdalena was too ill to travel; Julie, too, was unable to come, but her husband was present. Ferdinand and Constantin did not receive the telegram in time to be there, and only found out about her death when they arrived in St. Louis.

Walther describes the details of Emilie's last illness, death, and funeral in a letter he wrote to the Keyls in New York a few days after the funeral. The letter, written after he had regained his composure, indicates his profound love and deepest appreciation for her lifetime of faithful, self-sacrificial service, demonstrated daily in inexhaustible love and honor for their marriage.

August 30, 1885

My heartily beloved Stephanus,

> Her last illness began apparently as a result of a cold which she contracted after a bath on a cool evening. She got serious heart cramps, which caused her to have the most terrifying breathing difficulties for weeks on end, day and night with only short interruptions, which made virtually all sleep impossible. These difficulties always were a real wrestling of life with death, because it always seemed to her that the very next instant she would be completely unable to breathe and would choke to death. Her anguish was therefore great. Day and

night she sighed, groaned and whimpered. She would say, "O Lord Jesus, help me! O my most dearly beloved Savior, have mercy on me!" In this and similar matters she prayed without ceasing. She often complained, "Oh, I can no longer endure this!" But she never expressed one word nor even gave one facial expression of impatience. As patient as a lamb for the slaughter, she lay on her bed of pain.

Dr. Bosse, an excellent, experienced, conscientious, and involved physician, at first did not dare to give her any opiates to permit her to rest, since he feared that precisely this way she could lapse into the sleep of death. But since her pains and her anxiety increased constantly, Dr. Bosse finally did resort to opium as also some other means. This finally resulted in our good mother being freed suddenly from her breathing difficulties and pain, so that after the first sleep of several hours, she said, "I am as if in heaven."

Only now, a frightful, almost burning glowing fever set in with her, which did not want to yield to any medication. It became more and more difficult for her to speak till in her last days she lost the power of speech completely. But it seems as if all pain had left her and that she might not even feel the burning fever because of her weakness. As often as I leaned over her face, she regularly commenced to smile in a sublime way and did this till her death. The physician had soon noticed that the illness had also affected the kidneys, since there was evidence of albumin in the urine, which he examined chemically each day. So she became weaker and weaker till eight days ago today, about noon, also her consciousness faded.

Up to then she audibly repeated all the prayers said for her. It was highly comforting to see and hear how she busied herself with the Word of God and how she was refreshed thereby. She had soon realized that she would die, and she was prepared to depart with joy in the name of her Lord Jesus, then to be with Him eternally. She had no spiritual afflictions in all of this. She believed firmly that because of Christ all sins had been forgiven her and that she would be saved. When she had further serious attacks in the night from Friday to Saturday, I heard her confession and gave her absolution and the Lord's Supper.

Saturday evening the physician no longer gave her any medication. Then he said, early on Sunday, that the time of her departure was at hand but that the struggle for life might extend until Monday morning. But God heard our cries. Sunday afternoon her breathing became ever weaker and in the last hour even more soft, till finally five minutes of five in the afternoon her precious soul left her softly and quietly so that even for a little while we did not even know whether she had gone to sleep or whether she was still awake.

Heavily afflicted yet yielding humbly to God's guidance, I am yours,

C. F. W. Walther[49]

Franz Delitzsch, in his letter of condolence to Walther, expressed his deepest sympathy, also because he had known Emilie as a young girl in Etzdorf and referred to her as a "lovely little gazelle." In another letter he referred to her beauty.[50]

Martin Guenther, in his biography of Walther, wrote as follows about Emilie:

> She was a faithful disciple of the Lord, who adorned her faith with a quiet, devout life, and proved that especially through her love of God's Word and through works of love and mercy. She was in deed and in truth a helpmeet to her husband for 44 years.[51]

NOTES

[1] Roy A. Suelflow, ed., *Selected Writings of C. F. W. Walther* (St. Louis: Concordia Publishing House, 1981), 14–16.

[2] "Letters of Emilie Buenger to C. F. W. Walther," trans. by Roy A. Suelflow, *Concordia Historical Institute Quarterly*, Vol. XVII, No. 4 (January 1945), 106–07.

[3] Suelflow, *Selected Writings of C. F. W. Walther*, 17–18.

[4] "Letters of Emilie Buenger to C. F. W. Walther," 108–09.

[5] Theo. Buenger, "C. F. W. Walther," *Concordia Historical Institute Quarterly*, Vol. IX, No. 3 (October 1936), 70.

[6] Martin Guenther, *Dr. C. F. W. Walther: Lebensbild* (St. Louis: Concordia Publishing House, 1890), 68–69.

[7] *Alma Mater*, Vol. XIX.

[8] *Der Lutheraner*, Vol. 26, No. 14 (March 15, 1870), 110.

[9] For a detailed description of Walther's community, see Karl Kretzmann, "The Old Lutheran Neighborhood in St. Louis," *Concordia Historical Institute Quarterly*, XVIII (April 1945), 15–22.

[10] Marguerita Lenk, *Fünfzehn Jahre in Amerika*, 3rd ed. (Zwickau: Johannes Hermann, 1911), 41.

[11] Suelflow, *Selected Writings of C. F. W. Walther*, 31.

[12] Personal interview with Paul Lehmann, 87, on June 24, 1950. Lehmann was a grandnephew of Walther and lived in the Walther home 1886–87. The Lehmann interview is deposited at Concordia Historical Institute.

[13] David S. Schaff, *The Life of Philip Schaff: In Part Autobiographical* (New York:

Charles Scribner's Sons, 1897), 184.

[14] Ludwig Fuerbringer, *80 Eventful Years* (St. Louis: Concordia Publishing House, 1944), 75.

[15] Suelflow, *Selected Writings of C. F. W. Walther*, 149.

[16] Ludwig Fuerbringer, *Walthers Briefe*, I (St. Louis: Concordia Publishing House, 1915), 164–66. Trans. by this author.

[17] Fuerbringer, *Walthers Briefe*, I, 166.

[18] Fuerbringer, *Walthers Briefe*, I, 166–67.

[19] Fuerbringer, *Walthers Briefe*, I, 168.

[20] Fuerbringer, *Walthers Briefe*, I, 178–80.

[21] *Die Abendschule*, February 19, 1865. Trans. by this author.

[22] Letter of April 2, 1865 in *Die Abendschule*. After the apprenticeship in Altenburg, Constantin went to Collinsville, Illinois, in 1871. D. H. Steffens, *Doctor Carl Ferdinand Wilhelm Walther* (Philadelphia: The Lutheran Publication Society, 1917), 229.

[23] "Historical Sidelights," *Concordia Historical Institute Quarterly*, Vol. XXVI, No. 1 (April 1953), 46–47.

[24] Carl S. Meyer, *Walther Speaks to the Church* (St. Louis: Concordia Publishing House, 1973), 46–47. Trans. by Michael Moore.

[25] Suelflow, *Selected Writings of C. F. W. Walther*, 43–44.

[26] Walther to Ferdinand, February 20, 1874, Wadewitz. Trans. by this author.

[27] Walther to Ferdinand, February 22, 1876, Wadewitz. Trans. by this author.

[28] Carl S. Meyer, *Letters of C. F. W. Walther: A Selection* (Philadelphia: Fortress Press, 1969), 113–115.

[29] Walther to Ferdinand, February 22, 1876. Wadewitz. Trans. by this author.

[30] Ludwig Fuerbringer, *Walthers Briefe*, II (St. Louis: Concordia Publishing House, 1916), 172–73. Trans. by this author.

[31] Fuerbringer, *Walthers Briefe*, II, 226.

[32] *Der Lutheraner*, Vol. LXVI, 94 and Vol. LXXI, 481.

[33] Fuerbringer, *Walthers Briefe*, II, 49–52. Theodorchen died before he reached age two.

[34] Fuerbringer, *Walthers Briefe*, II, 60–62.

[35] Suelflow, *Selected Writings of C. F. W. Walther*, 37–38.

[36] Suelflow, *Selected Writings of C. F. W. Walther*, 39–40.

[37] Fuerbringer, *Walthers Briefe*, II, 136–41.

[38] See Theodor S. Keyl, "The Life and Activities of Pastor Stephanus Keyl," *Concordia Historical Institute Quarterly*, Vol. XXII, No. 2 (July 1949), 65–77.

[39] Suelflow, *Selected Writings of C. F. W. Walther*, 46–47.

[40] Suelflow, *Selected Writings of C. F. W. Walther*, 42.

[41] W. G. Polack, *The Story of C. F. W. Walther* (St. Louis: Concordia Publishing House, 1947), 163–164. Trans. by John Theodore Mueller. The original, in the Wadewitz transcriptions, dates this as July 21, 1844 and notes that the original is addressed to E. W. from F. W.

[42] Fuerbringer, *Walthers Briefe*, II, 46.

[43] Meyer, *Letters of C. F. W. Walther: A Selection*, 129–31.

[44] Walther to Emilie, May 13, 1881, Wadewitz. Trans. by this author.

[45] Suelflow, *Selected Writings of C. F. W. Walther*, 51.

[46] Fuerbringer, *80 Eventful Years*, 87.

[47] Walther to Stephanus Keyl, August 14, 1885. Wadewitz. Translated by this author.

[48] Walther to U. Koren, his "highly honored and beloved friend and brother in the Lord Jesus," August 18, 1885, Wadewitz. Trans. by this author.

[49] Suelflow, *Selected Writings of C. F. W. Walther*, 52–54.

[50] Delitzsch to Walther, October 3, 1885. Wadewitz. Trans. by this author.

[51] Guenther, *Dr. C. F. W. Walther: Lebensbild*, 152.

8

SOME GLIMPSES
INTO WALTHER'S LIFE

A MULTIFACETED MAN

In addition to lecturing in the classroom, at district conventions and pastoral conferences, Walther was a faithful pastor. He had a deep concern for other pastors also, encouraging them and at times offering them practical advice. In his *Pastoral Theology*, Walther noted that when there are loathsome and contagious diseases in a household, the pastor should not visit a patient on an empty stomach.[1] Walther made reference to Pastor George Volck of New Orleans, who had failed to eat breakfast before visiting a patient with yellow fever. He contracted the disease much more quickly and shortly thereafter died at the age of 22 years, after serving in the ministry for only three months. Walther firmly believed that the pastor should visit the sick and the dying to bring them comfort in the love and resurrection of Christ, pointing the patient to the open heaven.

Walther was an inspiring biblical preacher. It was written of him:

But as decidedly orthodox as Walther is in all doctrine, as certain as he is in his sermons, as certain as in his theological works, one must not suppose that his sermons seem to be mere repetitions of the doctrine of the sixteenth and seventeenth centuries. Walther always makes the impression that he tolerates much; that he values truth above all else; that he readily lays everything on the line for it; that he has tasted and recognized in difficult battles of life the doctrines of the Reformation as the only truth.[2]

In an article in *The Lutheran*, Henry C. Jacobs remarks about Walther's preaching:

These occasional discourses ... are the warm and living utterance of one who, while learned in the literature of theology, knows far more of theology as an imminently practical wisdom that has a technical science. They are not simple repetitions of what has been said very well, a hundred times before; but the individuality of the preacher and peculiar character of the relations of both preacher and people constantly color the sermon.[3]

When in 1874 August Crull of Ft. Wayne proposed that Walther's sermons be translated and published, Walther responded with total surprise, but did not object. He responded to Crull, "I did not see anything to hinder this." He elaborated that the sermons might serve as a response to those who had accused him and the Synod of "dead orthodoxy." In typical humility, Walther added, "The good that lies in these sermons is not mine; the worthless is mine."[4]

MUSIC

Walther had unique musical talent. He improvised constantly and seldom used the swell organ. His extemporaneous pieces were serious and held in honor. Johann L. Gruber, a parish school teacher in St. Louis, wrote about Walther as choir director and as organist and pianist. Walther started a choir consisting of members from various congregations who met in private homes. It was a special choir since only the best vocalists of the four congregations were selected. They performed at the dedication of Trinity Church, St. Louis, in 1865, where they sang Mozart's "Second Mass." At the 350th anniversary celebration of the Reformation they sang Haydn's complete "Third Mass" with organ accompaniment.[5]

PHYSICAL APPEARANCE

In his volume, *80 Eventful Years*, Ludwig Fuerbringer describes Walther's physical appearance as follows:

He was a rather small man, about five feet five or six inches, rather lean—I think he weighed no more than about 140 pounds.... He had quite a prominent nose and a remarkable head and this was noticed the more because when I first knew him he was quite bald. This was brought to my attention in a somewhat peculiar way. On some festival occasion celebrated in the open air, Walther had taken off his hat, either when he spoke or when prayer was said, and someone in the large crowd near me observed, "What a remarkable head!" Later I found out that the man who said it was a sculptor and had a special eye for remarkable features.[6]

Theodore A. Buenger, Walther's nephew, described his demeanor.

He always walked and bore himself erect. He was quite slender.... He had a large forehead, deep set, kind eyes, a hook nose, and a far protruding chin. He was always dressed in a black beaver-cloth dress suit, wore only high silk hats, a heavy white scarf necktie, and a standing collar of a peculiar cut, which reached to his ears on both sides of a fairly long, sparse goatee. In winter he wore a splendid mink-lined overcoat, which had been sent to him from Germany by a member of the Free Church, Fraülein Von Haugewitz....

His entire bearing and appearance were very distinctive. He was most punctilious in keeping appointments and expected the same of others. His address was polite to a fault. He did not seem to expect other people to accommodate themselves to him; quite the contrary. Whenever my thoughts revert to those days, I am overcome with amazement at the consideration and the politeness and the patience with which he met us youths. Walther had a personality that won the common people as well as the influential men.[7]

Julius A. Friedrich, the last seminary student to receive Walther's signature on his diploma, reminisced about Walther.

When he was ill and rather weak, we asked him to come to classes in his house slippers and his lounging jacket, but he was mortally insulted. He had always come to class in boots, black coat, silk hat, a big stand-up collar and almost a bed sheet of a tie.... Dr. Walther expected every student to be in his seat when he stepped into the classroom. They were all expected to be dressed in black.[8]

COMPASSION FOR OTHERS

An interesting sidelight reveals Walther's compassion and deep concern for others. One such example is a letter he wrote in 1873 to the mother of Henry Sieck, pastor in Memphis, Tennessee.[9] Memphis at the time was being threatened and infested with yellow fever. In response to Mrs. Sieck's request that her son be called elsewhere, Walther answered that he was extremely sorry to hear about the yellow fever that ravaged the area. He said he had been traumatized and "on my knees daily" praying to God that He would extend His protective hand over her son "whom I love deeply and value very highly." Walther continued:

Even if I urged him to leave, he would not do so, because he fears God in his heart and knowing that, a pastor does not flee in the face of problems. If he sees that he is no longer able to serve the Lord and would leave without my urging, I would leave this to his own conscience and not be judgmental of him.

Please remember that no sparrow drops from the roof without our Lord's will and not a single hair drops from our head. When your dear son received the call to Memphis, there was neither cholera nor yellow fever. To my knowledge, fever has never come to be an epidemic in Memphis. We could openly do what our Lord did in praying, "Remove this cup from me if it is your will." Please do not remove this faithful, greatly-gifted servant of integrity in mid-life. I do not doubt at all that with many Christians praying, crying and petitioning, God will hear them and preserve a proper preacher with the doctrine of the Gospel, serving as a true angel of God in the midst of Memphis. If God, the Lord of life and death, spares him, his experiences will provide incredible blessing....[10]

Walther comforted Mrs. Sieck by reminding her of Jacob wrestling with the Lord: "I will not leave you unless you bless me." The letter was signed "Your Fellow Sufferer and also a friend who hangs onto hope in the Lord." In 1886, Henry Sieck accepted a call to Zion, St. Louis and participated in Walther's funeral.

OVERWORKED

On one occasion Walther's good friend, Ernst August Brauer, invited him to come to his home in Crete, Illinois. Walther's response is interesting, saying it was imperative that he stay home and complete his work on the *Baier Compendium*. He admitted that he had finished only half and owed a huge debt to the subscribers who also had paid for the second half. He expressed his regrets that he did not have time to work on dogmatics during his lectures in the academic year. He assured Brauer that nothing would please him more than to "bum around" [*bummeln*]. He expressed the hope that he would find at least one week in the next three months to visit his daughter Julie. He wrote that he felt that he was constantly on a treadmill. In closing, he prayed that God would give him eternal rest: "That is my fervent wish."[11] Walther did not regularly take off the month of April and he taught his classes without interruption during the academic year.

Honors Received

It was a distinct honor for Walther to receive the Doctor of Theology degree from Capital University and Seminary in 1878. At a time when the Missouri and Ohio Synods were still on friendly terms, the Ohio Synod in October 1877 resolved to honor Walther by conferring the doctorate on him. The certificate has been preserved at Concordia Historical Institute.[12]

Already in 1855 Goettingen University of Germany had offered him the doctorate, but he felt he could not accept it because he did not agree with the theology of Goettingen. He observed that he would feel like a "crowned jackass" with such a degree.

The conferral of the degree took place in the *Aula* of Concordia Seminary in the evening of January 25, 1878. Martin Guenther recorded Walther's acceptance statement. In true Christian humility, Walther responded:

> You have put my knowledge of myself to a very strong test.... I wish it had been a totally private ceremony.... This is not merely hypocritical humility.... I am deeply ashamed to stand before you.... This confession comes out of the deepest depths of my heart.

Walther protested that he did not belong in the same category with Luther, Chemnitz and Gerhard in sharing the honored doctor's title. He adds that even Luther was hesitant to accept it in 1512. He further said:

> I am not worthy of this, the least of all the Doctors of Theology, to open the shoelaces of those who have it, and know of no better honor than to be able to sit at the feet of these great teachers, and I the least of their students.

> The highest honor which the church can confer on a theologian.... the teacher of teachers.... I would like to cover my head with shame. The moment I receive this doctor's title, I will not be any more pious or more intelligent, nor more learned, no more worthy, but I am and will remain a poor old sinner and an uneducated bungler, which I have been up to this time....

> Two things have lifted up my spirit in spite of my unworthiness and inability. First, it is not only the believing faculty, but an entire correct believing evangelical Lutheran synod which is giving me this honor....

> Another reason is this, that the holy apostle states emphatically in 1 Corinthians 12:23 that the church, if it really wants to adorn itself,

should give the greatest honor to those members who are considered most dishonorable.

May our God help that I, a poor, miserable person, may use this responsibility to God's honor, for the extension of His kingdom, and thirdly, that it may serve me to salvation by not dishonoring God, hinder the church, and work towards my own destruction. May my doctorate make me from this point a guardian of my truthfulness, but also in times of doubt, may I not be discredited before God, but, as this comforted Luther so often, so may it give me the same comfort!

Pray for me: that He would guard me against unbelief, doubt, sin, pride and arrogance and keep me in His truth and grace so that He, among other things, can make me strong to defend the truth until death and conduct boldly and victoriously the battles of the world against soul-damning false teaching, heresy, sectarianism, and all ungodly spirits and that He may acknowledge me on that great, frightening day for the world but a joyous day for the children of God, as one of His, accept me in His grace, through Jesus Christ, our Lord.[13]

DEFAMED AND RESTORED

In the aftermath of the extremely bitter Predestinarian Controversy, two members of the Ohio Synod, Johann H. Fruechtenicht and Gottfried Schmidt, viciously slandered Walther. They accused Walther of having committed sins against the Sixth Commandment while he had been a pastor in Dresden, Saxony. According to their account, the church authorities removed him from the clergy roster with the result that Walther escaped punishment by fleeing and abandoning his congregation. After several months, the account stated, Walther appeared at nearby Rochlitz, Saxony, and agitated for the separation of church and state. A muscular blacksmith in Spernsdorf used a heavy rope and flagellated Walther's back. Soon after, they claimed, Walther and his friends left Germany and sailed for America.

Walther was rightly incensed over these accusations and demanded retractions. In an article in *Der Lutheraner*, Walther reported that he had engaged a Fort Wayne, Indiana, attorney by the name of James Barrett in order to take legal steps to defend himself. In the article, Walther states that it is not consistent with Christian love to take someone before the secular courts, and that it is much more Christian to bear all injuries in patience and commit the matter to God. However, in spite of this, he gives his reasons for having taken the issue to court.

1. It is surely a serious sin to haul an offender to court out of hate in order to harm him and thus to avenge one's self against him. (Matthew 5:43–48)
2. It is totally unchristian to take legal steps against a brother in the faith and member of one's congregation before a secular authority because of an injustice experienced from him, instead of leaving the final judgment to the congregation. (Matthew 18:17; 1 Corinthians 6:1–8)
3. Further, it is not right if a person does not make attempts to settle the matter in a godly manner before he goes before a secular court with his opponent (or accuser). (Matthew 5:25)
4. Further, it is not right if a Christian inaugurates legal action because of a minor wrong done to him, and does not rather suffer the wrong. (1 Corinthians 6:7)
5. Moreover, it is shameful if a Christian or a servant of the Word sues someone in court who slanders him simply because of a truth he confesses, so as not to have to bear the ignominy. (I Peter 4:14; Luke 6:22–23)
6. Certain circumstances could occur, however, in which it is not only unchristian, but rather totally proper, yes, a holy obligation, no longer quietly to put up with certain insults experienced from one who is no brother, nor will be one and rather to call on help of the secular authority against the accuser. This authority has been instituted by God to protect its citizens and subjects against injustice, 'that they may lead a quiet and peaceable life in all Godliness and reverence.' (1 Timothy 2:1–2; cf. Romans 13:3–4; 1 Peter 2:13–14)
7. It is not merely permitted for a servant of Christ and of the church, but under certain circumstances it may become his duty to seek protection from secular authority against those who perpetuate such grievous charges against him as to make him publicly infamous and unworthy of the ministry and for the blessed administration of the same; for according to God's Word, a servant of Christ "must be a man who is respected by the people outside the church so that he will not be disgraced and fall into the devil's trap." (1 Timothy 3:7)

These, then, are the reasons which moved me ... as I found myself in this situation, to do as I did. I did not go to court out of hate against my opponents, nor to avenge myself against them, nor to add any harm to them, nor to derive personal monetary gain from it, rather only because of my office as preacher and father, only therefore for the sake of God and of my neighbor.[14]

Walther added a footnote to this explanation. His lawyer had demanded high compensatory damages. Walther explains that this was done only to fulfill the demands of the law. "Obviously," he wrote, "I would not have utilized one cent of it for myself, if it had gone to trial and such a compensatory damage had been granted me."

The retraction from the two men came almost immediately; Walther promptly withdrew his complaint. Walther was also permitted to publish the retraction in *Der Lutheraner*. [15]

ILLNESS

Perhaps it is miraculous that Walther, who had been ill frequently in his life, lived to reach age 75. In a letter to Gustavus Seyfarth in 1882, he complained about his old problem, *Leberleiden* (a disease of the liver) "that will not let me go."[16]

Walther regularly wrote birthday letters to all his children. In this one, written to "Dear Daughter" (Magdalene Keyl) for her 40th birthday anniversary, he wished her joyous days, encouraged her to rejoice, and reflected also on his own life:

> The Lord has done great things for you. The outward circumstances of our life are not so important as the inner or spiritual ones. May the dear God grant you a satisfied and joyful heart in the new year of your life. We cannot give that to ourselves, but all good and complete gifts come from above, the Father of lights and He will also grant peace and joy in our hearts....
>
> When I was younger, I was always somewhat sickly and weak and thought that I would never reach my 40th birthday. But God will continue to bless you in body and soul, your parents, your husband, and your dear children.... I pray that I may soon come to my evening rest.[17]

.   While most of Walther's illnesses and physical ailments during his lifetime were not of a serious nature, in 1873 he suffered from temporary memory loss. It occurred in Milwaukee, soon after Walther had finished presenting an essay at the district convention. He was staying at the home of his brother-in-law, Friedrich Lochner. While walking, the two men, Lochner and Walther, were physically attacked. Lochner successfully staved off the attacker. Later in the evening, they were invited to the home of a Dr. John for dinner. Around nine o'clock on their way home they were overcome by a severe thunderstorm and were totally drenched. Later when they arrived at the Lochner parsonage, Lochner checked on Walther and found him in a complete daze. Walther asked, "Where are we?" This was followed by several other questions indicating that Walther could not recall anything. When Lochner tried to calm him down and assured him that he was in his guest bedroom, Walther responded: "My bedroom? I have never seen this before!" Lochner told him that he had lived there for an entire week. Again Walther asked, "Where are we?" and Lochner responded, "In Milwaukee." Walther: "How did I get to Milwaukee?" Lochner once more comforted him and pointed to his travel bag. Walther asked, "Is that really mine? Why am I in Milwaukee?" Lochner's response: "We have had a convention here and you are the president of the Synod and attended it." Walther: "The convention is over? I don't remember anything about it."

Lochner, whose heart was fluttering, prayed in deep agony to God to convince Walther to lie down for some rest. Lochner continued that Walther did so and Lochner rested on the sofa nearby. Upon checking, Lochner found the patient sleeping peacefully and the entire night passed without further incident. Lochner relates that the next morning "The dear man still felt a bit dizzy but was in total control of his memory." The doctor who saw him that morning blamed extreme overwork as the cause of the problem and warned that it could occur again. He ordered Walther to put aside all of his work and to go on a journey to rest and relax. Thoughtfully, Lochner accompanied Walther to Addison, Illinois and a brother pastor accompanied him back to St. Louis.

Shortly after that, on July 11, 1873, Walther wrote to Wilhelm Sihler in Fort Wayne, Indiana on board the *Belle of La Crosse* at Comanche, Iowa:

My precious Sihler,

After longer inner tensions, I finally resolved to take a trip on the Mississippi in order, God willing, to regain my strength through fresh air and complete intellectual inactivity. I had exerted myself so hard intellectually at the last conventions that after the Northern District convention was ended and also the pastoral conference which followed thereupon, I suddenly lost my memory of the last 20 years. Suddenly I no longer knew where I was or that Lochner, with whom I was staying, was pastor in Milwaukee, that I had there attended a convention, etc., although otherwise I was fully conscious. This condition prevailed for about half an hour, after which my memory gradually returned.

The doctors whom I consulted stated that this kind of attack was very serious at my age. Two of the doctors without mutual consultation gave me their opinion that if I do not cut down my intellectual activity, softening of the brain will result. The attack, they said, resulted from insufficient blood flow to the brain. Thus it became clear to me that I had to take my condition seriously. As ready as I am, believe me, to devote the rest of my powers to the service of the church, yet I believe I have no right to continue in my previous manner after such a serious warning. The thought of an eventual softening of the brain with its tragic side effects is naturally a frightening one for me. I would rather remain useless till my death but have my proper senses than to remain active for a short while but end up with a loss of my senses.[18]

On July 24, Walther wrote a letter to G. E. C. F. Sievers to share his recent experience and decline an invitation to stay with Sievers at the meeting of the Synodical Conference. Walther responded, among other things, that his plans were changed because of the incident.

You, too, undoubtedly have experienced that when God's hand has hit us hard, it is so good when one, in such times, experiences great love from one's children and fellow servants. I sincerely thank you for your love. I undoubtedly would have accepted your invitation if I could have attended the Synodical Conference session, because I had long yearned to see the Franconian Colonies, a strong root of our Synod. Perhaps if God gives me a couple of more years, I may still be able to have the opportunity for such a visit.[19]

Walther's illness has been referred to as "edema of the brain." Adolph Harstad, a student at the seminary when Walther was ill earlier in March 1873, wrote:

Our teacher, Professor Walther, has been very ill for a time so that for three weeks we have missed many of our most important hours of instruction. But God caused it all to come out so that we received him back again. Last week he returned. It was a festive occasion when he, that morning, entered the classroom to resume his instructions according to Baier's Latin textbook which we used. When he had come in the door we all rose and sang with strong voices, "Now Thank We All Our God." One of the German students made a beautiful speech in Latin on behalf of us all, and expressed our joy for seeing him back with us again. Then he spoke of how our hands had been bound, so to speak, during his illness [Walther's]. We could only send our prayers and sighs to our heavenly Father. Another student made a speech in German welcoming him back. Thereupon Professor Walther answered in his usual humble manner and confessed his unworthiness.[20]

While on a river excursion, in efforts to regain his health, Walther wrote his wife Emilie a four-page letter on board the steamboat Minnesota. The letter, dated July 17, 1873, reads in part as follows:

The trip has been very acceptable. Again and again there has been, farther in the north, a very acceptable balsamic air. Only in our State Room it was so extremely humid. I have not been feeling all that well in St. Paul until last night. I had very little appetite and little sleep. It is better today in this respect. In a few hours we hope to get to Rock Island and stay there overnight and if possible to take another boat for the last part of our homeward journey at noon tomorrow. With God's help, I hope to be home in the early part of next week.

Even if I do not really feel it, I nevertheless do not doubt that the trip was beneficial since the results of such a trip really do not show up until one is home again.[21]

On September 10, 1873 Walther wrote in a letter to H. Fick in Boston: "I feel feverish at times, do not have an appetite, and I am tired in my bones. Besides there is my old ailment of swollen liver." The letter was written from Port Richmond, New York. Although Walther appeared to have recovered, he nevertheless asked the Synod, meeting in Fort Wayne in 1874, to be relieved of the presidency. However, this was not done until 1878.

LIFE-THREATENING EXPERIENCES

Walther encountered several narrow escapes during his lifetime. While still a young pastor in Dresden and Johannesburg, Missouri, he was driving his horse and buggy when a flash flood demolished the road. Bridges had not yet been built over the creeks; instead stones were laid in the creek bed so that in good weather these could be crossed. During a flood, the real job of the driver was to stay on the rocks. On one occasion Walther missed the rocks and almost came to an untimely death.

In the late 1840s in a much more serious accident, he visited the church in New Minden, Illinois, as part of his responsibility as president of the Synod to visit all congregations. A swollen creek obliterated a stone path that he was crossing. Eyewitnesses relate that the buggy fell over completely into the water and the horses ran off. Though soaked through and through, Walther crawled out of the swollen creek and onto the shore.

Quickly he removed his sopping wet clothes and changed into dry ones from his valise. He then swung his drenched clothing over a branch from a tree and carried it over his shoulder. He looked, from all appearances, like a tramp when he arrived at the church.

Even more serious was the near drowning in the Mississippi River when he joined a faculty colleague for a swim. Professor Adolph Biewend and seminarian Hugo Hanser were with him. In the treacherous water, Walther stepped into a sinkhole in the river and went down. Hanser witnessed this and with Biewend's help pulled him out and saved his life.

DECLINING HEALTH

During the later years of his life, Walther felt his strength and health diminishing. He was conscious of weaknesses in his body and on occasion wrote about the nearness of his death and his anticipation of being with Jesus his Savior. As early as November 1883 Walther expressed himself candidly about his declining strength:

> Apparently you don't know me in my great weaknesses. You would be witness to the energy it takes me to write a single article, including a sermon, since you would hardly trust your eyes. In the application and zeal in my work, I can honestly state that I will not fall behind anyone. I have to get down on my knees before God and thank Him for this sentence or paragraph that I'm planning to write. Usually, before I have finished writing, I am standing actually in fear of death. I can no longer recall anything from memory because that information is locked in. Even if there is something good in my sermons or in my essays, I can truly affirm that it is not mine, it is totally God's grace and work.[22]

In the midst of deteriorating health, nothing hit Walther more severely than the death of his wife Emilie in August of 1885. He was most anxious to follow her, to be with her in the realms of heavenly bliss, forever with Jesus Christ. A year after Emilie's death, in August of 1886, Walther visited his children in New York and in Cleveland. He returned home on August 16 feeling drained. Two months later, October 13–19, 1886 he concluded his series of thirteen lectures at the Western District Convention held at Trinity, St. Louis. In this final essay, Walther concluded dramatically with these words:

> Now we are at an end with our theses discussed during the past 13 years, in which it was shown that our Lutheran Church in all of these

doctrines gives all glory to God alone and never ascribes to the creature the glory which belongs to the great God. What belongs to God our church also gives Him fully. Now, may our dear God help us that we not only rejoice that we are members of such a church, but that we, too, may give Him all glory through our faith, confession, life, suffering, and death.

Our life's motto must be: *Soli Deo Gloria*! [To God alone the glory!] That's what the angels sang immediately after the Savior was born. That is the first and also the most important matter. God received back His honor through Jesus. We have incurred nothing but shame, but as God has reacquired His honor, we have received eternal life. Blessings to all who believe this from the heart! They will then see all the holy angels at the right hand and will sing God's glory, grace, and honor from eternity to eternity.

God help us, dear brothers, that some day we too may be found among that host and then, from our entire heart, really give all glory to God. Here we cannot do this, since our evil flesh clings to us. But there, after God has removed the old flesh from us, our doctrine will not be mere theory, but then we will also practice it. O Lord Jesus, help us all to that end. Amen![23]

Martin Guenther, present at this last session, tells us that Walther already showed great signs of physical weakness and even was fever-ridden and almost sobbing.[24]

SEVENTY-FIFTH BIRTHDAY

Walther observed his 75th birthday on October 25, 1886. As was the custom, colleagues, family and friends gathered at his home to extend personal greetings. Observers noted that nothing seemed different, except that Walther's energy was depleted more quickly than before.

Walther's teaching career of more than 37 years came to an end on November 3, 1886, when he asked to be relieved of all teaching responsibilities. His daughter, Lenchen, came from New York in early December to assist her father and to be with him. In the following months his son Ferdinand came three times. The housekeeper, Katharina Huesemann, and later a nurse assisted him in his home.

FIFTIETH ANNIVERSARY OF ORDINATION

One of the major celebrations for Walther took place in his home: the 50th anniversary of his ordination. It was celebrated on January 16, 1887. The local congregations conducted separate services of praise and thanksgiving that day. Early in the morning a delegation of students conveyed their congratulations to him, and in the afternoon friends and colleagues came to his home to wish him well. Seated in his chair, Walther welcomed each guest. Those who came from a distance for the event included F. A. Craemer from the Seminary in Springfield, Illinois, accompanied by a Mr. Uhlig; G. A. Schieferdecker, at that time pastor in New Gehlenbeck, Illinois; H. Sauer and Mr. Meyer from Fort Wayne, Indiana. In addition, the pastors and delegates of the four St. Louis district congregations came, as well as members of the faculty, A. F. Hoppe, editor of *Luther's Works*, and Martin Barthel, director of Concordia Publishing House. Another distinguished guest was Carl Gottlob Weise, age 73, who was present at Walther's ordination as a member of the Braeunsdorf (Germany) congregation.

Otto Hanser of St. Louis spoke words of comfort on behalf of all the pastors, followed by Rudolph Lange on behalf of the faculty. Then came an unexpected surprise. A leather bag containing $3,000 in gold coins was presented to Walther as a special 50th anniversary gift from various members of the Synod. The presentation was made by Wilhelm Achenbach, pastor of St. Trinity in St. Louis.[25] All those present expressed their hearty congratulations and well wishes. In his frailty, Walther responded:

> It is true that God has taken my miserable person and poor sinner and used me only out of unmerited grace in order to carry out His work. It would be ingratitude if I wished to deny that God has done great things. To Him and to Him alone give all honor.... I have received a lot of praise as well as much criticism during my life, but you can believe, my dear brothers, that I have become immune [*gleichgültig*] to them. Thank and praise God for the great deeds He has done....[26]

The next day after the festivities Walther dictated a special note of thanks for publication in *Der Lutheraner*:

> In the last days and particularly on the day of my 50th anniversary of ordination, [I] received an almost untold amount of wonderful letters of congratulations, partially from entire congregations, partly from pastors and teachers, partly from faculties together with their pupils and students, which have humbled me profoundly. I would much

rather have crawled into the earth, and yet I feel rejuvenated and express my gratitude to God over the overwhelming love of my brothers.

My heart requires it that I express my gratitude. Regrettably, to do this in greater detail has become impossible because of my physical illness. From time to time it has been reported in papers that I have been improving daily from my physical illness; this is not at all true. God's goodness I express with humble thanks! Naturally, my illness is not of the type that is followed by physical weakness, but the depletion of all my physical powers is the very sickness itself which adds to the suffering in the last months. This my weakness is so great, I carry out only one objective [*Einzige*]. Without support I can only walk three steps; and, when I am being assisted by others and attempt to take ten steps, my breath is gone and unconsciousness threatens.

In deepest humility and a heart overflowing with gratitude, signed in St. Louis, January 17, 1887.

C. F. W. Walther, Pfarrer of the Evangelisch Lutherische Gesamtgemeinde, St. Louis, Mo.[27]

This was Walther's last longer article for the paper he had founded. The exceptions were four brief acknowledgments of monies received for poor students. Throughout the years, he had assumed the responsibility of acknowledging such gifts publicly. Even until a month before his death he urged his children to regularly support this work.

Towards the end of his life, Walther withdrew from all activities and prayed daily for a blessed end in Christ. When he first became ill, he still had hoped that he might recover and resume his work. But this was not to occur. He received many visitors during his last month of illness. Apparently he did not experience the temptations or vexing [*Anfechtungen*] by the devil as he had earlier in his life.

On one occasion C. C. E. Brandt, pastor of Ebenezer, together with H. Bartels of St. John, came to visit Walther. After they had shared the Gospel with him, they noted tears of joy running down Walther's cheeks. He remarked:

Oh, what would happen if we didn't have the godly comfort? The faithful Savior! Oh, that will be marvelous when we see Him, whom we have not been able to see here, but have loved Him nevertheless. Oh, if only I were there! But I submit to what God wills![28]

NOTES

1. *Pastoral Theology*, 4th ed. (St. Louis: Concordia Publishing House, 1890), 283.

2. For details, see *C. F. W. Walther: The American Luther* (Mankato, MN: Walther Press, 1987), 137, where Donley Hesse translated and abridged an earlier article by A. R. Broemel (1815–1885), 67.

3. William H. Cooper, "C. F. W. Walther's Pen," *The Lutheran* (October 6, 1937), 12.

4. Walther to Crull, December 8, 1874. Wadewitz. Trans. by this author.

5. Johann L. Gruber, *Erinnerungen an Professor C. F. W. Walther und Seine Zeit* (Burlington, IA: Lutheran Literary Board, 1930), 13–14.

6. Ludwig Fuerbringer, *80 Eventful Years* (St. Louis: Concordia Publishing House, 1944), 81–83.

7. Theodore A. Buenger, "C. F. W. Walther," *Concordia Historical Institute Quarterly*, Vol. IX, No. 3 (October 1936), 73.

8. Julius A. Friedrich, in an interview with Gerhardt Mahler, editor of the *St. Louis Lutheran*.

9. She was the grandmother of L. J. Sieck, later president of Concordia Seminary, St. Louis.

10. Walther to Mrs. Sieck, October 28, 1873. Wadewitz. Trans. by this author.

11. Walther to E. A. Brauer, May 13, 1882. Wadewitz. Trans. by this author.

12. The text appears in Martin Guenther, *Dr. C. F. W. Walther: Lebensbild* (St. Louis: Concordia Publishing House, 1890), 130.

13. Guenther, *Dr. C. F. W. Walther: Lebensbild*, 131–133.

14. *Der Lutheraner*, Vol. 40, No. 14 (July 15, 1884), 109.

15. *Der Lutheraner*, Vol. 40, No. 14 (July 15, 1884), 109. Just before the retractions were made, the case had gone to the United States Circuit Court 7813, and recorded on No. 36, page 570 in a civil action, which was dismissed on July 1, 1884.

16. Walther to Seyfarth, January 9, 1882. Wadewitz. Trans. by this author.

17. Walther to Magdalene, November 18, 1882. Wadewitz. Trans. by this author.

18. Walther to Sihler, July 11, 1873, in Roy A. Suelflow, *Selected Writings of C. F. W. Walther* (St. Louis: Concordia Publishing House, 1981), 129–130.

19. Guenther, *Dr. C. F. W. Walther: Lebensbild*, 124.

20. Adolph Harstad, "*An Autobiography*" (Madison, WI: [publisher information unavailable], 1891), 1.

21. Walther to Emilie, July 17, 1873. Wadewitz. Trans. by this author.

22. Walther to Sihler, November 19, 1883. Wadewitz. Trans. by this author.

23. August R. Suelflow, *Convention Essays* (St. Louis: Concordia Publishing House, 1981), 184.

24. Guenther, *Dr. C. F. W. Walther: Lebensbild*, 198.

25. The leather bag has been preserved and occasionally is displayed at Concordia Historical Institute.

26. Guenther, *Dr. C. F. W. Walther: Lebensbild*, 201.

27. *Der Lutheraner*, Vol. XLIII, No. 3 (February 1, 1887), 25.

28. Guenther, *Dr. C. F. W. Walther: Lebensbild*, 204.

9

Forever with the Lord

Walther's Last Days and Death

During the last weeks of his life, Walther was sleeping most of the time and may have been only semi-conscious. His biographer, Martin Guenther, assured him at another visit: "The Lord will not forsake you nor leave you, and will give you mighty support, the best of all strengths." Raising his tired head, Walther responded: "Particularly in the last hour!" Frequently he prayed: "God be merciful to me!" and "Jesus, Thy Blood and Righteousness, my beauty are, my glorious dress...." When Otto Hanser visited him, he asked Walther whether he was eagerly looking forward to the heavenly glory. Walther responded with an emphatic "*Ja!*"[1]

Walther was bedridden at his home when the 1887 convention of the Missouri Synod began on May 4. When his son Ferdinand reminded him of it, he added that soon Walther would be a part of the gathering of patriarchs, prophets, and apostles. Walther responded, "That will be marvelous!" Two days before his death on May 5, when a member of the congregation visited him and started speaking the 23rd Psalm, Walther joined in immediately and prayed the entire psalm from memory. Dr. Louis Bosse, an old friend and physician, visited Walther frequently.[2]

At Walther's request, Georg Stoeckhardt, his pastor, came to conduct evening prayer with the family on May 6. He prayed, "Should this night be the last for me in this vale of tears, then lead me, Lord, into heaven with all the elect." Walther responded, "May God grant this!" Then Stoeckhardt asked him whether he was, like Luther, now also dying in the firm confidence of the Gospel of the Lord Jesus Christ, which he had preached throughout his life. Walther answered with a loud and expressive "*Ja!*"

After some severe pains, suffered at midnight, Walther sighed, "It is enough!" Then he seemed to be suffering no longer. The next day he was, so to speak, lying at death's door, but was totally conscious and indicated that he fully understood what Stoeckhardt, Schaller, and son Ferdinand were saying. He died, softly and gently, at 5:30 p.m. on Saturday, May 7.[3] He had reached the age of 75 years, six months, and twelve days.

Son Ferdinand carried the frail body of his father from the upstairs bedroom to the parlor downstairs, where it was embalmed and prepared for burial.

The precise cause of death is difficult to establish. Contemporary German resources call it *"Nervenschwindsucht."* It is also referred to as "Tuber Dorsalis" or "Spinal Tuberculosis" which developed into "Tuberculosis Meningitis" and ultimately affected the brain.

The death certificate was signed by Louis Bosse. It stated, "I certify that I attended the person above named in his last illness, who died on the date stated above the name."

Date: May 7, 1887–Tuber Dorsalis

Place of burial: New Saxon Cemetery now known as "Concordia Cemetery"

Undertaker: B. F. Haenichen

Embalmer: W. S. Clement

THE 1887 CONVENTION OF SYNOD

The convention of the Missouri Synod meeting in Fort Wayne from May 4 to 14 was anticipating news of Walther's death. In his opening address, the president, H. C. Schwan, stated:

> Walther is extremely ill.... Several times we had hoped that he would recover, but then his health deteriorated and his death is anticipated....

> Even though we have expected his death for some time, nevertheless, it will hit us extremely hard. He was the one who laid our Synod's foundation; he did more for our growth and expansion than anyone else; he was our leader, both with regular work and in conflicts. The words of Elisha at the parting of Elijah ... apply to this servant of God with even greater excitement, 'My Father, My Father, chariots of fire and their horsemen!' In his words and in his actions he was our spiritual father. How much we are lacking now that he is not present. How very much we will miss him! Who could ever forget him? Yet— God desires to take him from us. We humble ourselves under His almighty hand. He is the Lord, and may do whatsoever He pleases. To Him be all honor! For Him there is no person who cannot be spared.[4]

The convention was informed of Walther's death by telegram on Saturday, May 7. By Sunday morning the news was made known to the synodical delegates. Though prepared, they were "terribly shaken" by it. Soon after the news broke, the members of St. Paul's Church in Ft. Wayne, where the convention was meeting, proceeded to drape the interior of the church in black.

On Sunday evening the convention met in a special session to determine the details of how the "precious body" of Walther was to be buried. The Synod adopted the following resolutions:

1. To request the relatives and the St. Louis congregations to postpone the funeral until Tuesday, May 17, after the conclusion of the convention;

2. To express the desire that the body be buried in the old cemetery of Holy Cross so that all who come to St. Louis would be able to visit the grave of "our beloved and honored Doctor";

3. To ask that the Honorable President Schwan serve as representative of the Synod and deliver the funeral sermon, and F. A. Craemer [former missionary to the Indians in Michigan] represent the faculties with an address at the coffin;

4. To postpone a lengthy memorial service at the present time, [since much work remained], but on the following day [Monday, May 9] to hold a brief memorial service.

At the close of the session on Sunday evening, the delegates sang "From Depths of Woe I Cry to Thee." Psalm 90 was read and the Litany was sung with all the delegates kneeling. The Ft. Wayne students formed a choir and sang in four-part harmony, "Kyrie," under the direction of Johann H. Ungemach.[5]

Walther's family and congregations in St. Louis honored the requests of the Synod. The funeral service was not held until Tuesday, May 17. By then the delegates who wanted to come to St. Louis for the funeral had an opportunity to arrive in time.

PREPARATIONS FOR FUNERALS AND BURIAL

As soon as the news of Walther's death reached the four district congregations and the Seminary student body in St. Louis, meetings were held so that the necessary arrangements could be made for the funeral. The first meeting of the St. Louis congregations [*Gesamtgemeinde*] was held on Sunday, May 8, at the Barry Street School. Since the voters were waiting for input from the synodical convention in Fort Wayne, they simply elected three men from each congregation—a total of twelve—to arrange for the details.

The Seminary student body met on Monday, May 9, at 8:00 a.m. and again on Wednesday, May 11 to prepare for their participation. They elected two committees, one for the flowers for the funeral and the second for draping the buildings. They also had several chorus rehearsals.

The local congregations, part of the *Gesamtgemeinde*, also met to resolve various details of the funeral. They determined that all the buildings were to be draped, including the Seminary itself, the classrooms, Walther's home, faculty homes, and Trinity Church. They also decided that at the beginning of the funeral, the bells of all the churches were to be rung. Further, they agreed to purchase a metallic casket of a deep mahogany color, and to place a catafalque over it with a high canopy "crowned with an orb and cross."

Draping all of the buildings took the entire week—from Monday, May 9, to Friday, May 13. A total of 1,133 yards of black calico were used. Walther's home was done first and was completed by May 10, the day the Keyl family arrived. A painter with long ladders helped with the draping along the high walls. The next room to be draped was Walther's lecture room.

A seminary student, J. D. Matthius, kept an excellent record of the details pertaining to the involvement of the students in the funeral preparations.[6] After hearing that Walther had died, Matthius went to the Walther home to offer his services. On Friday afternoon, May 13, the student body, headed by the pallbearers, walked to the Walther home. There they sang a hymn, and Stoeckhardt, who did not attend the Ft. Wayne convention so that he could minister to Walther in his final days, offered a prayer. At 12:45 p.m. the student pallbearers carried Walther's body "laid in a coffin richly ornamented with silver" to the center corridor of the Seminary, near the lecture room, where it remained with a student honor guard around the clock.

A large display of flowers surrounded both the head and the foot of the coffin. At the foot end were two gates, standing open, referred to as "gates ajar," symbolizing the open heaven. Also at the foot of the casket was a laurel wreath, a custom which has been retained for the funerals of Seminary faculty members throughout the years. The wreath was placed by the students and bore the inscription, "Our Professor." Behind it was a tablet with the inscription, "I lie and sleep fully at peace." Palm branches were placed by the Young Ladies Society of Holy Cross Church.

The places where Walther had labored in the Lord were now quiet in death. His lecture room and chair were draped in mourning. Walther had learned over the course of his ministry that there was no human wisdom, no human ability or worthiness except the cross of Christ. In this truth, he faced death joyfully and was comforted by the blood of the Lamb slain for sinners. He was certain of his salvation in Christ—a certainty he had also taught his students.

During his last illness, Walther told his son that all the students at the seminary ought to prepare a paper on the theme: What must a young pastor preach above all else if he wants to bring salvation to his congregation? During his last days Walther cut short discussions dealing with matters of the congregation and the church, and prayed only that God would make him righteous assuring him of his salvation.

THE FUNERALS

A total of four funerals, including the burial service, were conducted for Walther in St. Louis. The first, held at the request of the English-speaking community, took place Saturday evening, May 14, in the Seminary chapel. About 600 people were present. The hymns sung included "My Life Is Christ, the Savior," and "I Fall Asleep in Jesus' Wounds." At the close of the service the students sang, in four-part harmony, "Nearer My God to Thee."

H. Birkner, pastor of Christ Church in St. Louis from 1885 to 1890, preached the sermon. He stated:

> [We] are obliged to confess: His [Walther's] gain is an irreparable loss to us. There is, indeed, not a shadow of idolatry or undue adoration, if I call Dr. Walther the "Luther of our American Lutheran Church," and say, his loss is irreparable, since it is a well-established fact, that since the time of the Reformation there has been no teacher adhering closer and firmer to the doctrines of the Gospel as expounded in the Confessions of the Lutheran *Book of Concord* than he, whose lips are now sealed and whose eyes are closed in death. And furthermore, it is a well-established fact, that God has only at certain times given unto his church men eminently qualified to lead the van in the battles the church of Christ is obliged to encounter. In speaking of the profound learning, of the greatness and of the eminent accomplishments of him whose death we mourn, we therefore only acknowledge the grace and kindness of our Heavenly Father, who has thus blessed us for so many years by suffering a man such as Dr. Walther to live among us.
>
> Ah, truly, he has gone to receive his final reward. This college, the monument of his untiring labors, is hushed in death-like silence....

His eyes are closed, his lips are sealed, the hand so well-accustomed to wield the mighty weapon, the pen, is resting from its labor....

May his memory be cherished among us as the memory of one dear to the church of Christ, as a teacher of the most eminent gifts and as a servant of God of greatest prominence...."[7]

The second funeral service was held at 3:00 p.m. on Sunday, May 15, also in the Seminary Chapel. Stoeckhardt preached "a short, fervent sermon," using as his text 1 Corinthians 2:2: "I determined not to know anything among you except Jesus Christ and Him crucified." The service began with the hymn "For Me to Live is Jesus." In his sermon, Stoeckhardt emphasized how Walther's entire life had been a testimony for Christ: in his church, his family and on his deathbed.

After the sermon came the anthem "Beethoven's Burial" by F. W. Sering. Stoeckhardt then pronounced the blessing and with the singing of the chorale, "I Fall Asleep in Jesus' Wounds," the service came to a close.

When the service concluded at 4:15 p.m., eight seminarians served as pallbearers to carry the coffin out of the Seminary into the hearse. Among the students were Friedrich Adams, Edward Albrecht, F. Julius Klingmann, Wilhelm Kohn, John Dietrich Matthius, Michael Mikkelson, and Eivind Olson Vik.

In spite of the stormy weather, it is estimated that some 3,000 people took part in the procession. It was some six or seven blocks long, moving along Jefferson Avenue towards Miami Street and to Trinity Church. About 200 Seminary students preceded the hearse, which was drawn by four horses blanketed in black. On either side were eight students walking with uncovered heads. First in line following the hearse were family members, followed by the Seminary professors, then out-of-town pastors, local pastors, and countless dignitaries, friends, and congregation members. All along the route the church bells were tolling. The procession took about an hour.

Upon arriving at Trinity Church, the casket was placed before the altar, which had been draped in black. After a hymn was sung and the benediction pronounced by C. J. Otto Hanser (pastor of Trinity), the mourners viewed Walther's body and left the church through its north entrance. The body lay in state at Trinity Church from Sunday to Tuesday, May 15–17. Thousands came to pay their last respects.

A St. Louis newspaper gave the following vivid description of the Sunday afternoon:

Seldom in the history of St. Louis has a concourse assembled to do honor to the memory of any member of the community in any way comparable to the multitude that gathered at Concordia Seminary yesterday to pay the last sad tribute to the late Dr. C. F. W. Walther. In spite of the storm the streets leading to the Seminary were thronged by those thousands on the way to the hall where lay the body of the renowned and revered father of the German-Protestant churches of St. Louis, and long before the hour the great hall of Concordia Seminary was filled to overflowing by the throng of mourners. At the west end of the chapel, upon a catafalque heavily draped in black, was the body of the deceased. The chapel and corridors were heavily hung with crepe and around the coffin were placed masses of flowers sent by the friends and the parishioners of the venerable pastor, who for more than half a century had led the devotions of the parents and grandparents of many of those present.[8]

The third and largest funeral service was held on Tuesday, May 17, at Trinity Lutheran Church, located at Eighth Street and Lafayette Avenue. Extensive arrangements were made for this funeral, which began at noon. All the participants were asked to gather on Eighth Street at 10:30 a.m. at the Barry Street School. A detailed set of "Rules and Regulations" for those participating were published in all the local newspapers the day before, with a notation that they would be strictly enforced. These rules included instructions for the order of the carriages in the procession. Carriages were available to those who applied; tickets for coach seats sold for $1.25 each. For those arriving Tuesday morning, lunch was provided by the arrangements committee at the Seminary. Anyone wanting to stay overnight was asked to get in touch with the offices of the daily paper, *Rundschau*, on Texas Avenue.

Trinity Church was heavily draped in black, including the pillars, the organ, the pulpit, and the choir loft. Pastors of the Synod came from all areas of the country for the funeral. Some 250 pastors traveled from the synodical convention in Fort Wayne to St. Louis for the service at Trinity. Other synods were also represented: the Minnesota Synod by its President, Pastor Albrecht; the Wisconsin Synod by two of its seminary professors, Notz and Graebner; and the Norwegian Synod by its president, as well as Professor L. Larsen of Decorah, Iowa. Guenther states, "At no other funeral of a theologian in America did so many theologians participate. The city of St. Louis has rarely seen such a big funeral."[9]

The service at Trinity began with the hymn, "From Depths of Woe I Cry to Thee," sung by the congregation. H. C. Schwan, President of the

Missouri Synod, preached the sermon, and F. A. Craemer, professor at the Springfield Seminary, spoke on behalf of all the seminary and college faculties of the Synod.

Schwan's sermon was based on Psalm 90. He pointed out that the message Walther's coffin conveys to us is that all men must die, even a giant in the kingdom of God like Walther. Death, he said, is God's sign of sin in our world and a reminder that everyone, even the "high and mighty," are only mortal. About Walther he stated:

> He laid the foundation for our ecclesiastical fellowship, and worked harder than anyone else for the edification, expansion, and maintenance of our church. He was our father, the spiritual father of our souls. He was our leader in the construction, and battled for us in combat.... And yet he had to succumb to death, and must now become dust and ashes.

> This dear man was a gift to us. Did we acknowledge him as a gift from God? Yes, we acknowledged him and honored him, but was this honor actually based on the right reason in the proper way? Did we always accept God's Word from his mouth as indeed God's Word? ... Did we sometimes minimize the Word because it came from the mouth of a human being? Or, on the other hand, have we sometimes accepted the Word only because it came from his mouth? Have we at times perhaps considered him too much or too little as a person?

> How important it is for us that we reflect that the Lord blesses us and is gracious unto us and our descendants! Through Christ, the same God whom Moses worshipped has come into our life, and has taken death captive. And through the Gospel God has brought us life.... May the Father of all comfort raise up our weak knees and tired arms so that we may move ahead in the life that has been ordered for us and each one go forward in the fear of the Lord, in the strength of His almighty power! ... So He will bless the work of our hands. To Him be the glory in all eternity. Amen.[10]

The service continued with a choral selection by the seminarians, followed by the hymn, "Jerusalem, Thou City Fair and High" sung by the congregation. F. A. Craemer, a long-time friend of Walther, then stood before the altar to give his address, as the synodical convention had requested, using as his text 2 Kings 2:12. In dramatic fashion he began with the words of Elisha: "My father, my father, the chariot of Israel and the horsemen thereof." He spoke in a loud, at times sobbing voice. The audience was in tears and in visible pain. Comparing him to Luther, Craemer called Walther the father of the true Lutheran church in this country, having saved the church from rationalism which was so rampant in Europe. Reflecting on the past fifty years, Craemer stated firmly:

[In the past] many in the church calling itself Lutheran, in theological books and periodicals, considered the Scriptures to be outdated, as outlandish roots which did not fit into the American culture. The truth of God's Word was being replaced with hollow rationalism, half-heartedness, and weak, powerless Lutheranism which had illicit relationships with the sects, sometimes even with reformed 'enthusiasm' [*Schwaermerei*]. Now look at the wide boundaries of this land: in the East and West, North and South not only the name and fame of the Lutheran Church has been restored, but also almost 1500 pastors, churches and schools are professing again the doctrine of Luther, and this was mainly the God-given result of Dr. Walther's faithful labors.[11]

Craemer continued:

We did not always recognize Walther's greatness as we should have. Did we not often think that we were more wise than he? Were we as thankful as we should have been for the rich blessings we received through him? ... For this let us cry to God for forgiveness, to wash us clean through the blood of His Son. Above all, let us be thankful that He chose this man to raise up the Gospel again in all its purity. Let us prove this thankfulness by our actions, that with all our might we promote and carry on Walther's work in the battle against our enemies. Let us not be unfaithful or ungrateful for God's goodness, so that some day our end will be like that of our spiritual father. Let us earnestly beg our Savior to preserve us in His true faith and lead us to the glorious goal.[12]

After Craemer's address, the choir sang a choral selection, and a chorale was sung by the congregation. The service was concluded in exactly two hours.

Writing about the funeral the following day, a local newspaper reported as follows:

So impressive and dignified a funeral St. Louis has not seen in a long time. There were about 2,000 persons in the church, and the streets and alleys near the church at Eighth Street and Lafayette Avenue were so dense with people for blocks around that Captain [Henry] Frangel and his police detail had difficulty keeping a path open for the mourners.[13]

The pallbearers who carried Walther's coffin out of Trinity Church to the hearse were Professors M. Guenther, F. Pieper and C. Lange, and Pastors W. Achenbach, G. Wangerin, H. Sieck, C. C. E. Brandt, C. Janzow, and H. Bartels. Police were stationed at various points throughout the procession route. The marshals and police had a difficult time keeping the crowd away so that those processing could get to their carriages and buggies at the various predetermined spots. There were eight police on horseback, led by a sergeant. The four marshals, on horses, were dressed in black and wore white gloves. They carried a staff in their right hands. The hearse was followed by four black horses. The bells of Trinity were softly ringing.

The procession, about two miles long, stopped briefly in front of the Seminary en route to the cemetery. Ninety carriages preceded the hearse, and 87 followed it; 61 buggies also joined the procession, for a total of 238 conveyances. Streets were lined with people, and many watched from their houses. The weather was very mild. Just as the procession passed the Seminary at 3:00 p.m., the sun peeked out through the clouds. The bells of Holy Cross Church and the Seminary bells were ringing alternately, long after the procession had passed. As the hearse passed by, every head was bared out of respect for the deceased. As the procession approached the cemetery, bells tolled there also.

The Committal and Burial

Walther was buried in the cemetery at 4209 Bates Avenue in St. Louis which he himself had dedicated thirty years earlier. Because it was so new, only a few had been buried there. The cemetery was referred to as "the new Saxon Cemetery." Only later, in 1896, was the name "Concordia Cemetery" officially adopted.

For the graveside service a speaker's stand was specially built and was draped in black. C. J. Otto Hanser delivered the address on Daniel 12:1–3. With great emotion he said:

> We are standing at an open grave. Each grave preaches a profoundly serious message of deep sorrow. In a penetrating way it preaches that it is the end of fallen man's glory, the end of all earthly joy. An open grave, further, is also the place for painful sorrow, an irreplaceable loss for those who must bring a loved one to his final resting place on earth.

But for the grave by which we are surrounded today this is true in a very special measure. It is not only the grave of our dear father whose children are standing in tears surrounding it, but also the grave of a great person, a prince in Israel of God's church. It is the grave of the shepherd who has served his congregation for almost half a century with the richest gifts of the Spirit, with never-tiring faithfulness and self-sacrifice even in times of great heat of battle, as well as in times of blessing. It is the grave of a Doctor of Lutheran theology whose thousands of students all over the world proclaim the pure Lutheran doctrine....

A grave is a place of slumber, a chamber of rest.... Our deeply beloved Dr. Walther has found his resting chamber and a sleeping room in this open grave, which he had sought and wished for. He is resting from all his work.... For 50 years he has dedicated in deepest love to his Lord Jesus all the powers of body and soul.... He is resting from all suffering and pain of this poor life. As a chosen worker of his Lord, he had to endure much as a Christian. There was poverty, heavy painful illness with great spiritual temptation; then there were the sorrowful deaths of the members of the family, and finally his life's companion. There were the attacks of his enemies, thanklessness and slander ... and ultimately his seven months of suffering until his death. There is hardly any pain or trouble in this life which he did not experience....

Thank God that he is resting from all of this. The text [Daniel 12:1–3] gives us a marvelous promise that those who are sleeping in the earth will be awakened. What blessed hope! Just as a person after undisturbed rest awakens refreshed, and with joy greets the light of a new day ... so also the believers will awaken from their graves with glorified bodies. In the same way the disfigured, fallen body of our dear Dr. Walther will awaken from his grave to this blessed life.... Therefore, dear mourners, let us remember our Dr. Walther with gratitude. Let us remember his peaceful end and follow him in his victorious faith until we see him again face to face in eternal joy and blessed life in Jesus Christ. Amen, that will be true for all of us, Hallelujah. Amen, Amen.[14]

After Hanser's address, the seminarians sang the hymn by F. Sering entitled *"Bei Walthers Begraebnis"* ["For Walther's Burial"]. The arrangement of the hymn was by Wilhelm Achenbach, pastor of St. Trinity Church in St. Louis. The hymn contains the beautiful message that Walther came to rest and after long battles put his sword away when the

Lord called him home. For us there is severe pain and sorrow, but we have the comfort that God's grace continues to help and protect His church.

The Norwegian Synod was represented by several men, including Professor L. Larsen, who felt constrained to speak at the burial service. In touching words, he expressed deep gratitude for the ministry of Walther and the benefits the Norwegian Synod had received from his labors. He ended by expressing the wish and prayer that all would remain faithful "in the great trust committed to our care."

The burial service continued with Pastor H. Sieck approaching the grave and reading 1 Corinthians 15. As the coffin was being lowered, the assembly sang the hymn, "This Body in the Grave We Lay." Pastor G. Wangerin led the Lord's Prayer. Pastor Achenbach alternated with the audience in singing responsive stanzas of the hymn, "How Blessed Are Ye Saints." At the end the seminary students again chanted a beautiful dirge, and as the body was laid to rest, the mourners dispersed one by one.

In order to prevent any possibility of desecrating the grave, the inside opening was lined with brick masonry all around. The casket was covered with a heavy stone slab, six inches thick. Gravel was added, and cement poured over the entire grave. Finally, the mound was covered with flowers, palms and evergreens.[15]

WALTHER'S WILL

By any financial standard of his time, Walther died a poor man. He never kept money given to him for his literary contributions; he gave it to charities. His will was written on February 26, 1887, ten weeks before his death. By that time he had given up hope of recovering his health.[16] Witnesses to the will were Louis Lange, August Gast and Benjamin C. Hoffmann.

The will is a simple one, as one would expect from a man who is seriously ill and near death. It is written in English, in good handwriting, and begins with the words: "In the name of God. Amen." The will requires that his executor pay all his final debts and funeral expenses. He bequeathed his entire library to Concordia Seminary, St. Louis. To the faithful housekeeper for several decades, Katharina Huesemann, he left $100. All the rest of his estate, real, personal and mixed property, he left to his four surviving children: Magdalena Christiane Keyl (Port Richmond, Staten Island, New York), Constantin (Norborne, Missouri), Ferdinand (Brunswick, Missouri) and Julie Emma Niemann (Cleveland, Ohio).

Walther's assets at the time of his death were as follows: $2,285 cash on hand (probably the amount left of the $3000 given to him at his 50th anniversary of ordination), a non-interest bearing note of $720 for a house and lot in Norborne, Missouri, and goods and personal property appraised at about $750. His total assets were $3,755. It is interesting to note the appraisal of several items: revolving bookcase, $5; grand piano, $25 (both at Concordia Historical Institute); an "ice box," $2; and the "rubber bed," $25. The most expensive item of furniture was the bedroom set, valued at $60.

Walther's library consisted of 333 titles, including boxes of manuscripts and letters. A *Book of Concord* published in Dresden in 1580, a Polyglot Bible, Krauth's *Conservative Reformation*, Morris' *Bibliotheka Lutherana*, Hazelius' *History of the Lutheran Church*, were among his prized books. The library contained mostly works of systematic and exegetical theology, representing sixteenth and seventeenth century authors, as well as a good collection of American Lutheran writers.

The house which the Synod had given Walther in 1870 reverted back to synodical ownership. It was dismantled in 1906. The impressive Seminary building which Walther had dedicated with such joy in 1883 also was demolished after the Clayton campus was constructed in 1926.

Each of the four children inherited $900 in cash when the estate was settled in June 1888. A year later each of them received an additional $16.61. Ferdinand purchased the house and lot in Norborne, Missouri.[17]

Walther's body was laid to rest, and his property distributed to his children. But the legacy of this servant of Christ who restored in America the teachings of Martin Luther lives on.

NOTES

[1] Martin Guenther, *Dr. C. F. W. Walther: Lebensbild* (St. Louis: Concordia Publishing House, 1890), 204.

[2] Bosse was born in Germany in 1823 and died less than a year after Walther in 1888. He had been very involved in the great cholera epidemic of 1849 and dispensed medicine from his own pharmacy. He also served on the staff of Lutheran Hospital without compensation.

[3] Guenther, *Dr. C. F. W. Walther: Lebensbild*, 206.

[4] *Proceedings, Missouri Synod,* 1887, 176–77. Trans. by this author.

[5] *Proceedings, Missouri Synod,* 1887, 3–4.

[6] See *Lutheran Witness,* Vol. LVI, No. 14, 230–31.

[7] *Lutheran Witness,* Vol. VI, No. 1 (June 7, 1887), 5, 8.

[8] *Globe-Democrat* (May 16, 1887), 6.

[9] Guenther, *Dr. C. F. W. Walther: Lebensbild*, 208.

[10] *Zur Erinnerung an Dr. C. F. W. Walther* (Zwickau: Johannes Herrmann Verlag, 1887), 13–18. Trans. by this author.

[11] *Zur Erinnerung an Dr. C. F. W. Walther*, 20 and *Lutheran Witness* (June 7, 1887), 8.

[12] *Zur Erinnerung an Dr. C. F. W. Walther*, 23–25.

[13] *Anzeiger des Westens*, May 18, 1887.

[14] *Zur Erinnerung an Dr. C. F. W. Walther*, 25–31.

[15] For a detailed account of Walther's death and burial see Erich B. Allwardt, "Death and Burial of C. F. W. Walther," *Concordia Historical Institute Quarterly*, Vol. 60, No. 2 (Summer 1987), 52–64.

[16] A photostatic copy of the will is in the files of Concordia Historical Institute under "Walther's Legal Papers." The original text is located in the Probate Division of the Missouri Circuit Court, in file 16281.

[17] Allwardt, "Walther's Will," 85–86.

EPILOGUE

THE WALTHER MAUSOLEUM CONCORDIA CEMETERY, ST. LOUIS, MO.

Five years after the death of C. F. W. Walther, the four congregations constituting the *Gesamtgemeinde* decided to build a memorial at Concordia Cemetery in honor of their beloved pastor and teacher. This decision, made in January of 1889, was the last official action taken by the joint congregation before it was dissolved. Soon after the resolution was passed, a building committee was named. It included Pastors C. J. Otto Hanser and Charles Obermeyer, and Messrs. Charles Wehking, F. Sanders, Alex. Rohlfing, Friedrich Dette, Herman Ellermann, C. F. Lange and F. Quirl. In a short period of time the necessary funds of almost $9,000 were gathered and construction was begun. The local firm of Schrader and Conradi designed the octagonal Gothic building, and Joseph Conradi, a 29-year-old Swiss immigrant, executed the statue of white Italian marble.

Originally the plan was to dedicate the memorial on May 7, 1892, precisely five years after Walther's death. Because of delays, however, this was not possible, and the dedication took place on June 12, 1892.

The edifice itself is constructed of gray granite (Dark Barre from Vermont), except for the pillars which are of black "Quincy" granite. The pillars stand on eight constructed pedestals and rise to a height of eleven feet, where the window arches begin. Over each window is a gable. An eight-sided pyramid rises above to a height of 28 feet, leading to a cross. The entire structure is 33 feet high, including the cross which is five feet tall.

Eight granite steps lead up to the bronze door of the mausoleum, with a window of French plated glass. Inside are eight slender pillars, hewn out of carrara marble, also resting on pedestals. On the inside one can see the rims of an intricately-fashioned starry sky. The walls on the inside are covered with one and one-half inch finely polished marble slabs of various colors. The windows are made of French cut glass, except for the one in the rear, which is of light blue glass. The dark brown vines in the four corners represent the four evangelists. The upper rear window depicts a flying angel (Rev. 14:6–7) which also appeared on the masthead of *Der Lutheraner*.

On the floor are colored mosaic slabs which indicate the spots where Walther and his wife are buried. At the head of each grave there is an inlaid star giving the birth and death dates of each, in letters laid deep into the marble.

The life-size statue of Walther (5 feet 11 inches) portrays him at the age of 45–50. His pose is that of a speaker at a synodical or district convention. To Walther's left stands a pillar with a Bible resting on it. In his left hand he holds the *Book of Concord*, which rests on the Bible. In his right hand he holds notes such as he would have used when presenting a theological essay.[1]

The pedestal on which the monument stands bears the inscription of Romans 3:28: "Therefore we conclude that a man is justified by faith apart from the deeds of the law."

The service of dedication of the mausoleum took place at 4:00 p.m. on Sunday, June 12, 1892. It was attended by a large number of people, including pastors, professors and students of the Seminary, members of the local congregations and many friends. Rev. Herman Barthels gave a few introductory remarks. Francis Pieper was the main speaker. He said, among other things:

> We stand at the grave of a man with whom Christian doctrine and Christian faith were not mere theory, but practice—he finished the course and kept the faith to the end. So may God give all of us the grace that this earthly life and finally also death will be for us the entrance into eternal life, where we, as for all blessings, so also for the gift of this great and faithful teacher want to thank God from everlasting to everlasting. Amen.[2]

It is possible that the white marble bust of Walther, now on a pedestal in the Board Room of Concordia Seminary, was done by Joseph Conradi and given to the Seminary. Pieper in his address at the dedication of the mausoleum, states that there is a marble bust in the Aula (chapel) of the South Jefferson Avenue Seminary.

Over the years considerable damage was done to the mausoleum by vandals. With the help of countless friends, the structure was restored by Concordia Historical Institute and rededicated on October 16, 1988. The plot of ground on which the mausoleum stands was deeded to The Lutheran Church—Missouri Synod on May 20, 1987.

NOTES

[1] *Der Lutheraner*, Vol. 48 (March 1, 1892), 40–41.

[2] Erich B. Allwardt, "Dedication of the Walther Mausoleum," *Concordia Historical Institute Quarterly*, Vol. 61, No. 1 (Spring 1988), 46–48. On June 14, 1892, the daily paper, *Anzeiger des Westens*, printed Pieper's entire address on page 12.

INDEX